TEMPLES, TOMBS & HIEROGLYPHS

ALSO BY BARBARA MERTZ

NONFICTION

Red Land, Black Land

FICTION

Writing as Elizabeth Peters

THE AMELIA PEABODY MYSTERY SERIES

Crocodile on the Sandbank

The Curse of the Pharaohs

The Mummy Case

The Deeds of the Disturber

The Last Camel Died at Noon

The Snake, the Crocodile, and the Dog

The Hippopotamus Pool

Seeing a Large Cat

The Ape Who Guards the Balance

The Falcon at the Portal

He Shall Thunder in the Sky

Lord of the Silent

The Golden One

Children of the Storm

Guardian of the Horizon

The Serpent on the Crown

Tomb of the Golden Bird

TEMPLES, TOMBS & HIEROGLYPHS

A Popular History of Ancient Egypt

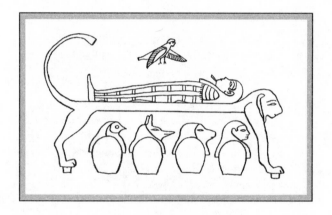

SECOND EDITION

BARBARA MERTZ

WILLIAM MORROW

An Imprint of HarperCollins*Publishers*

This book was originally published in 1964 by Dodd, Mead & Company.

Jacket image: Pair statue of Merire, High Priest of Aton at Memphis, and his wife, Inyuia, from Sakkara. Photograph by D. Forbes. Courtesy of the Cairo Museum.

Designed by Jennifer Ann Daddio

ISBN: 978-0-06-125276-1

Book Club Edition

To John A. Wilson

1899–1976

Scholar, teacher, humanist

Contents

Foreword to the First Edition   xi

Foreword to the Second Edition   xv

A Note on Names   xvii

Ancient Egyptian Chronology   xix

List of Black-and-White Illustrations   xxiii

List of Color Illustrations in Photograph Insert   xxv

List of Maps   xxvii

ONE: THE TWO LANDS   I

Geb the Hunter   I

The Wagon or the Mountain   I6

Troubles with Time 24

Wearers of the Double Crown 33

Wars of Religion? 41

TWO: HOUSES OF ETERNITY 46

King Djoser's Magician 46

Good King Snefru 54

The Missing Queen 64

Children of Re 75

THREE: THE GOOD SHEPHERD 95

Despair and Deliverance 95

Binder of the Two Lands 107

FOUR: THE FIGHT FOR FREEDOM 126

Invasion 126

Liberation 132

FIVE: THE WOMAN WHO WAS KING 142

Hatshepsut the Queen 142

The King of Upper and Lower Egypt 145

The Hatshepsut Problem 162

The Other Hatshepsut Problem 164

SIX: THE CONQUEROR 168

SEVEN: THE POWER AND THE GLORY   190

Amenhotep II   190
Amenhotep the Magnificent   198

EIGHT: THE GREAT HERESY   205

NINE: THE BROKEN REED   240

Look on My Works!   240
Ramses II   244
Peoples of the Sea   257

TEN: THE LONG DYING   269

Adventures of a Man of No Consequence   269
The Quick and the Dead   274
Tomb Robbers and Royal Mummies   277
Mummy Musical Chairs   282
The Third Intermediate Period   283
Horsemen from the Holy Mountain   286
Back to the Drawing Board   295
The Final Humiliation   299

Additional Reading   309
Sources of Quotes   313
Index   315

Foreword to the First Edition

My affaire de coeur with ancient Egypt began in remote childhood, when I first encountered James Henry Breasted's *History of Egypt* at the local library; it is still flourishing, although many years and many distractions have intervened. It is necessary to make this highly subjective statement, I think, both to explain the reason for this book and to justify some of the statements which appear herein. There are occasions in the following pages when serious Egyptologists may be offended by what strikes them as a frivolous or fantastical tone. Frivolity there may be; but it should not be taken for disparagement of the field of Egyptology in general or of particular scholars and their pet theories. Few academic subjects are improved by being approached in a spirit of deadly seriousness. I suspect, in fact, that most of them can profit by a bit of kindly mockery, particularly if it is self-administered. That I venture to smile at a field to which I personally adhere above all others should be proof that I act from a general principle, and not from particular malice. "They do but jest, poison in jest; no offence i' the world."

It is only fair to warn the reader that this is not a history book. It is, rather, an informal study of Egyptology—a study of all things Egyptian. My criterion for selection of material has been very simple: I have included anything I found interesting. Hence you will encounter straight archaeological reporting, gossip, and historical theorizing in uneven quantities. You will also encounter—I hope—people. The individual has been rather out of fashion in serious history, although the trend is swinging back in his favor of late. I follow the fairly conventional viewpoint, which holds that events are the product both of The Man and The Background, but I do believe that the shape of events is fashioned by the particular man or woman who holds the reins of destiny at a particular moment in time. Therefore I have frankly and unashamedly talked about people when I was able to do so: about kings and queens for the most part, but also about artists, magicians, and even civil servants.

Any attempt to evaluate, or even describe, the character of a historical personage is difficult and highly subjective; often the biographer inadvertently tells more about himself than about the subject of his biography. In the case of ancient Egyptian individuals it is virtually impossible— in fact, you can leave out "virtually"—to do more than speculate. Our knowledge even of events is scanty and incomplete; insight into motives and influences is completely lacking. I have tried to indicate the points at which I leave solid ground and sail off into happy flights of fancy, but undoubtedly I have forgotten to label all the pertinent cases. My consolation is that the same error has been, and is being, committed by professional historians.

I have often speculated as to why so many people are attracted to the study of archaeology. Certain appeals, such as the lure of buried treasure, are fairly obvious; it is to this imaginative human urge that most popular books on archaeology cater. But there is another type of problem involved in archaeology, and in history in general, which also appeals to a wide audience—the people who like puzzles, riddles, and exercises in simple logic. When we, as students, read a history textbook, we are presented with a series of statements that we accept, with more or less indifference, as true. We do not see the skillful patchwork, the blending together of data from dozens of different sources, which creates a coherent picture of events; and we miss the fascination of following the mental processes by which the patches are matched and hooked together. To follow out these processes in detail is not only entertaining but also profitable, for in the end we find ourselves questioning the sources of certain statements, and even disagreeing with the conclusions which are drawn from them. Here is a consummation devoutly to be wished; the questioning mind should be developed by any person who reads a daily newspaper. I have tried to indicate some of the sources and some of the methods which we apply in order to derive what we call Egyptian history. Many of them transcend Egyptology but are seen just as clearly in this context as in others.

Foreword to the Second Edition

When I first set out to revise this book, I was naive enough to believe several kindly friends, who must have been blinded by affection, because they assured me that I wouldn't need to do very much. As I immediately discovered, I had to do quite a lot. Not only have (good heavens) forty years passed, but they have been years full of new discoveries and new interpretations, and even new characters in the story of ancient Egypt, some of whom were not known when I wrote this book. Contrary to the opinions of the uninformed, revisionism is an integral part of good historical scholarship. It may seem at times that revisionists have gone overboard in their attempts to find new ways of looking at old material, but it is a necessary process.

Despite my disingenuous disclaimer that I had included only material

I found interesting, it became obvious to me that I had given short shrift to certain periods and certain topics. Another complication arose from the fact that in the interim I had written another book about ancient Egypt which covered some of the same material. I had to decide what to put in which book.

Having made my excuses I should add that producing a second edition of this book and the other, *Red Land, Black Land*, has been a great adventure. I have kept up with the field to the best of my ability and made a number of trips to Egypt, but condensing the new material and fitting it into place presented a number of challenges. I hope I have met them adequately; if I have succeeded even in part, much of the credit must go to my many friends and colleagues in the field, not only for their publications but also for the generous advice they have given me. I owe a special debt to Dennis Forbes, editor of *Kmt*, who took time from his busy life to go over the entire manuscript with his indispensably lethal marking pen. I am also indebted to Roxie Walker for tactfully correcting my misstatements on the subjects of bones and dating skeletons. Kristen Whitbread and Loretta St. John dealt with the electronic issues, if that is what they are called. Thanks to those ladies, I didn't have to call them anything.

This is a traditional, even "old-fashioned," history that focuses on people and events rather than on social change. In a way it can be read as a detective story, which sifts through a multitude of clues in order to determine what really happened. There are red herrings, the usual suspects, and detectival historians, for written history is, or should be, a synthesis and analysis of myriad, often contradictory, clues. I might—indeed, I will—reiterate my belief that learning to question and analyze so-called facts is the most important lesson a student can learn. It is especially important in today's world, when we are barraged by information from so many disparate sources.

A Note on Names

I have avoided the Greek renderings of certain names, such as Khufu instead of Cheops. Ancient Egyptians didn't write the vowels, therefore you will find various spellings of names and other words: Amen, Amon, Amun; ushabti, shabti, shawabti; Harmhab, Horemheb; to mention only a few. There are also variations in the way certain consonants are transliterated: Cush or Kush, Saqqara or Sakkara, and so on. My versions are arbitrary, but so are those of most other people.

Ancient Egyptian Chronology

Dating based on William Murnane, *The Penguin Guide to Ancient Egypt*, Penguin Books, rev. ed., 1996.

AUTHOR'S NOTE

You will find different dates in different books; the further back in time, the greater the uncertainty. Chronologies are based on a number of sources, some more reliable than others. The general outline of dynasties comes from the Greek writer Manetho, who divided Egyptian history into families of rulers. Modern scholars have cast doubt on certain details, but the system is more or less fixed in stone.

You will sometimes encounter the terms C.E. (Common Era) and B.C.E. (Before the Common Era) instead of B.C. (Before Christ) and A.D. (Anno Domini). There is a reason for this, but I can't see the point of changing terms that have been in use so long.

ARCHAIC PERIOD. 3150–2686 B.C.
    Dynasty O. Scorpion, Aha, Narmer
    Dynasty I. Unification. Menes, Djer, Djet, Den, Queen Merneith
    Dynasty II. Peribsen, Khasekhemui

THE OLD KINGDOM. 2686–2181 B.C.
    Dynasty III. Step Pyramid. Djoser, Khaba, Huni
    Dynasty IV. Pyramids of Dahshur, Medum, Giza. Snefru, Khufu, Khafre, Menkaure
    Dynasty V. Userkaf, Sahure, Unis
    Dynasty VI. Teti, Pepi I, Mernere, Pepi II

FIRST INTERMEDIATE PERIOD. 2181–2040 B.C. Breakdown of central government
    Dynasties VII–X. Some partially overlapping.

MIDDLE KINGDOM. 2040–1782 B.C. Reunification
    Dynasty XI. Intefs and Mentuhoteps
    Dynasty XII. Amenemhats and Senuserts, Queen Sobekneferu

SECOND INTERMEDIATE PERIOD. 1782–1570 B.C.
    Breakdown of central government.
    Dynasty XIII–XVI. Some overlapping. Hyksos
    Dynasty XVII. Sekenenre Tao II, Kamose 1663–1570 B.C.

NEW KINGDOM. 1570–1070 B.C. Reunification
    Dynasty XVIII. Ahmose, Amenhoteps and Thutmoses, Queen Hatshepsut, Akhenaton, Tutankhamon, Ay, Harmhab
    Dynasty XIX. Seti I, Ramses I and II, Merneptah, Queen Tausert
    Dynasty XX. Ramses III–XI, Herihor

THIRD INTERMEDIATE PERIOD. 1070–525 B.C.

Dynasty XXI Smendes, Psusennes, Pinudjem

Dynasty XXII Libyan. Sheshonks, Osorkons, Takelots

Dynasties XXIII–XXIV. Libyan. Country divided.

Dynasty XXV. Cushite. Piankhi, Shabaka, Taharka

Dynasty XXVI. Saite. Psamtiks, Necho, Apries

LATE PERIOD. 525–332 B.C.

Dynasty XXVII. First Persian

Dynasty XXVIII–XXIX. Egyptian dynasts

Dynasty XXX. Nectanebo I and II

Dynasty XXXI. Second Persian

PTOLEMAIC. Conquest by Alexander the Great, 332 B.C.

Succeeded by Ptolemies and Cleopatras.

ROMAN. Conquest by Julius Caesar, 30 B.C. Egypt a Roman

province.

List of Black-and-White Illustrations

The Nebti name of Menes I

Crowns of the king of Egypt 23

The Narmer palette 34

The royal titulary, cartouche, and *serekh* 35

Serekhs of Sekhemib and Peribsen 43

Serekh of Khasekhemui 44

Cartouche of Khufu 46

Types of Old Kingdom mastabas 47

Building stages of the Step Pyramid 48

The pyramid complex 59

The mummy and its equipment, and the ba 82

Hippopotami and crocodile 84

Cartouche of Senusert   95

Cartouche of Ahmose   126

Cartouche of Hatshepsut   142

Titles of the Egyptian king   145

Senenmut's name and title, steward of Amon   147

Cartouches of Thutmose III   168

Cartouche of Amenhotep II   190

Cartouche of Akhenaton   205

The god Aton in original form   210

Aton as a sun disk, with rays ending in hands   211

Cartouche of Ramses II   240

Cartouche of Psamtik   269

List of Color Illustrations in Photograph Insert

Hemiun the Vizier
Queen Hetepheres' burial chamber
Pyramid texts
Hatshepsut
Senenmut
Temple of Deir el Bahri
Hatshepsut's Red Chapel, Open Air Museum at Karnak
Thutmose III
Thutmose III's tomb, decoration of burial chamber
Fat Amenhotep III
Canopic chest of Tutankhamon
Colossus of Akhenaton

Kiya, Hermopolis

Amenhotep, son of Hapu

Temple of Ramses II, Abu Simbel

Temple of Ramses III, Medinet Habu, Luxor

Pyramids of Meroe

List of Maps

Ancient Egypt   II

Nubia   86

The Near East During the New Kingdom Period   170

Three Roads to Megiddo   172

Setting of the Battle of Kadesh   246

One

THE TWO LANDS

The Nebti name of Menes

GEB THE HUNTER

One bright summer afternoon in the year 5263 B.C., a man stood on the cliffs high above the Nile Valley. He was slightly built and only a few inches over five feet in height; his brown body was naked except for a kilt of tanned hide. But he held himself proudly, for he was a tall man among his people, and a leader of men. The people he led clustered about him— women peering timidly out from a tangle of black hair, hushing the children in their arms; men bearing their weapons, bow and arrow and stone ax. The wind blew hot behind them; they had turned their backs on the desert. Once it had not been desert. Once, in the time of their ancestors, there had been water, and green growing things, and animals to kill for food. Now the god had withdrawn his hand from their homeland. And so they looked with bright apprehensive eyes into the new land below, a green slash of life cutting through the growing desolation all around. The leader's keen vision saw the gleam of water and the flicker of birds' wings; his hunter's ears caught the far-off bellow of a hippopotamus. There was food below, and water; yet still the leader of the tribe hesitated. He knew the old life, with all its perils. Could he face the more chilling peril of the unknown and, unaware of destiny, take the first step toward the pyramids?

It is a pity that this picturesque episode must belong to fiction rather than history. Some of the details may be true. The first prehistoric cultures in Egypt are dated to around 5500 B.C., but not even the miracle of carbon 14 could give a date so specific as the one mentioned above. At some point in the remote past, man came out of the desert into the valley of the Nile and settled into small villages. He may have looked something like the leader of the tribe who, in a historical novel, would be christened Geb or Ab, or something equally monosyllabic and prehistoric. But it is unlikely that a single man with a vision initiated the transition from nomadic hunters to village farmers. The change took place over long centuries.

Admittedly, the signs of the great change are not dramatic when they are seen in dusty museum cases—flint knife blades and arrowheads, not very different at a casual glance from the crude tools of the hunters; tattered scraps of a woven basket that once held grain; the bones of a dog, appearing, to an untrained eye, like the bones of any wild beast. Yet the transition is more important than the pyramids and more exciting, in its implications, than the golden treasure of a Tutankhamon. We find ourselves here at the beginning of a long and momentous chapter in the great book of man. As the pages turn, we will meet kings and conquerors, poets and inventors. We will conjure up visions of treasure unsurpassed by the most luxuriant forms of imaginative fiction; we will encounter the darker aspects of the human spirit as well as its bright triumphs. Yet never again, perhaps, will we see the human animal take a step so gigantic as this first one, little known and poorly recorded as it is.

Scholars usually place the first "revolution" in man's way of life between the Paleolithic and Neolithic eras. These terms, which mean "Old Stone Age" and "New Stone Age," were coined to describe a change in the techniques of working stone implements, but it is the least significant of the differences between the two periods. The wandering hunters of the Old Stone Age became the farmers and shepherds of the Neolithic. The permanent settlement of a tribe implies agriculture and domesticated animals, and perhaps pottery—though there is considerable variation from place to place—and people continued hunting and fishing even after other means of food production were developed. The evidence of the transitional period in the Nile Valley is almost nonexistent—so far. One suspects that something is bound to turn up eventually, but perhaps not in the Nile Valley itself; there were hunter-gatherers wandering around the Western Desert, and possible signs of at least semipermanent habitation there as early as nine thousand years ago. For our purposes, however, the oldest known predynastic cultures of Egypt date from approximately 5400 B.C.

Life in the early village cultures was not exactly luxurious. The houses were built of mud and sticks and consisted of a single dark room, unfloored and unventilated except for a smoke hole in the roof. The bodies of the dead were laid in shallow holes scooped in the sand, with no covering except straw mats or skins. But in the goods buried with them we may see the groping of the human spirit toward the concept of immortality. They could only postulate a continuance of the life they knew; so the hunter has his spear, the woman her beads (*vanitas vanitatum*, against the fleshless skull), and the pitiful child bones sometimes huddle against the dust of a once-cherished toy.

The bones and their belongings can speak to us, sometimes with poignant clarity. And the mute stone and baked clay can speak as well, to those who know how to listen. So meager are the remains from this distant time, before the dawn of history, that archaeologists have developed ingenious techniques for wringing the greatest possible amount of information from each scrap. They rely upon the skills of many specialists—biologists, who can identify the species of the gnawed bones in the kitchen middens, geo-chemists, who analyze pottery, and paleobotanists, who ponder the with-ered grains left in the bottom of the granary basket by a thriftless ancient housewife. (Contrary to popular report, none of the "mummy seeds" found in Egypt has ever produced a living plant; there is a limit to the preservative qualities of even Egyptian soil.)

Most of the archaeological evidence from prehistoric Egypt comes from graves. There are a few village sites, and also the kitchen middens, an archaeological euphemism for garbage dumps. The prehistoric equiva-lents of beer cans and melon rinds are fish and animal bones, worn-out flint tools, and scraps of broken pottery. There must have been settle-ments of some sort near these ancient garbage dumps, but not many have survived. From these scanty remains Egyptologists have defined a num-ber of predynastic cultures, interrelated, but each having its own typical assemblage (the collection of objects produced and used by the people of a given culture). In this period, such an assemblage might include flint weapons, beads and amulets, baskets, and pottery.

I have never been able to decide which is duller, flints or pottery; but I distinctly remember the appalling blankness that used to seize my mind when I was asked to identify bits of pottery during an examination. Probably this attests to my underdeveloped imagination, for pottery has been one of the most useful tools of the archaeologist. The ordinary household pot has no intrinsic value, so people throw it away when it breaks, and tomb robbers sneer at it. Though a pot can be smashed, its fragments are virtually indestructible. For this reason pottery is an in-valuable clue to chronology, since it is seldom removed from the spot in which it was originally dumped. But it is fair to say that no one ever dreamed of the far-reaching implications of potsherds until Sir William Flinders Petrie started thinking about them.

It is fitting that Petrie's should be the first name we mention, for he was truly *the* formidable figure in Egyptology. Some scholars call him the father of "scientific" archaeology (for certain dark reasons of my own, I prefer the adjective "critical"). To list his accomplishments in the methods of excavation alone would take pages, but even his pioneering work in technique was less important than his approach, rigorously logical and painstakingly exact. The new approach came from Petrie himself, not from his training; as he plaintively remarks, there was nobody around to train him. He arrived in Egypt at a time when Gaston Maspero, the dedicated French director of the Egyptian Antiquities Department, was beginning to insist upon rules and regulations in excavation, thus destroying all the fun of what had been a joyous free-for-all of plunder and wanton destruction. But Petrie, who carried on a loud private war with both native and foreign thieves, did not even think much of Maspero. Petrie had a marvelous gift of invective; his blasphemous comments upon inefficiency and crooked dealing were uttered in an elegant scholarly style, which gave them even greater force. In his autobiography, Petrie inveighs against other archaeologists, the Department of Antiquities, Maspero, the British Museum, the French in general, and a good many Egyptians in particular. This may suggest that it was Petrie, and not the rest of the world, who was out of step. He was; but only because he was leading the parade, and his contemporaries had not yet learned the precise and intricate measure of the movements he set. Very little of Petrie's passion is personal; the people he damns to the lowest pits are those who, through stupidity or venality, allowed his precious antiquities to suffer. He liked most of the Egyptians he worked with, and won their affection and loyalty so completely that the men he trained in excavation, inhabitants of a village called Quft, supplied archaeological expeditions with headmen and diggers for many years.

The aspect of Petrie's character that astounds us even more than his fanatical insistence on detail is his fantastic energy. He ranged over Egypt from the Delta to the cataracts of Nubia like a mythological dragon, gulping in raw material and ejecting it in the form of neat volumes that cataloged bones, stones, beads, and pots. The real proof of his genius is that stories are beginning to collect about him, as is the case with the absentminded scholars in other fields whose passion for their work leaves them little time for the unimportant amenities of everyday life. Petrie himself describes, with characteristic gusto, how he used to work naked in the stifling corridors of the pyramids like "the Japanese carpenter who had nothing on but a pair of spectacles, except that I do not need the spectacles." He thought nothing of walking ten or twenty miles across the desert to collect the weekly payroll for his crew; and on one dig in Palestine he and his assistants had to get their drinking water from a well whose contents, in color and consistency, resembled thick split-pea soup. This was all to the good, Petrie comments blandly; in one dish they were getting not only water, but vegetables and meat as well.

Working for Petrie must have been rather a strain. His eating habits, which he expected his students to emulate, were particularly difficult. A row of tin cans and a can opener were set out on a slab in the tomb, which served as the expedition dining room, and when Petrie had finished he left what remained in the can for the next diner. It is rumored that two of his students fell in love while nursing each other through simultaneous bouts of food poisoning.

I have no compunctions about repeating these tales, because in my opinion they add to, rather than detract from, the stature of a great scholar. Most of the major contributions to the sum of learning have been made by men who had something else on their minds besides the amount of salt in the soup.

Among Petrie's many accomplishments was the classification of the prehistoric Egyptian cultures. He had no written material, and even the most basic chronological tool of the archaeologist, a stratified site, was lacking to him. Such sites are rare in Egypt but common in other parts of the Near East, where they have provided the best source of relative chronology. The best examples occur in the area between the Tigris and Euphrates, once the kingdom of Babylonia. Here the flat land is broken by steep-sided mounds, or tells, which were long regarded as man-made even before archaeologists started digging into them. The tells are city sites, representing centuries of continuous occupation. The earliest settlement was built on ground level. When it was destroyed, by armed conflict or by the natural processes of decay, the succeeding inhabitants leveled the ruined walls and built on top of them. Over the centuries the town grew higher and higher, perching upon the ruins of its ancestors. When an archaeologist digs such a site he can therefore assume that the town on the top of the heap is the latest in time, and the remains on the lowest level are the earliest. He can thus derive a "floating" chronology, which gives the sequence of the different cultures but not their absolute dates. He may number the cultures in order, or give them letters of the alphabet, working from the top down or the bottom up; and I, for one, wish he would get together with his associates and decide on a consistent method. The third level from the top of a mound called Tell Asmar may be referred to as Asmar III, or Asmar C—or Asmar VI, if the mound has nine levels. In order to pin down his floating chronology in terms of absolute time, the archaeologist must have at least one object that can be dated, either by an inscription upon it or by cross-reference with another culture whose absolute chronology has been fixed.

Petrie had no such site, and no reference books for cross-checking. A pioneer has to write his own books. All he had were graves—hundreds of them, scattered, and lacking any obvious relationship to one another or to anything else. The graves were only pits scooped out of the sand. They contained a variety of objects, though most of them had two things in common: bones and pottery. Yet Petrie dared to ask himself whether these holes in the ground could be arranged into a time sequence. That he ventured to ask the question at all is proof of his talent; that he could answer it, comes very close to genius.

The bones did not look promising, so Petrie turned to the pots. There were a lot of them, and—more important—they were not all alike. Pottery has another handy quality, in addition to the ones we have mentioned. It is subject to the dictates of fashion; it changes.

Taking a group of some seven hundred graves, Petrie, who had begun as a statistician, made an index slip for each grave. The slip was ruled in columns, one for each type of pot found in the grave. These had already been divided into a number of general categories by their appearance—red-polished ware, blacktopped ware, rough ware, and so on. As his starting point Petrie chose a type called "wavy-handled" (because it has wavy handles). These pots are derived from foreign types; we can trace their development from primitive prototypes in Palestine, but they appear fully formed in Egypt. The waves are ridges pressed into the ledge handle by the fingers of the potter; they enabled the carrier to get a better grip on the vessel.

In the earliest stage, these pots are globular, with pronounced handles and well-defined ridges. Later they become slimmer, with less prominent handles. In the last stage, the wavy-handled pot is a tall cylinder with a simple waved pattern—the remains of the original handle—around its upper section.

In defining these stages, Petrie made an assumption: that, as time went on, the features of a pottery type "degenerated" from functional to purely decorative. This assumption was supported by the change in the contents of the jars. At first they contained an aromatic ointment covered by a thin layer of clay. Then the ointment was replaced by scented clay. Last of all were the jars containing only solid clay. Here the notion of degeneration is more obvious, and it does not speak well for the predynastic Egyptians. As the relatives of the dead became more sophisticated, they decided that while they could certainly use the precious ointment themselves, its utility to the dead was only problematical. The poor corpse was not really cheated. Its needs could be served by magic, and the proper incantation could turn the clay into ghostly ointment. In later periods, this process of magical substitution reached its logical culmination; the dead were equipped for the hereafter by means of models, or even pictures, of the objects they would need.

Having established the earlier and later types of this particular pottery class, which he called "W," Petrie had the beginning of a chronological sequence. Now he could begin to tie in the other pottery classes that were found in company with the wavy-handled examples. Some of the graves that contained wavy-handled pots also had pottery of a class that Petrie designated "L," for "late," because it continued in use up to historic times. This gave him a terminal point, since the examples of the "L" type that occurred in First Dynasty graves could be dated. In all Petrie worked with nine classes of prehistoric pottery. Besides the "L" and "W" classes he had a blacktopped red group (B), a red-polished (P), a rough (R), and others. Not all the graves contained all nine classes of pottery, but each grave contained at least two; if a grave did not have more than one class, it was useless for a comparative methodology, and Petrie did not include it within his corpus of examples.

Through correlation with the wavy-handled types Petrie was able to work out sequence patterns for the other classes of pottery. Of course, the chronological developments of various classes had to be consistent. For example, let us assume that subtypes 9–12 of wavy-handled pottery are consistently found with subtypes 1–3 of the red-polished ware. Then subtypes 4–6 of the red-polished ware cannot occur with the wavy-handled subtypes of an earlier date—subtypes 1–9. If they do, then something is wrong with the internal arrangement of one class or the other—or both. This is a very simplified example of the sort of cross-check Petrie had to make with nine different classes of pottery and seven hundred graves. And he had no computer! The logical processes involved are not especially profound, but the scope of the material is so broad that one's imagination reels in considering it.

However, this was precisely the sort of problem at which Petrie excelled; as a recorder of multitudinous details, he was probably without a peer among archaeologists. He gave numbers to all the subtypes within his nine classes and wrote the numbers on his index slips, one slip for each grave. Having transformed his pots into mathematical symbols, he could juggle bits of paper rather than objects; we can picture him hovering over a big table spread with an intellectual meal of seven hundred index slips, rushing from one side of the table to the other in order to find the right spot for a particular slip, and feasting his eyes on a particularly consistent arrangement, like a gourmet at a seven- (or seven-hundred-) course dinner.

In the end, Petrie had a series of grave groups whose pottery formed a consistent and logical pattern. The pottery classes overlapped in time, naturally; one category might be in its last stages of development before another category came on the scene, and the oldest class might have vanished altogether before the latest one appeared. Yet the overlapping of classes was continuous, and there was never a point at which a comparative method, involving at least two types, could not be applied. Petrie had forced his scattered graves into a sequence, and the numbers he assigned to the grave groups were called "sequence dates," for they had no connection with years B.C. There were fifty numbers in all, running from thirty to eighty; it was typical of Petrie that he left a range open for future discoveries that might antedate his earliest graves.

Petrie had developed a framework into which newly discovered graves could be fitted by a simple comparison of pottery types. There was still no way of dating prehistoric objects in terms of absolute time. However, the framework did provide a comparative chronology, and it was more capable of being broken down into broader subdivisions than single sequence dates. Certain groups of graves, and hence of sequence dates, formed distinctive assemblages, which had enough in common to be labeled as separate "cultures."

The criteria used to distinguish cultures involve materials other than pottery—stone tools, weapons, ornaments, and so on. An increasing number of prehistoric village sites have turned up; the objects found at these sites also form coherent assemblages. At one of these sites, a discovery made in 1925 took Petrie's work out of the realm of theory. Gertrude Caton-Thompson, working at Hememieh, found a stratified site, and there were Petrie's prehistoric cultures in the sequence he had postulated. Below the earliest he had identified she found a still earlier culture, which was assigned sequence dates from the numbers the great pioneer had left open for just such an eventuality. Since Petrie's day his work has been refined and to some extent revised, but the basic sequence remains.

Thanks to the work of Petrie and Caton-Thompson and their successors, we now have a very general picture of prehistoric life in ancient Egypt. Even at this early period we must distinguish between the two major geographical subdivisions of the country—Upper Egypt and Lower Egypt.

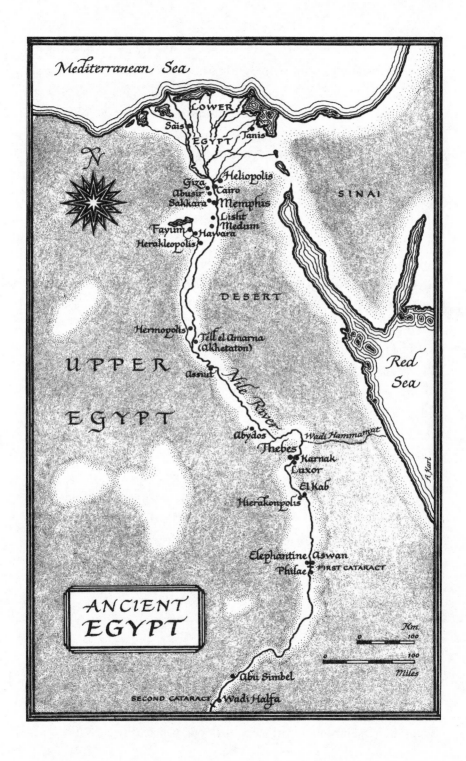

Mediterranean Sea

LOWER

Sais

EGYPT

Tanis

N

SINAI

Giza
Abusir
Sakkara
Heliopolis
Cairo
Memphis
Lisht
Medum
Fayum
Hawara
Herakleopolis

DESERT

Hermopolis
Tell el Amarna
(Akhetaton)

Assiut

UPPER

EGYPT

Nile River

Red
Sea

Abydos
Wadi Hammamat
Thebes
Karnak
Luxor
El Kab
Hierakonpolis

A. Karl

Elephantine
Philae
Aswan
FIRST CATARACT

ANCIENT
EGYPT

Km.
0   100
0   100
Miles

Abu Simbel

SECOND CATARACT   Wadi Halfa

In order to comprehend this terminology, the reader must adjust to what may seem a piece of striking illogic: Upper Egypt is the valley of the Nile, from the Cairo region south, and Lower Egypt is the Delta. The illogic is only illusory; it arises from the fact that the Nile flows from south to north, and the region nearest the source is properly "upper" in relation to the mouth of the river. Since the Delta is at the top of modern maps, with the river hanging down like a tail, most people find the Upper Egypt–Lower Egypt concept hard to keep in mind. I don't blame them. It was years before I could read "Upper Egypt" without making a conscious mental effort to remember where it was. All I can do, however, is sympathize, because the names are often used by archaeologists, and there is no changing them now. To confuse the issue still more, some scholars believe that in ancient times Upper Egypt ended near Assiut, with Lower Egypt being everything north of that city.

The two regions differ from each other in many ways, the most obvious being that of physical topography. Upper Egypt is a fantastic country—five hundred miles long by perhaps five miles wide. On either side of the river is a narrow strip of fertile black soil, bounded by sand and by the steep cliffs of the desert plateau through which the river has, through immemorial ages, carved and deepened its channel. The line between living and dead land is sharply defined; one may stand today with one foot on the sand and the other on the green-growing fields. The ancient Egyptians were keenly conscious of the difference between the "black land" and the barren "red land," and these two terms occur frequently in their literature. The black land was precious and cherished. Temples, palaces, and towns were built whenever possible on the wasteland of sand, which lay between the fertile strip and the barrier of cliffs, so that not an inch of cultivable soil would be wasted. The two narrow ribbons of black land, one on either side of the river, have always supported a disproportionately large population, when one considers the actual acreage under cultivation. In ancient times this situation was possible because of the unfailing fertility of the soil, which was the result of a unique phenomenon—the annual flood, which deposited not only water but also nutrient silt upon the fields. Other rivers perform this obliging service, but never with the regularity of the Nile; so predictable was the Nile rise that the ancient Egyptians called one of their seasons "Inundation," for during those months the land was always under water, soaking up the life-giving nutrients that the river had taken up in its northward flow.

The idea of automated irrigation may sound paradisaical to a farmer, but it was not so easy as one might suppose. The height of the river varied from year to year, and a difference of inches might mean the difference between famine or prosperity. Further, the water had to be directed to the proper place during the dry months, which are very dry indeed.

When the Nile nears the Mediterranean, it breaks up into several branches whose beds form the large river Delta. In ancient times this land was swamp, thick with reed and papyrus and teeming with bird and animal life. There was no need for irrigation or inundation here; the problem was that of too much water.

There was a contrast between the Delta and the river valley in psychological, as well as physical, terms. The Delta bordered on the sea, which was the ancient highway of commerce and conquest; the valley was isolated on both sides by wild deserts and wilder people.

It would seem logical, then, that the Delta region developed earlier, and more quickly, than did the south. This doesn't seem to have been the case. However, we know more about Upper Egypt than about the Delta. Material that survived in the hot, dry air of Upper Egypt rotted away in the Delta swamps. This fact affects archaeological knowledge in two ways; not only is there less material to be found in Lower Egypt, but also less work has been done there. It is frustrating to excavate in a region where you have to work in water up to your knees, and infuriating to get only indistinguishable lumps of rotted material for your pains. It is no wonder that archaeologists prefer to breathe the salubrious desert air of the south, which has preserved even such fragile objects as textiles and painted reliefs. However, long-suffering scholars have in recent years worked extensively in the Delta, and the picture is constantly being revised.

The sea—the "Great Green," as the Egyptians called it—may be a high road for contacts between peoples, but it may also be a barrier. An island is hard to invade, and in one sense all of Egypt was an "island" society. The sea protected it on the north, and inhospitable deserts deterred invasion on both sides. Conquest from the south was hampered because of the nature of the river upstream from Egypt. From Aswan north to the Mediterranean the Nile was and is easily navigable, but south of Aswan there was a cataract region, a stretch of river filled with rocks and waterfalls, which rendered the passage of ships difficult and peril-filled. This situation has changed since the construction of the Aswan dams, but during the period that is the subject of this book there were five more cataracts south of Aswan, some even more dangerous than the first. The first cataract was, for many years, the southern boundary of ancient Egypt.

Barriers, of water or desert, can keep out other things besides invading armies—trade, and new ideas, for instance. One theory of the beginning of history in Egypt maintains that the valley was developed more quickly than the Delta. If Egyptian civilization owes something to external stimulation, the stimuli could have been transmitted via the Red Sea route and brought overland across a well-known caravan route that leads from the sea to the region around modern Luxor. So far, excavation in the area has not turned up any physical proof of such contact. Another theory holds that the predynastic cultures of Nubia were much more advanced than earlier, Eurocentric scholars believed, and that they interacted with their kin to the north. A cemetery at Qustul, in Lower Nubia (that's the region closer to Egypt than Upper Nubia), contained graves so large and so rich that the excavator, Bruce Williams, considered they must have belonged to great chiefs, or even kings. There is no sneaking around this by claiming that the graves belonged to Egyptians or Egyptian vassals; the artifacts were typical of the A-group Nubian culture, which in its later phases (you might have known there would be phases) was contemporaneous with the late predynastic in Egypt. Williams even put forth the daring suggestion that these Nubian rulers conquered southern

Egypt and were the stimulus for, if not the actual founders of, pharaonic civilization. This theory is considered pretty far-out, and the sad thing is that with much of what was Lower Nubia now buried fathoms deep under Lake Nasser, there may never be a definitive answer.

When I was a graduate student—back in antedeluvian times—we were given neat lists of prehistoric cultures, one succeeding the other like steps on a ladder: Tasian, Badarian, Amratian, Gerzean, and Semainean in the south; Fayum A, Merimde, and Maadi in the north. Each culture had a few more amenities than the one that had preceded it, and the latest, Gerzean-Semainean, had achieved a fairly high standard of living for a predynastic society, with painted pottery, beautifully worked flint tools, stone vessels, metal, and neat houses.

These cultures were named after the type site, the place where that particular culture was first unearthed. This is a time-honored and hideously confusing device, as anyone who has encountered the Aurignacians and Levalloisians of European prehistory knows to his sorrow. It becomes even more confusing when archaeologists change their minds about the names—as they almost always do. Semainean was always a suspect culture; it is now generally believed to be a variant of the Gerzean. Tasian may not exist either, except as a form of the Badarian. Amratian is now generally referred to as Naqada I, and Gerzean is Naqada II and III, each with internal subdivisions; so according to some dating systems, late Gerzean (from about 3500 B.C.) is equivalent to Naqada IID–I and D–2. You will be happy to hear that so far Badarian is still Badarian. It is the one Caton-Thompson found at Hememieh, underneath Petrie's two major cultures—Amratian and Gerzean.

We may as well get all the names in while we're at it; Naqada III is also known as the Protodynastic—as compared with the Predynastic in general—and in some quarters Naqada IIIC is referred to as Dynasty O. More about this ambiguous period later. (If you happen to run across a reference to Dynasty OO, take my advice and ignore it.)

Perhaps the most useful remark we can make about the predynastic cultures is that they are related to one another, not only chronologically but also causally; each has certain things in common with the one that followed it. In general, the nearer in time to the First Dynasty, the more complex the society—the more "civilized," in our terms. Yet conventionally the beginning of civilization in Egypt does not occur until historic times, with the beginning of the First Dynasty. We are cautiously tiptoeing around the edges of a problem that is, in part, one of terminology; scholars are not as precise as they might be in defining words like *culture* and *civilization*. The two words are sometimes used interchangeably, but not all cultures are civilizations. *Civilization* itself may be used specifically, as in the phrases "Egyptian civilization" and "Chinese civilization," or it may be used as an abstraction, to describe a state of affairs that is contrasted with barbarism. The lack of precision is regrettable; however, we may avoid a certain amount of confusion by restricting ourselves, at this point, to the second of the two meanings. We have been talking about prehistoric, or predynastic, cultures. Gerzean, Amratian, and the rest are not civilizations, nor are they "civilization." At what point, then, does a culture acquire the traits that enable it to be considered a civilization?

THE WAGON OR THE MOUNTAIN

After the phenomenal leap from nomadism to settled village life, prehistoric culture shuffled along rather placidly for a few thousand years. Then something peculiar happened.

Scholars who concern themselves with the broader problems of history often anthropomorphize the cultures they are comparing. The man-shaped figures that represent civilizations may be pictured as climbing a ladder or a mountain slope, progressing ever higher on their way to—what? Us? But if we are determined to have an analogy, we might say that the process of civilization more closely resembles the acceleration of a wheeled vehicle on a downward slope; slow at first, then ponderously gaining speed until it rushes headlong across the level plain beneath. Momentum carries it on for some distance, initially at a speed so great that it may seem as if acceleration were still taking place. But eventually the heavy vehicle slows . . . and slows . . . and stops. And there it remains, in a state of rest, until some unknown force returns to push it toward another slope, or until it decays and disappears.

We cannot really compare a culture to a wagon any more than to a human being climbing a mountain. But analogies are fun, and this one gives a mental picture that may be useful to us. For something did give the Egyptian prehistoric culture a shove, during the late period we call Naqada II. The picture of society we see then is noticeably different from that of the earlier cultures. People lived in houses with windows and doors, and wore clothing woven out of flax. The flint tools are elegant, even to an antiflint observer; and copper is increasingly used for artifacts which had been made of stone. Graves are deeper and more carefully built, sometimes lined with wooden planks. There are differences in the graves now, some still small, some larger and more pretentious, and the grave goods of the larger tombs are richer—sure signs of class differentiation. People had more time for activities that were not directly related to the struggle for existence; they played games and they painted pictures on their pots. The old brown and red pottery continues, but a new type enters, made of a new kind of clay and decorated with quaint little figures of men and animals and boats. The boats carry insignias, which may be the standards or devices of small political units; we assume that in this period the land of Egypt consisted of many communities, each governed by a local chief. These changes are striking, but they are not so striking as the further changes that are about to occur. We are very close to the First Dynasty now—to the beginning of history and of civilization, properly speaking. We are curious, not only about what happened, but also about why it happened.

Let us go back to the wagon on the slope. We might carry the analogy one step further and ask: Does the wagon creep along (we will grandly ignore the fact that neither a culture nor a wagon can be said to "creep") until it reaches the point at which the ground drops away from beneath its wheels; or does someone come up behind it and give it a shove? More pedantically: does civilization arise naturally out of a primitive culture because that culture has, by slow accretion, reached a critical stage of development; or does an external stimulus serve as the catalytic agent?

I would like to avoid the term "primitive," because it implies a certain value judgment. I can't do it, though. Alternatives like "preliterate" and "prehistoric" are at once too explicit and too vague. You know what I mean, and I know what I mean, so let's stick to "primitive."

We may argue about exactly what distinguishes a civilization from a primitive culture, or even about whether such a clear-cut distinction can be made. Let's not argue about it. Let us merely agree that certain new elements are necessary to define a civilization: monumental architecture, centralized government, a division of labor resulting in social classes, and, perhaps most important, writing. If we think about these elements, we see that each of them implies more than it says about the society in question. Monumental architecture, for instance, requires advanced techniques in the preparation of materials, and some understanding of architectural and mechanical principles; it also suggests that the state can spare some of its members from the basic work of food production to work on labor gangs; further, it implies that there is an elite group within the state that has the power to order and supervise such labor. The keeping of records becomes necessary—for purposes of taxation, if for no other reason.

So when and where did all this begin? Did the idea spread outward from the original center to other societies, or did it occur independently in various parts of the world? If it did occur only once, where was the cradle of civilization?

The problem of Diffusion versus Independent Invention is still being debated by scholars, and also by people whose scholarship is, to put it nicely, goofy. The latter believe in a single source, but they don't agree on what it was. Some give the credit to the hypothetical geniuses of the lost continent of Atlantis. However, the most popular current theory favors visitors from outer space. I don't want to get started on this, because it makes me lose my temper.

A slightly more believable version of the Diffusion scenario holds that all advanced civilizations derived from a single terrestrial source, with Egypt being the leading contender. It is only slightly more believable, really. Despite superficial similarities such as pyramids and sun worship, the advanced civilizations of the Americas have no provable, direct connection with the much older civilizations of the Middle East.

It's not as simplistic as that, of course. There is always communication among cultures; the closer they are geographically, the more frequent the contacts. Enterprising merchants have been around since prehistoric times; some such trader might have seen a pot whose shape took his fancy and brought it home to be imitated and improved upon. He might have watched, openmouthed, as a priest scribbled weird symbols on a piece of stone or stamped equally weird symbols into a clay tablet; once the purpose of the exercise had been explained, its usefulness would have been apparent to a keen-minded man. This process is sometimes referred to as stimulus diffusion—the copying of a concept instead of an object.

Ancient Sumer and Ancient Egypt aren't that far distant physically. Egyptologists and Sumerologists have been arguing for years about which of their pet civilizations was the first to invent writing. For a long time the Sumerologists were ahead. Their arguments went like this: Despite the fact that elements of the two cultures appear dissimilar—the mud-brick ziggurats of Mesopotamia and the stone pyramids, the pretty picture writing of Egypt and the bird-track cuneiform—there are signs of Mesopotamian influence in Egypt at the very end of the predynastic period. Cylinder seals are typical of Mesopotamia and atypical of Egypt, but there are cylinder seals in late predynastic graves. Building stone is scarce in the flat plains of the Land of the Two Rivers, so the natives of that region built in brick; the earliest large-scale architecture of Egypt is in the same brick, and it imitates a well-known Mesopotamian style, recessed brick niching. Even when the Egyptians began to quarry their numerous fine sources of stone, they cut it up into brick-size pieces.

These traits died out early in Egypt and were replaced by "Egyptian" ways of doing things. Stone architecture began to employ the monolithic blocks we can see in the Giza pyramids; seal impressions were made with stamp seals—scarabs—instead of with the cylinder type. And the writing, of course, is completely dissimilar. The pictures of objects, which became the hieroglyphic symbols of Egyptian writing, were all Egyptian objects. But who got the idea first, the citizens of Sumer or those of Egypt?

Not that it really matters. However, since some people think it does matter, the reader should be informed that in recent years discoveries at the holy city of Abydos in Egypt have turned up examples of writing—typically Egyptian writing—that are earlier than anything found in Mesopotamia. So there.

Let's get back to the wagon. The analogy isn't bad, actually. The achievement of civilization, however arbitrarily we define it, was not an event; it was a process, and a complicated process at that. A number of factors were responsible. The concept of stimulus diffusion, which we mentioned above, was undoubtedly one of those factors, but the idea of writing wouldn't have caught on unless the borrowing culture had reached a stage of development in which the new concept was understood and desired. In terms of our analogy, both a change in terrain and a push are needed to get the wagon going; the stimulus would not be felt if the circumstances were adverse.

Because people like simple answers, scholars once postulated a "dynastic race" whose people entered Egypt at the end of the prehistoric period, bringing with them the gifts of civilization. They unified the land and, like the Normans in England, ruled the conquered indigenes as a racially distinct noble class, before interbreeding produced a single people. The dynastic race came from Asia—a large place, but one cannot summarize the conflicting theories of origin more precisely than that. They spoke a Semitic language, which mingled with the Hamitic (African) tongue of the natives to produce the Egyptian speech.

The term "race" is out of favor, and rightly so. Anthropologists use it to delimit certain groups of human beings in terms of "nonessential" differences—skin color, hair texture, shape of skull, and so on. Study of predynastic skeletons suggest that they may belong to several different physical subtypes, but we can't be sure who these people were, where they came from, or what they actually did. All sorts of people came into Egypt, from prehistoric times onward—merchants, traders, invading armies, immigrants, envoys. We will see them coming, and sometimes going, as we follow the long centuries of Egyptian history, and once we get well into history proper we can document foreign influences more accurately. But in preliterate cultures we don't have written records, or even much material. Often the evidence for a "race of invaders" consists of cultural changes, which, in prehistoric societies, primarily means new kinds of pots. I have a prejudice against this sort of argument. I get idiotic mental images of invading armies brandishing pots, which they thrust threateningly into the trembling hands of the conquered indigenes. Current thinking, I am pleased to report, denies the dynastic race and the waves of invaders. Cultural change can result from trade as well as conquest, and the more we learn about predynastic cultures the more we see continuity and interrelationships.

This has been an unsatisfactory sort of discussion; instead of answering questions, it raises new ones. But this is the subject matter of prehistoric archaeology, when it goes beyond the simple cataloging of bones and pottery. The questions raised are important questions. If they are ever answered, we will learn much, not only about Egypt, but also about the human animal in general. The scope of the problem is universal, and the answers deal with man himself.

The beginning of history in Egypt is signalized by a noteworthy event—the unification of the country into a single nation, whose boundaries ran from the sea in the north to the first cataract of Aswan. We know very little about political organization before this consolidation. We assume that the small tribal units of the early predynastic gradually amalgamated and formed larger social and political groupings. At one time Egypt may have been made up of several dozen little states, each ruled by a prince or a chief. Through conquest and marriage and the other techniques of imperialism the smaller units were eventually joined into larger kingdoms. We have now ambled into the late predynastic period, aka the Protodynastic, Naqada III, or according to some people, Dynasty O.

A lot more is known about this period than was the case thirty years ago. One of the most fascinating sites is that of Hierakonpolis, which is about thirty miles south of Luxor. (As the reader may have guessed, I have selected it from among several other places because I've been there.)

There have been sporadic excavations at Hierakonpolis for over a century. Early expeditions turned up some of the best-known artifacts of the late predynastic—the Narmer palette, the so-called painted tomb, the Scorpion mace head, and so on. In the late 1960s an expedition settled in for the long haul, and it has laid bare innumerable cemeteries, a town site of considerable extent, and the remains of one of the first temples found in Egypt. The temple was dedicated to the god Horus, who became the symbol of kingship and one of the most popular deities of Egypt throughout dynastic history. The fact that Horus was apparently the local god, the sheer size of the town, and the existence of various royal artifacts suggest that Hierakonpolis was the capital of an Upper Egyptian kingdom—one of several, perhaps, with Thinis (Abydos) and Naqada as rivals. Eventually, to make a long story short, the kingdoms became one. Whether diplomacy and royal intermarriage were factors is and probably always will be unknown, but there certainly was a lot of fighting. Scenes of battle and the ceremonial bashing of captives appear on carved objects dating from this period—knife handles, mace heads, and stone palettes.

Presumably a similar process was going on in the Delta, so that eventually there were two kingdoms, one in the north and one in the south. Each kingdom had its own set of symbols and insignias and its own pro-

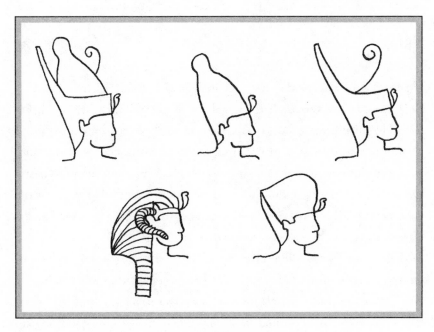

Crowns of the king of Egypt
Above, right to left: red crown, white crown, double crown
Below, right to left: blue crown, Nemes headdress

tective gods and goddesses. The king of Upper Egypt wore a distinctive White Crown and the king of Lower Egypt a Red Crown.

We know that there were kings of the southland, for one of them was the Unifier, who conquered the north and became the first king of the Two Lands of Egypt. We know his name—Menes. We know when this signficant event happened. It was in 3400 B.C.; or 3110 B.C.; or maybe 2850 B.C.

A relative chronology like Petrie's presents problems of one order; absolute dating has its own difficulties, and they are not minor ones. The adjective "absolute" may sound misleading. How can a system be absolute when we can give three alternative dates for an event like the beginning of the First Dynasty? We would expect one date, or none at all. Let us now consider some of the techniques used in Egyptian chronology. It is a complicated subject and deserves a section all to itself.

TROUBLES WITH TIME

If the reader is up-to-date on archaeological matters, he may expect a short, snappy answer to all the problems of chronology: carbon 14. He would be mistaken, on two counts: there is nothing short or simple about the radiocarbon process, or its applicability to historical problems; and, in fact, it did not solve the major chronological questions about dynastic Egypt. The process is certainly fantastically useful in other parts of the past, particularly in those very remote eras that are the province of the archaeologist-anthropologist rather than the archaeologist-historian. But in the case of Egypt, the previously established dating system helped to establish the validity of the carbon 14 process rather than the reverse.

The savage reader (to plagiarize Mark Twain) may reasonably ask at this point, "Why talk about it, then?" There are several good, logical answers to the question. One is that the radiocarbon process is very useful in dealing with Egyptian prehistory; another is that carbon 14 is only one of a number of related methods, the great gift of the physical sciences to history, which deserve a more than cursory treatment. But the real reason I want to discuss carbon 14 is because it delights me by its inherent improbability. Eighty years ago, the suggestion that a physicist could tell an archaeologist the age of a piece of wood by purely physical, laboratory techniques would have struck said archaeologist as completely preposterous. This is the real excitement of archaeology, and of life in general: that the horizon of what may be known is not bounded by what is known. And, of course, the development of the radiocarbon process is a fascinating intellectual adventure in itself.

In 1945, Willard F. Libby of the University of Chicago was studying the effect of cosmic ray neutrons upon the nitrogen of the atmosphere. The result of the meeting was a genuine, if tiny, nuclear reaction; the product was radioactive carbon. Libby argued that since its chemical behavior is the same as that of ordinary carbon, this carbon 14, or radiocarbon, should form carbon dioxide molecules and mix in with the ordinary carbon dioxide of the atmosphere. Every high school student of biology knows that carbon dioxide is taken in by plants in the process of photosynthesis. Since animals live off plants, the conclusion was logical, though rather startling: all living matter should be weakly radioactive, from the tiny proportion of carbon 14 that it absorbs.

The first verification of Libby's theory came from a decidedly inglorious source—the methane gas given off by the city of Baltimore's sewage. Not only did this decaying organic material give off radioactivity, but it contained exactly the proportion of carbon 14 that Libby had predicted. Subsequent tests were performed on samples of wood, oil, and other material from all over the world. The proportions were as predicted.

This was a good confirmation of the theory, but it was more than that. Libby immediately saw the possible application of the process to dating. Among his samples had been wood from the tombs of Snefru and Djoser, kings of the Fourth Dynasty. The dates given by radiocarbon checked out with the calculations Egyptologists had made independently.

How does it work? Obviously the laboratory apparatus did not contain a neon coil that lit up and read 4,500 years. Before the laboratory results could be translated into years of time, a lot of work had to be done.

Let's take a specific organic object as an example—an oak tree, perhaps. When the tree died, it of course stopped taking in carbon 14. As it lay in the earth, or in the walls of a building in the form of planks, the radiocarbon it contained at its demise, being unstable, began to disintegrate. Libby calculated that the rate is about one percent each eighty years. The process of decay is exponential; that is, in the first eighty years one percent of the total decays, in the next eighty years one percent of the remaining total, and so on. Scientists talk about decay rate in terms of its "half-life"—the length of time it takes for half the original radioactive content to decay. At the latest measurement, the half-life of carbon 14 is 5,568 years.

Thus, by measuring the amount of carbon 14 remaining in our oak tree, or any piece of it, we can calculate (and if that sounds simple, it is not) how many years have passed since the tree stopped living. Truly, the process is brilliantly conceived. But it has certain limitations.

These limitations arise from various causes. One is the problem of the increase of error. You may have seen radiocarbon dates given in various publications; they look something like this: 3,325 years +– 150. The "plus or minus" indicates the range of possible error. The older the date given, the greater the range. Why the lack of precision? Well, for one thing, it is very difficult to get an uncontaminated sample, free of modern organic substances. If the sample we are working with is fairly recent in age, it still contains a large part of the original radiocarbon; hence, the intrusion of a chunk of modern carbon 14 represents only a small proportion of the total and does not affect the results too much. But if our object is thirty thousand years old, it has lost all but a tiny amount of the carbon 14 it contained at its demise; the amount is so small that it is hard to detect, even with precise laboratory instruments, and any intrusion, however minute, affects the results enormously. The problem of contamination was a serious one at first, when the process was new and unfamiliar; field-workers packed samples in straw or allowed bits of root from living trees to get into the container. Another source of contamination is the atmosphere itself; laboratory instruments must be carefully shielded against cosmic rays and must themselves be completely free from radioactive contamination. The composition of the atmosphere has been changed in the past century, not so much by atomic explosions as by the "old" carbon released by the combustion of coal and oil since the Industrial Revolution.

All these factors affect the accuracy of radiocarbon dates. Then there is the pleasingly mysterious "systematic uncertainty," the causes of which seem to be unknown, which gives errors of one hundred to two hundred years. Further limitations come from the fact that only certain materials are suitable for processing. Charcoal and well-preserved wood are best; bone, for various reasons, has given unsatisfactory results. The sample must be burned to be tested, which means that choice specimens are not readily relinquished. And, because of the rapid (in geologic terms) decay rate of carbon 14, the process cannot be used with any material that is over 70,000 years old. This is plenty long enough from our point of view, but it frustrates archaeologists who work with fossil man and his immediate ancestors.

Several other physical techniques are employed in chronology. Thermoluminesce analyzes the decay of certain elements in pottery. Dendrochronology counts tree rings, and in some parts of the world scientists have constructed overlapping series of such rings which cover extended periods of time. Both techniques have their limitations, which I do not intend to discuss. Suffice it to say that although they have been of some use in establishing prehistoric chronology, their use in the dynastic periods of Egypt is limited. By the time these techniques were developed the chronology had already been fairly well established—though like everything else in Egyptology, it is constantly being revised.

One of the people who worked on chronology back at the beginning of the present century was James Henry Breasted, who is arguably the United States's most famous Egyptologist. Born in the small midwestern town of Rockford, Illinois, Breasted had a long way to go to get to Egypt. In his day it was essential for an Egyptologist to study in Berlin, where the monumental figure of Adolf Erman was placing the Egyptian language on a sound philological basis for the first time. Breasted's family was not wealthy, but he got to Berlin, and later to Egypt. Like Petrie, the American Egyptologist was a man of tremendous energy, but his talents lay in philology and administration rather than in excavation. His *History of Egypt* is still a wonderful read, though his interpretations are out-of-date. Breasted's magnum opus was the translation of every known historical text from Egypt; the result fills five thick volumes, and required the personal inspection and copying by Breasted of almost every text included—many of the pre-Breasted copies of inscriptions look as if they were made at twilight by a myopic scholar who had lost his glasses.

The book, *Ancient Records of Egypt*, is Breasted's great work in terms of published material, but many would say that his true monument is an institution, not a book. This is the renowned Oriental Institute of the University of Chicago, the first department for the study of Egyptology on American soil. Its expeditions have worked for many years in other parts of the Near East as well as in Egypt, and its publications number in the hundreds.

The first volume of *Ancient Records* contains a lucid summary of basic methods of Egyptian chronology. These methods have been refined since Breasted's time, but the essential sources remain relatively unchanged.

The nearest thing to a contemporary history of Egypt we possess is the work of an Egyptian priest named Manetho, who wrote and lived under Ptolemy II Philadelphus, in the middle of the third century B.C. "Possess" is a misleading term, for we do not have the text of Manetho's history. What we have are quotations and synopses made by later historians of Roman times. The quotations come mainly from Josephus, a Jewish historian who was trying to make a case for the antiquity of his people; the superior attitude of his Greek fellow scholars had riled him. Josephus is a biased source; he had an ax to grind, and even if he was too honest to misquote consciously, his bias would probably affect his choice of material.

The other sources merely summarize Manetho, giving lists of kings and sometimes a sentence of description. The copies do not always agree with one another, and they garble names and dates most horribly. How much of the error is due to the copyist, and how much to Manetho himself—who was, after all, a long way in time from the beginnings of Egyptian history—we do not know. But we know that Manetho is not to be trusted blindly, at least not in the copies we have. Speaking of dynasties, we should note that they are derived from Manetho, who was trying to distinguish separate royal houses or families. In view of the fact that Manetho is damned with such faint praise, one might ask why we rely on him for this breakdown. The answer, as most Egyptologists admit, is because Manetho's concept has been used for so long that it would be inconvenient to discard it. His dynastic breakdowns work well enough, though in some cases it is hard to see why he started a new dynasty when he did.

Painstaking archaeological spadework and the study of hieroglyphic inscriptions have enabled scholars to check Manetho's list of kings against contemporary records, and to construct lists of their own that sometimes differ drastically from the Greek's. By the time of the Middle Kingdom the Egyptians were dating events by the years of a king's reign. If a mass of dated objects gives year 23 as the last year for a particular monarch, we assume that he probably ruled no longer than twenty-three years. The records are fairly complete for the later period of Egyptian history; so, counting back from 525 B.C., when the Persians invaded Egypt, we can estimate the length of the later dynasties with fair accuracy.

Records from the earlier dynasties are still fragmentary. The Old Kingdom, which includes Dynasties One through Six, was followed by a period of confusion, when the country broke apart into smaller units ruled by local princes, some of whom continued to claim the titles of pharaoh. This First Intermediate Period, as it is called, causes chronological problems because dynasties Seven through Eleven, which comprise the period, were, in some cases, overlapping or contemporaneous. By the end of the Eleventh Dynasty the kingdom was again united under kings who kept good records. This is the Middle Kingdom, which includes dynasties Eleven and Twelve. Another period of disunion followed the Twelfth Dynasty, and again there is disagreement about the length of dynasties Thirteen through Seventeen. The Eighteenth Dynasty marks the beginning of the New Kingdom, or Empire, as it used to be called; documentary evidence from this period is good, but here the chronological problem is confused by possible coregencies, which have provided Egyptologists with some of their most exciting and inspiring sources of argument. There are other chronological confusions between the end of the Nineteenth Dynasty and the end of Egyptian history proper, so we cannot simply add up the known years of various kings' reigns to find out when the First Dynasty began. Fortunately, there are other methods.

Everybody knows that the Egyptians invented the calendar. However, this is one of the pleasant oversimplifications that appear in high school history books; the Egyptians had not one calendar, but several. Probably the earliest was a lunar calendar whose months ran from one new moon to the next. A number of "primitive" peoples have lunar calendars, since the changes in the phases of the moon are conspicuous; but in Egypt the rhythmical activity of the river soon suggested another method of dividing the year—a division into seasons. One of these seasons was called "Inundation," and the rise of the Nile at the beginning of the annual flood was an event eagerly awaited and anxiously noted. During the third millennium B.C. an event of quite a different character occurred at about the same time as the beginning of Inundation—the reappearance after a period of invisibility of the brightest star in the heavens. Sirius, the Dog Star, which the Greeks called "Sothis," came to be regarded as the harbinger of the Inundation, and its heliacal rising was named *wp rnpt,* the "Opening of the Year."

The lunar calendar worked admirably for a simple agricultural people; but as society became more complex, it was seen to have disadvantages. Every new month had to be established by observation, and no one knew in advance whether it would have thirty days or twenty-nine. At the end of the lunar year there would be a space of days, even weeks, before the opening of the new year, which was signalized by the rising of Sirius. So some busy bureaucrat decided, with royal approval, to set up another year whose exact length would be known in advance. This is called the "civil calendar," and it is the distant ancestor of the one we use. It had twelve months of thirty days each, with five "intercalary" days at the end of the year. We don't know how this unknown genius arrived at the number 365; he might have counted the days between successive risings of Sirius or he might have averaged out the number of days that elapsed between Inundations over a period of years.

Even this solution to the problem of time has a difficulty, which the reader has probably noticed. The true solar year does not have 365 days, but 365 and a quarter and then some. Hence, if the "Opening of the Year" occurred on day one, month one, when the civil calendar was first set up, four years later it would fall on day two, month one. A period of 1,460 years (four times 365) constituted what we call a "Sothic cycle" and brought the rising of Sirius back to "day one, month one" of the civil calendar once again.

There's a lot more one can say about the calendars of ancient Egypt, but I am not that one. What really matters for our purpose is the Sothic cycle. From time to time the Egyptians saw fit to mention the rising of the Dog Star in connection with a date of their civil calendar. Now we know, from Roman sources, that a Sothic cycle—the coincidence of the rising of the star and the first day of the civil calendar—began in A.D. 139. By a simple process of arithmetic we can calculate that the previous cycle started in 1322 B.C., and the one before that in 2782 B.C. (Bear in mind that there is no year zero.) We have a mention of a Sothic rising, with date, in the Twelfth Dynasty, and another in the Eighteenth. Hence we can establish these events in terms of our own time scheme with relative accuracy. Why not absolute? Because we don't know where the observations were taken. It makes a difference. Still, the variance is only a few years one way or the other. Knowing the dates of the Twelfth and Eighteenth Dynasties enables us to fix the approximate length of the confused period between these two stable periods.

We do not have, as yet, any astronomical reference from the Old Kingdom. There are two major documents that attempt to give a king list, with dates, for the Old Kingdom. One of them is in pieces and the other is in fragments.

The fate of the Turin Papyrus is told in a story that may be apocryphal, but whose general spirit is unhappily too typical of the early days of archaeology. The papyrus was complete when it was discovered in 1823 by a gentleman named Bernardino Drovetti, who stuck it into a jar that he tied around his waist. He then rode off to town on his donkey. The gait of a donkey being what it is, Egyptologists have been pushing the pieces of the papyrus around ever since, and cursing Drovetti as they do so. The other document, the Palermo Stone, is equally fragmented, though its material would seem so much more durable. Several bits of it have been found, and the absence of the remainder is all the more frustrating because it gives year-by-year accounts of events for every king of the first five dynasties.

If the reader finds the foregoing discussion confusing, let me assure him that I have simplified the various problems to a degree most Egyptologists would consider unscholarly in the extreme. There are several other king lists from later dynasties, but they aren't complete, perhaps because they were never intended to be historical documents. Names like those of the so-called heretic pharaohs of the Eighteenth Dynasty are omitted. There are references to Egypt in various foreign documents, but the chronologies of these countries have their own internal problems. Even if we were able to pin down a specific year for the beginning of the First Dynasty, this would be misleading; the unification was more likely a process than a single event.

So, although most authorities agree that the Twelfth Dynasty began around 1985 B.C., they differ by as much as four hundred years when it comes to the beginning of the First Dynasty. However, the evidence seems more and more to confirm the date of approximately 3110 B.C. as the start of history in Egypt, so we may as well stick to that for the time being.

Which brings us back, in case you thought I'd forgotten, to Dynasty O. The Palermo Stone lists several kings preceding those of the First Dynasty, and certain fancy tombs at Abydos have been attributed to these individuals. They were not rulers of a united Egypt, so they can't belong to the First Dynasty, which starts with Menes, the man who brought both parts of Egypt under a single ruler. Hence Dynasty O. I wouldn't worry too much about it, if I were you.

WEARERS OF THE DOUBLE CROWN

For a long time historians were inclined to place Menes among the shadowy heroes of legend, in the company of Roland and King Arthur. Tradition, to be sure, named him as the Unifier; but Tradition, scholars feel, is a tricky wench, to be handled with caution. Archaeological evidence confirmed the assumption that a conquest did take place and that it was initiated by a king of the south, but the name of the conqueror was long in doubt. There was even a question as to whether a single king might claim that distinction.

We know of the conquest, and of conquering kings, from a series of carved stone objects dated to the end of the predynastic—mace heads, knife handles, and slate palettes. The most useful is the Narmer palette, which was found at Hierakonpolis. Stone palettes are common in predynastic graves; they were used for grinding cosmetics. As time went on they got bigger and their surface became a ground for bas-relief. The palette of Narmer shows a quaint little king, dressed in a kilt and wearing the White Crown of the south, coolly preparing to bash a kneeling captive on the head. Above the prisoner is a curious symbol depicting a hawk (which signified the king) in triumph over the Delta region. Behind the predatory king is the diminutive figure of his sandal bearer (sizes in Egyptian relief indicated relative importance rather than actual stature). At the top, between two heads of a cow goddess, are the signs that spell the king's name—Narmer. On the back of the palette, Narmer, with his faithful sandal bearer still in attendance, wears the Red Crown of the north.

It does not require too much imagination to interpret the reliefs on this palette as scenes of conquest—conquest of north by south. King Narmer, then, is a likely candidate for the title of Unifier.

What about Menes, tradition's candidate? Some scholars would like to identify him with King Narmer. The Menes-Narmer equation is a fetching bit of logic. It goes like this: (I) On the palette, Narmer is shown

The Narmer palette

conquering people from the Delta and wearing the two crowns; (2) There-fore, Narmer unified the country; (3) Menes unified the country; (4) Menes = Narmer. QED.

There is nothing wrong with this argument, so far as it goes. Egyptian kings had more than one name, and Menes could have called himself Narmer if he had wanted to. However, there is another equation that makes better sense. It would identify Menes with a king named Aha, whose tomb has been found.

Among the objects dated by archaeologists to the First Dynasty are small tags of ivory or wood, insignificant in appearance but all-important in that they bear some of the earliest Egyptian writing. Unfortunately, we cannot read all the signs; they are extremely primitive, and not all can be identified with hieroglyphic symbols of later periods. Scholars are making progress with the decipherment of these tags, however, and we can make some deductions about the names and titles of the period in question.

The full "titulary" of the Egyptian king was not developed until much later. In its final form it consisted of five titles and five names; two of the names were surrounded by the oval figures called "cartouches," which were used only by kings and queens. During the first two dynasties the titulary had only three elements; the most popular was the one called the "Horus name," written not in a cartouche but in an oblong box called a *serekh*, which is a simplified representation of the facade of the royal palace. On the "roof" stands the hawk-god Horus, who was identified with the king, and his figure is read as a title: the Horus So-and-So.

Aha is the Horus name of a First Dynasty king; it has been found on many labels, or tags. In the course of the excavation of the tomb of Aha's

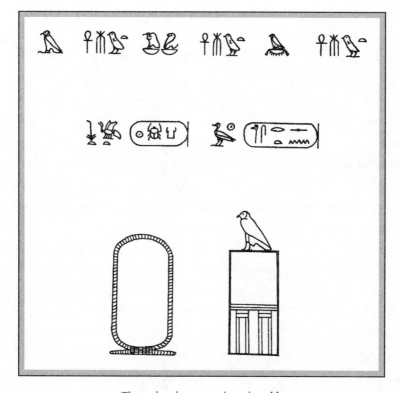

The royal titulary, cartouche, and serekh

mother, the queen Merneith, at the site of Naqada, a piece of an ivory label turned up that bore the king's Horus name and beside it another name—Men. The Men name was written under the so-called Nebti title, just as Aha was written under the Horus title. The word *Nebti* means "the Two Ladies," and refers to the two great goddesses of north and south; logically it could only be claimed by a king of both areas. But, more important, Men and Aha may be names of the same king.

The excavator of the tomb, John Garstang, was so excited about the broken label that he redug the entire tomb, looking for the missing pieces. The usual frustration of the archaeologist searching for one particular needle in a haystack was not Garstang's; he found the pieces, and the two names and titles are there.

Most scholars think that the two names belong to one individual, and believe that the Naqada label actually does bear the name of fabled Menes. I think so too, for what that is worth. We do not need to worry about a missing *s* here or there; the name "Menes" is a Greek form. However, another label has the name of Narmer alternating with the "men" sign; so it is possible that Narmer is Menes, and Aha is his successor. Another, far less romantic, theory holds that the scenes of fighting between north and south that appear on the Narmer palette and on other carved objects of the period indicate a long period of warfare between the two regions that may have extended over several reigns. The assumption of the crown of the conquered region before the conquest was actually complete could have been an example of political propaganda (similar examples are not unknown in our time).

Having verified the claims of tradition for consideration in one respect at least, we may return to that source for further information about Menes the Conqueror. He is supposed to have built a new capital at Memphis, not far from modern Cairo. This was the boundary between the Delta and the valley, and the location was shrewdly selected. Menes may have been a skillful politician as well as a great warrior; instead of suppressing the conquered North he assumed its insignia, its gods, and its customs—not to mention its women, for there is reason to believe that his mother or his wife was a princess of the Delta. From Menes onward the parallelism based on the notion of the Two Lands is a fundamental aspect of Egyptian thought. The king wears the Two Crowns (whose combined appearance makes it evident that they were not joined for aesthetic reasons). He calls himself King of Upper and Lower Egypt, and Lord of the Two Lands, and he is protected by the Two Ladies. If Menes deliberately adopted this procedure, we may see why he succeeded where others, perhaps, had failed; for there are tales of a predynastic union of the two areas that was impermanent. As a technique it has proved useful to many a succeeding conqueror.

We don't know a lot about Menes, but actually it is more than we might expect to know about a legendary character. Indeed, as we proceed we will find ourselves saddled with that archaeological rarity, an *embarras de richesses*. In Holmesian terms, it might be called "The Perplexing Problem of the Duplicate Tombs."

Two hundred miles north of Luxor lies the very ancient holy city of Osiris, god of the dead. It is called Abydos, and it was a place all the kings of Egypt delighted to honor. Before Osiris came to dwell there, it was the sanctuary of another, even older, mortuary god, and pilgrims from all over Egypt laid their bones in that sanctified ground in order to win greater glory in the world to come. The tomb of Osiris himself was there; its exact location was well known to the devout Egyptians.

When archaeologists began to excavate at Abydos, they were not expecting to find Osiris, nor did they. What they did uncover was almost equally unexpected—tombs of the kings and queens of the First Dynasty, including the tomb of King Aha. The excavators must have felt almost as much awe as they would have felt at finding Osiris himself.

One of the first people to excavate at Abydos was—correct. William Flinders Petrie. He won permission to dig at the site only after some difficulty, for the concession had been given by the Department of Antiquities to another archaeologist, a Frenchman named Emile Amelineau. It is considered courteous these days to give the early excavators a polite tip of the hat, in tribute to their intentions if not their methods; but it is hard to say anything very complimentary about Amelineau. He drove Petrie to distraction. Indeed, most people drove Petrie to distraction, for few of them could live up to his high standards, and he did not brook fools lightly. In the case of Amelineau we can sympathize with Petrie, because after the French excavator had dismembered the site of Abydos, Petrie was given the pieces. Amelineau had removed all the interesting items he found, without—to Petrie's fury—keeping records of how and where they were found. He had also ruthlessly destroyed much of the material he could not carry away. Yet Abydos was to show Petrie's ability in all its glory. His publication is still a standard reference work.

Petrie's thoroughness led him to one spectacular discovery, which Amelineau had missed—the mummified arm of a long-dead king or queen that still wore a set of exquisite bracelets made of gold, amethyst, turquoise, and lapis lazuli. Tomb robbers had rifled the coffin in remote antiquity and ripped off the jewels, arm and all. But something disturbed them in the midst of their job, and they had to run for their lives. In so doing, one of them stuck the mummified arm into a crack in the rock, planning to come back for it later when the heat was off. We may reasonably hope that the ancient gendarmes caught up with this particular member of the third or fourth oldest profession, for he never retrieved his loot. It is surprisingly attractive, this jewelry, and surprisingly well made. It gave Petrie an impression, which is borne out by other research, that the First Dynasty, so near in time to the primitive, was much more complex and sophisticated than one might expect.

This same Abydos tomb, which belonged to a king called Djer, provided a clue to a darker part of Egypt's past. Most readers know of Sir Leonard Woolley's discoveries at Ur, in Mesopotamia—the great royal tombs with their treasures of gold and the slaughtered bodies of hundreds of courtiers and slaves, who went to serve their masters in death as they had in life. Egyptologists have been mildly smug about the more civilized habits of their people, who supplied dead kings with wooden servant figures and painted pictures of slaves instead of the real article. Unfortunately for these assumptions of superiority, the Abydos excavations turned up a large tomb with surrounding rows of smaller graves that appeared to have been contemporaneous with the principal burial. Most of the victims were women.

Similar suspicious burials surround other First Dynasty monuments at Abydos. One of them, which belonged to a queen, had not only the bodies of her servants but the implements with which they had rendered service—vases with the potter, paints with the artist, needles with the court ladies.

In all fairness to the Egyptians it must be said that the First Dynasty tombs are the only ones that have these sacrificial burials, though there are hints of the practice in some of the predynastic burials at Hierakonpolis. Such extravagance with human life is more typical of barbaric periods (at least we civilized folk like to think so). More sophisticated cultures tend to develop magical substitutes.

When the Abydos royal tombs were discovered, everyone shook hands all around and checked one point off the list: First Dynasty royal tombs, okay. Then somebody began digging at Sakkara.

Every tourist to Egypt knows Sakkara. It is one of the ancient cemeteries of Memphis, conveniently close to modern Cairo. The said tourist is dragged to Sakkara by his guide in order to see the Step Pyramid of the Third Dynasty, the private tombs of the Fifth and Sixth Dynasties, and the Serapeum of the late empire. He spends a morning, or a day, and comes away with aching feet and the correct impression that there is a lot to see at Sakkara.

Since Memphis was founded by Menes, we would have every reason to expect that he and his successors would choose to be buried near the new capital. If the First Dynasty tombs had not been discovered at Abydos, it would have been a safe bet to look for them at Sakkara.

So, when someone looked, there they were—more First Dynasty tombs, of a size and complexity that strongly suggested they were royal. Even a divine king has only one body; why should he require two tombs?

A possible answer is that one was a real tomb, and one a cenotaph. Cenotaphs are sometimes erected when the body of the person to be memorialized is missing, as in the case of sailors lost at sea. The great sarcophagus of Dante in the church of Santa Croce in Florence is a cenotaph; the Florentines tried to add Dante to their collection of great men by every means up to and including body snatching, but the authorities of Ravenna, where the poet chose to be buried, and where his bones still lie, foiled the attempts. The Egyptian kings of the early period might have built two tombs in order to be represented, funereally speaking, in both sections of the country, which they called the Two Lands.

Another theory, now gaining in popularity, is that the Sakkara tombs belonged to high officials rather than kings. The argument still rages—if one may use such a violent expression about the courteous discussions of scholars—and the fun of archaeology is that a new discovery may overturn the whole structure.

A prominent political figure once referred to "revisionist historians" in a manner that implied: (I) he had coined the phrase; (2) these people were doing something underhanded. Neither is true. Revisionism is an essential process in history (and of course other disciplines). Like most things it can be used improperly—shaking things up just for the hell of it, or to get newspaper headlines. We see a certain amount of that in Egyptology. But new discoveries and new interpretations require a reassessment of the evidence—revisionism, as I like to call it. That's what history is about, and you'll find plenty of it in this book. Without apologies.

If Menes was Aha, we have a tomb at Abydos that belonged to him. Other First Dynasty royal tombs at that site belonged to his successors, and an ivory label confirms the sequence. Unlike the multisyllabled names of later dynasty kings, these are easy to commit to memory, supposing anyone would want to: Aha, Djer, Djet, Den, Anedjib, Sekhemib, and Qa'a, plus a queen, Merneith, whose title, "King's Mother" instead of Horus, indicates that she was probably acting as regent for a young son.

WARS OF RELIGION?

Contrary to the general rule—that our knowledge increases as we move forward in time—we know less about the Second Dynasty than we do about the First. We lack a basic source, the tombs of the kings. There are only two Second Dynasty tombs at Abydos, and they date from the very end of the period. Excavations at Sakkara have produced two large underground galleries that may belong to the Second Dynasty—but not to the two kings who have tombs at Abydos. If these Sakkara tombs had superstructures, they have vanished, but in the galleries were found seals bearing the names of the first three kings of the Second Dynasty—Hetepsekhemwi, Raneb, and Nynetjer. It's not necessary to remember these names; they will not turn up again in these pages. I just put them in to show how thorough I am.

We don't know why Manetho started a new dynasty with the Second. There are definite signs of dissension, and they take an unexpected form. The country had only been unified for a few generations, and we might expect that the conquered had not completely given up their dreams of independent power. But the rebellion against the central authority was not solely a matter of political conflict. It was tied in with religion.

Of all the gods and goddesses of Egypt, the best known are probably Isis and Osiris. Osiris was regarded as the earliest king of Egypt, who brought the Egyptians out of savagery, giving them laws and teaching them how to cultivate the land. He married his sister Isis, and their wise and benevolent rule was praised by gods and men alike. But Osiris's jealous brother Set murdered the king and usurped his throne. The body of Osiris was recovered by his devoted wife, whose laments so moved the gods that they restored Osiris and gave him kingship over the land of the dead. The posthumous son of the royal pair, Horus, finally defeated his wicked uncle Set in a bloody hand-to-hand combat and regained the throne. Hence the king of Egypt was called "the Horus." When he died he became Osiris and was buried by his son, the new Horus, with the same pious devotion that the god Horus had shown his father.

This myth has been interpreted in a number of ways. The followers of the "Dynastic Race" idea regard Horus as the patron deity of the conquerors and Set as the god of the indigenous population. The events were narrated by the winners, so their god became the avenging son and Set became the manifestation of evil; as someone has pointed out, the devil has never had the story told from his point of view either.

Another theory views Set as the god of the south (he was originally the local god of a town called Ombos in Upper Egypt) and Horus (Set's opposite number) as the god of the north. If we are determined to make political hay out of the story, this identification leaves us stuck with an unrecorded conquest of the south by the north, the exact opposite of Menes's conquest. This overly simplistic notion disregards the fact that Egyptian gods cannot be tidily restricted to a single place. Horus was also top god at Hierakonpolis in Upper Egypt. To confuse the picture still further, he was a sun god as well as the son of Osiris.

There is a third interpretation, which is that the story is theological in import, representing a rather naive version of the conflict between good and evil, light and darkness. The protagonists in the battle are not Osiris and his brother, but Horus and Set. The "Contendings" of this belligerent pair were a favorite motif in folklore and literature. Horus's symbol is the hawk; the little picture of the bird is the hieroglyph used to write the god's name. The symbolic animal of the Antagonist, Set, is a more mysterious beast. The squatting or standing quadruped with the long, drooping snout and upstanding ears has to be a composite or a complete fiction, so we just call it the "Set-animal."

The Egyptian duality of good and evil is not so clear-cut as are other versions. Unlike Lucifer and Ahriman, Set did not become a devil after he fell. He was a good god and a bad god, and he could turn from one to the other with a speed that makes Dr. Jekyll look like a tyro. When Set was defeated by Horus he was not cast into outer darkness. Even Isis pleaded for him, and he was given the desert and foreign lands as his domain. As the murderer of Osiris, Set was evil, and the pilgrims to Abydos used to watch his defeat, which was reenacted in a great annual mystery play, with happy cries of "Go to it, Horus!"—or something like that. But in his other manifestation, Set was a perfectly good god and was worshiped like any other. Other cosmologies knew a similar dichotomy; the Aztec Tezcatlipoca was both a sun god and the sun god's diabolic opponent; the slim huntress Diana could also be the frightful triform Hecate, goddess of witches and black magic.

Horus the falcon is so thoroughly identified with the king that it comes as something of a shock to see a heretical monarch rejecting Horus in favor of his bête noire, Set. This Second Dynasty iconoclast was named, originally, the Horus Sekhemib. We mentioned, while discussing the kings of the First Dynasty, that the Horus name was written in a *serekh* with a falcon on top. When King Sekhemib changed his Horus name he changed the whole structure. His name became Peribsen, and his *serekh* was topped by the Set-animal instead of the Horus falcon.

This change of ritual, which looks so small on a stone seal or stela,

Serekhs *of Sekhemib (left) and Peribsen (right)*

must have signified far-reaching and dramatic events. Many of the First Dynasty royal monuments, both at Sakkara and at Abydos, were set afire in ancient times, perhaps during this very period. The next king, Khasekhem, is known for his military exploits, and several campaigns were fought in the north. There is certainly a suggestion of a battle for the crown, if not outright civil war. The last king of the dynasty, Khasekhemui, has a name that means "Appearance of the Two Powers." The two powers, in this case, may well have been the old enemies Horus and Set; the king's name is, uniquely, surmounted by both gods standing in amity upon the *serekh*. Possibly Khasekhem and Khasekhemui are the same king, with the change of name signalizing a reconciliation—forcible or diplomatic—between the two factions that had been in opposition. The

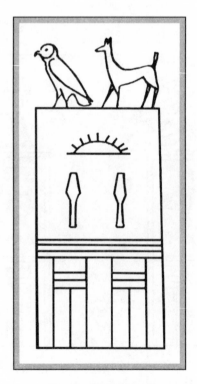

Serekh *of Khasekhemui*

fact that no tomb has been found for Khasekhem at Abydos, although the tombs of Peribsen and Khasekhemui are there, supports this theory.

The wars of religion in our own era are adequate proof that men may take up weapons over an idea, but it is rather startling to find the easygoing, tolerant Egyptians fighting about their gods when they could, and did, accept new additions to the pantheon without a murmur of complaint or confusion. Was the Set rebellion, like Akhenaton's later heresy, an attempt at exclusiveness—an attempt, in short, at monotheism? Well—no. There is no evidence for such a conclusion. We may never know the details of, or the reasons for, the religious upheaval of the Second Dynasty, and one must always bear in mind that religion can be, and often is, a cloak for more cynical power struggles. The more things change, the more they remain the same.

Two

HOUSES OF ETERNITY

Cartouche of Khufu

KING DJOSER'S MAGICIAN

One of the advantages of armchair travel is that we can spare ourselves the physical discomforts attendant upon the real thing. Let us, then, avoid the dusty paths of Sakkara and imagine that we are already at that site looking up—and I do mean up—at a fantastic construction called the Step Pyramid.

It comes at the very beginning of the Third Dynasty, this large architectural achievement; and at first glance it seems unbelievable that the people who were playing around with mud bricks and holes in the ground during the Second Dynasty could have leaped so swiftly out of the hole and into the sky, with cut stone as their ladder. There is a lot of sand in Egypt that has never been shifted. But even if we moved all of it we would still be left with the wonder of the accomplishment in so short a time; and we might find, even then, that the greater part of the credit must be given to the genius of one man.

Tradition, that much maligned handmaiden of history, had long credited the construction of the Step Pyramid to a certain Imhotep, the vizier and architect of Djoser, first or second king of the Third Dynasty. His name has been found in the Step Pyramid area, and there is little doubt but that tradition was correct. Imhotep was one of those talented people who captured the popular imagination; by Greek times he had become a godling and was credited with astounding accomplishments in medicine, magic, and scribal lore as well as in architecture.

When his lord and master asked Imhotep what sort of tomb he ought to build, the architect's first notion was to construct a huge mastaba—the

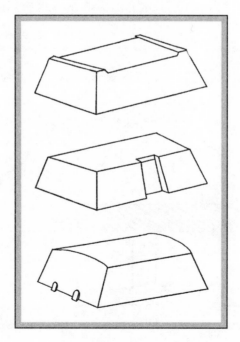

Types of Old Kingdom mastabas

type of tomb that was built by kings and nobles alike during the First and Second Dynasties. It continued to be used by commoners after their rulers had soared in ambition to the splendor of the pyramid. In shape a mastaba is a low, flat-topped rectangle, something like a shoe box.

It would be fascinating to have the tomb autobiography of Imhotep, as we have the autobiographies of later officials; to know when and how he first got the idea of superimposing another, smaller mastaba on top of the first, and a third on top of the second, and so on, forming a four-step pyramid. Later the design was enlarged to a six-step pyramid by broadening the base and building on along one of the extant faces of the structure. The Step Pyramid differs from later pyramids in that it was never filled in with stone to give a smooth, uninterrupted slope. But it served as an inspiration for a thousand years, and we are happy to be able to give the architect his due instead of crediting Anonymous, as we must do so often in ancient Egypt.

The first pyramid did not stand alone. A French architect, Jean-Phillipe Lauer, spent most of his long working life at Sakkara exploring

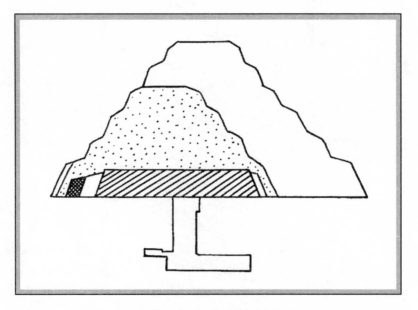

Building stages of the Step Pyramid

and restoring the structures that surrounded the Step Pyramid, so we can visualize, with only a moderate straining of the imagination, what the immense tomb complex of King Djoser looked like in the days of its pristine glory.

All the buildings, including the pyramid, were enclosed by a wall built of small white limestone blocks. The size of the stones was a survival of the older brick construction; the Egyptians had yet to learn how to exploit the new building material properly. Inside the wall lay courts and buildings and tombs of various types; so complicated is the structure that archaeologists are still finding things within the Step Pyramid enclosure. The broken remains of the buildings are important for the study of domestic architecture, since some of them reproduce the actual living quarters of the king, which were built of less durable materials than stone. Others are replicas of structures used in various ritual performances.

The pyramid itself is solid (we think); the burial corridors and chambers were underground, entered through a passage from the funerary temple next to the pyramid. This is not typical of later pyramids, and the Step Pyramid substructure is more elaborate than later Old Kingdom examples. Some of the walls had reliefs, done in a subtle and skilled style; others were covered with small blue-green glazed tile in imitation of matting. A badly battered though once magnificent statue of Djoser was found in the serdab of the pyramid, but the body of the king has long since disappeared. A few bones, flung irreverently on the floor of the burial chamber, may be all that remains of him—though there is no way of proving it.

Of the master architect Imhotep even less has survived. A few years ago, the world of Egyptology was more or less electrified by the discovery of what might have been the tomb of Imhotep. Unfortunately we can't be more specific than that. The tomb is—or isn't—at Sakkara, one of a group of large Third Dynasty mastabas—those of important people, to judge by their size. Not only were all these tombs thoroughly plundered in antiquity, but they were also virtually destroyed by later builders. Walter Emery, who first excavated in the area, believed that Imhotep's tomb was there somewhere, and that it served as the cult center for a Ptolemaic temple dedicated to the deified vizier. Ensuing excavations uncovered a fantastic labyrinth of underground galleries containing the mummies of hundreds of thousands of ibises and baboons. These animals were sacred to Thoth, god of learning, who was regarded as the divine father of Imhotep. Perhaps one of the desecrated tombs was his. Perhaps it is yet to be found. People are still looking.

A statue base in the Step Pyramid area bearing his name confirms Imhotep's connection with that structure, which is in itself a sizeable substantiation of one of Imhotep's reputed talents; and we are entitled to wonder whether tradition may not have been equally accurate about his other abilities. Imhotep's age, the Third Dynasty, was a formative period. An efflorescence of creativity took place, paving the way for the massive accomplishments of Egyptian culture that we will see fully developed during the next dynasty. Djoser's statue shows that the fumbling attempts of earlier sculptors had been replaced by a technique that was to become the traditional method of carving stone. In the realm of abstract ideas, equally significant discoveries were being made. I want to talk about one of these discoveries now.

Those of us who have reached the years of wisdom and dignity are perhaps fortunate enough to remember the farm kitchen of a grandparent or an uncle: the black wood-burning stove; the basin and ewer where the men washed up when they came in from the fields; the long table covered with oilcloth; the heavy sideboard, which held souvenir cups from the World's Fair and the family library—a Bible, the Sears Roebuck catalog, an almanac, and a leech book.

The leech book I own is not my grandmother's; I bought it for fifty cents at a secondhand bookstore, in a fit of nostalgia. When I hold it in my hands I can tell myself, if I am feeling sentimental, that I am holding the direct descendant of an ancient Egyptian book of medical science. We can trace the lineage of these works, through the Greeks to the Romans to medieval Europe, and then across the seas to America. They are not what we would call scientific books. Mixed in with practical remedies for rheumatism and spavins and "fits" are many incantations of a purely magical character. The distinction between science and magic is a relatively modern one. The Egyptians, like many of their descendants all over the world, saw only the effect. When the effect was an obvious one—a hole in the head following a blow with a mace—no people were more pragmatic about explaining the cause and dealing with the results. But when the cause of the trouble was less clear they did not hesitate to ascribe it to demons.

There are half a dozen major papyri from pharaonic Egypt that are basically medical in purpose. One contains diagnoses of diseases of the stomach, another deals with gynecology, and a third with ailments of the anus and rectum. Perhaps the most famous of the medical books is the Edwin Smith Papyrus, which was found in 1862. Its subject is the surgical treatment of wounds and fractures. Most of our copies of the medical papyri were written during the New Kingdom. But it is in cases like this that the painstaking, plodding labors of the philologist contribute to historical study. So thorough is modern knowledge of the Egyptian language that scholars can tell the probable date of a manuscript by internal evidence alone—by stylistic, grammatical, and epigraphical details—just as a student of English literature can distinguish a work of the fourteenth century from one of the seventeenth. The Edwin Smith Papyrus is very old; it was probably composed during the Fourth Dynasty, or even earlier.

Like the leech books, Egyptian "medical" texts contain two distinct types of material. The great majority is medical in intent; the purpose is to cure, but the methods are those of magic. Normally these methods involved two elements: an incantation, calling upon the demon to give up its hold upon the body of the sufferer, and a ritual act. Often the ritual was as painful for the patient as for the hypothetical demon; the afflicted member might be burned with hot irons or jabbed with needles. We know of these techniques from many lands and many ages; indeed, so widespread and so consistent is the belief in demonic possession that if unanimity of belief were a valid criterion of truth, we would be forced to give it more credence than we do. However, we have learned—and it took us time to learn it—that hot irons are not as effective as penicillin, nor incantations as curative as quinine.

What makes us catch our breath is a hint—only a hint—that some Egyptian leech of the third millennium B.C. may have learned the same thing. In the Edwin Smith Papyrus there are forty-eight long sections, which differ drastically both in format and in approach from the magical spells that fill the rest of this papyrus and most of the others. The approach is rigorously matter-of-fact; there is no mention of supernatural causes. To be sure, the cases in the Edwin Smith deal with wounds and fractures, in which the cause of the injury is apparent even to a superstitious eye. But there is one case of partial paralysis resulting from injury to a section of the brain, which surely involves analysis one step removed from the simple observation of a broken bone. The ancient observer here makes a revolutionary statement. This is not, he says, a question of something entering from outside of a man; it is something which his own flesh has produced. In other words—no demons.

Some scholars believe that other medical papyri contain excerpts from the same ancient surgical treatise that was the source of the forty-eight sections in the Edwin Smith Papyrus. The Edwin Smith Papyrus is a hodgepodge, a collection of material from various sources; if it was put together during the Old Kingdom, the surgical sourcebook must be even older—perhaps as old as the Third Dynasty.

The spirit of inquiry did not flourish. Down the centuries the magical formulae persist and multiply, and if any leech did get the eccentric notion that all illnesses, like the paralysis resulting from the brain injury, were caused by physical agents rather than diabolic ones, he never, to the best of our knowledge, voiced such heresy. Medicine and magic, sorcerer and leech—except for rare periods in the history of the human mind, they have been identical. It is indeed odd that we should be able to see a suggestion of scientific inquiry at so early a period in Egypt—odder still that it may have occurred at about the same time as the life span of the legendary wise man Imhotep. To the Greeks, Imhotep was not only the builder of the Step Pyramid and the patron saint of scribes; above all he was a master physician and was identified with Aesculapius. So great was Imhotep's renown as a doctor that in Ptolemaic times a young wife would say:

> With my husband I prayed to the Lord God Imhotep, son of Ptah, the giver of favors, who grants sons to those who have none, and he answered our prayer, as he does for those who pray unto him.

Perhaps her prayers had a sounder basis than she knew.

If Imhotep's scientific insights fell on sterile soil, his architectural innovation was accorded the most sincere form of flattery—imitation. Djoser was not the only Third Dynasty king to begin a pyramid. Air photographs, a useful modern aid to archaeological mapping, had shown that there was some sort of construction on the desert sands close to the Step Pyramid complex; it was rectangular in shape, but there did not appear to be anything inside it. In 1953 to 1954 this strange structure was excavated by Egyptian archaeologist M. Zakaria Goneim, who found unmistakable evidence that another step pyramid had been begun. It was meant to be as big as Djoser's, but it never got beyond the second level of building, perhaps because the ambitious king died too soon. The aerial photo had brought out the shape of the enclosure wall. There was also a substructure with many galleries where the excavators found vases and jar stoppers and, more thrilling, a number of gold bracelets. Generations of conscientious tomb robbers had somehow missed the gold, though they had removed the other contents of the tomb, which must have been fabulous—there were over 120 storerooms in the subterranean galleries. But the most momentous find was a sarcophagus in the burial chamber. Unlike the usual sarcophagus, whose top lifts like the lid of a box, this one had a sliding panel at one end. And, wonder of wonders, the panel was still sealed with plaster; on top of the sarcophagus lay the withered remains of a funeral wreath.

A Third Dynasty royal burial would have been a unique find indeed. The small world of Egyptology waited with some excitement until May

1954, when the sealed panel was raised. The sarcophagus was bare; it still remains one of the unexplained mysteries of Egyptology and has led some archaeologists to suspect that this pyramid has surprises in store even yet. If the empty sarcophagus was a trick to fool thieves, the real burial may still lie hidden.

This pyramid is attributed to one of Djoser's successors, a king named Sekhemkhet. Then we have two peculiar tombs at the site of Zawaiyet el Aryan, near Giza, which are also ascribed to the Third Dynasty. Neither was finished, but from the little that remains archaeologists have deduced that they were meant to be step pyramids of considerable size. One of these structures, called the Layer Pyramid, was never used for a burial; perhaps its royal builder died before it was finished. The second Zawaiyet el Aryan pyramid, appropriately named the Unfinished, is even more mystifying; work on its superstructure never even began, but the substructure contained an oval sarcophagus, sealed—and empty. Some scholars believe the empty sarcophagi served a religious purpose—a ritual burial for the king's ka, or spirit. I can't help wondering, though, where the actual body was placed.

These vanished pyramids, monuments to the failure of human vanity, are not spectacular in themselves; but they fill in the historical gap between the Step Pyramid, at the very beginning of the Third Dynasty, and the series of true pyramids, which were built during the Fourth Dynasty.

GOOD KING SNEFRU

We are mildly baffled by Manetho's reasons for starting a new dynasty, the Fourth, here. Snefru was probably the son of Huni, last king of Dynasty Three, and there is nothing to indicate usurpation or conflict.

The majority of Snefru's accomplishments were in areas that we would consider proper for a talented Egyptian ruler of this period. He sent fleets to Lebanon for cedar, some of which was used in his pyramids;

he fought in Nubia and worked the turquoise mines of Sinai with such success that he became the patron deity of that region, and later kings boasted of their expeditions that "nothing like it was seen since the days of Snefru." But in one respect Snefru differs from his fellows. In Greek times he was regarded as the kindest and most benevolent of all the ancient kings; he was the only one who was honored by the epithet "beneficent."

Battiscombe Gunn, a British scholar, suggested that these attractive character traits are depicted in an ancient text that claims to have been composed in the time of Snefru. In the story, the king is shown as a jolly good fellow; when he calls in a prophet to entertain him with tales, he himself takes pen in hand to write the words, calling the commoner prophet "my friend" and addressing his courtiers with the word *comrades*, which was used by laborers and artisans as a mode of address to one another. "Make thy name to endure through the love of thee," advises one Egyptian sage, and Snefru evidently succeeded. The names that most often survive the centuries are those of warriors and conquerors; it is pleasant to be able to honor one man for a virtue less conspicuous and more attractive than brutality. A tip of the hat, then, to "good King Snefru."

Tales like these have no historical basis, of course. There isn't much from these early periods in the way of historical "facts." Few written records, in other words. That is why this book and most of the ones that discuss Egyptian history in the Old Kingdom and earlier talk primarily about tombs and statues. They are almost all we have, aside from the ubiquitous pottery, which isn't particularly useful during this era. Hence the most interesting thing we can say about Snefru is that he seems to have had a penchant for pyramids. He built six or seven, or maybe eight of them (we can't be sure about the attribution of several). Only three of them are relevant to the present discussion, thank goodness.

The earliest is a peculiar structure at Medum, not far from Giza. It is a conspicuous landmark today, though it does not look much like a pyramid, owing to the fact that its outer casing has fallen away and the lower courses are buried in sand. For a long time Egyptologists thought this tomb was built by Huni, or at least started by him, and that his pious son Snefru finished the job. They knew that Snefru had two tombs, because of an ancient inscription which mentioned that king's "North" and "South" pyramids. They also knew that the Medum pyramid was believed by the Egyptians to be one of Snefru's tombs, but they discounted this because they knew, or thought they knew, where the other two of Snefru's tombs were located.

Admiring students of ancient Egypt have credited the Egyptians with the invention of many interesting and useful pursuits, but no one has ever given them their due as the originators of the pernicious habit of scribbling on tourist attractions. It is a habit that must arise from some basic human urge, for it has continued unabated till the present day. When the Egyptians of the Eighteenth Dynasty—a thousand years after Snefru—came to visit Medum, they carved their names on the temple walls and added comments. Age, which sanctifies many things, has legitimized even tourist scribbles, and the ancient scribbles are dignified by the name of graffiti. It is from the graffiti at Medum that we learn that Snefru was believed to be the builder of the pyramid there.

However, there are also two pyramids at Dahshur, another of the burial grounds of ancient Memphis. One of them is a very strange shape indeed. It is known as the Bent or Rhomboidal Pyramid, since it changes the angle of its slope about halfway up. The other Dahshur tomb is a true pyramid, the first ever built.

Formerly the Bent Pyramid was attributed to King Huni, and the Medum pyramid, whose attribution seemed so sure, was considered to be Snefru's southern tomb, with the true pyramid of Dahshur as his northern. Why the confusion? Because, with all the thousands of square yards of stone surface used in such a pyramid, in no place was the name of the man who built it to be found. This is one of the most astonishing facts in archaeological research—the scanty, almost negative, evidence upon which the ownership of the great stone tombs is based. In some cases the identification is based on references found in the surrounding tombs, for it was customary that a king's servants and courtiers be buried near him.

In recent years, careful excavation at the pyramid sites has turned up conclusive evidence, but one can understand why the free and easy "hurrah-for-the-dynamite" methods of the early archaeologists failed to find kings' names in the pyramids. In the Bent Pyramid, Snefru's name appears in the quarry marks hastily scrawled in red chalk on the undersides of certain blocks, for the convenience of the workmen. This discovery was made in 1947, and it settled the ownership of the Bent Pyramid. Similar marks on the stones of the true pyramid at Dahshur make it certain that this is Snefru's northern tomb. Thus we have discovered the two tombs mentioned in the ancient text. So what about Medum? Well, none of the records says Snefru had only two pyramids. It is generally accepted today that he was responsible for most, if not all, of the Medum pyramid, though some people still think that structure was finished by Snefru for his father, Huni.

It may seem extraordinary to the lay reader that Snefru, however virtuous, needed three tombs, not to mention the much smaller pyramids scattered around Egypt. It seems extraordinary to an archaeologist too. Didn't the man know when to stop?

But let's be sensible. The Medum pyramid, which appears to have been Snefru's first attempt, started out as a step pyramid. Then somebody decided to fill in the steps and smooth off the sides. However, the slope was too steep and the additional layers weren't bonded into the main structure. The whole thing started to slip. Snefru decided to start all over again, at Dahshur. His second attempt was the Bent Pyramid. The builders got that wrong too. The change in slope was an attempt to lessen the weight on the internal structures. (This is an oversimplification, but it's the best I can do.) Cracks began to develop.

We can safely add persistence to Snefru's other character trait. He moved a half mile south and started another pyramid. The result was the first true pyramid, one of the largest in Egypt, second in size only to the pyramids of Giza. Whew. Finally, he must have thought.

This is the accepted theory for Snefru's plethora of pyramids. He kept trying till he got it right. It's possible. I have to mention, though, that I've been inside both the Medum pyramid and the Bent Pyramid. The interior passageways are still functional. Maybe Snefru gave up too soon.

Of the two Dahshur pyramids, the Bent is the more intriguing. When John Perring and Richard Vyse, the first Europeans to work systematically around ancient Memphis, cleared this pyramid in 1839, they reported a strange and suggestive incident. Conditions within the deep passages of the pyramid were very bad, and the workmen suffered intensely from heat and foul air. On October 15, 1839, when the perspiring laborers were gasping for lack of oxygen, suddenly a strong cold wind began to blow through the choked passages. It blew for two days, so fiercely that it was difficult for the men to keep their lamps lit; then, just as abruptly, it stopped. Ahmed Fakhry, one of Egypt's most distinguished archaeologists, heard odd noises in one of the passages when he worked there in 1951. In view of these occurrences, it is distinctly possible that there are passages and chambers within or under the Bent Pyramid that have never been found. Perhaps the real burial chamber of Snefru is still hidden. The interior of the pyramid, though not so complex as those of later periods, is complicated enough, with heavy portcullis stones blocking the passages, hidden corridors, and other devices intended to confuse and distract.

Yes, there is still work to be done, even in areas that have been searched and researched. We know, for instance, that every pyramid had several other buildings connected with it. So standardized are the various elements of the "pyramid complex" that we can look for one structure or another with confidence even when no traces of its walls show above the ever drifting sands. The pyramid was usually enclosed by a wall and had a chapel near the northern entrance to the burial chamber. A smaller, subsidiary pyramid within the enclosure walls is also a standard feature, though its precise function is still uncertain. There might also be smaller pyramids for the burials of the king's chief wives. The wooden "solar boats" found near the Great Pyramid apparently represent another standard part of the complex, since boat-shaped pits have been found at other places, and an entire buried fleet accompanied the royal tombs at Abydos. Against the east side of the pyramid was the mortuary temple. In this building the soul of the dead king was tended by priests, who presented offerings and recited prayers for his well-being in the Land of the West, the abode of spirits. From the entrance to the mortuary temple a long causeway led down to the edge of the cultivated land. Here it joined the Valley Temple, whence the body of the king was brought by boat.

This is the Pyramid Age—more properly called the Old Kingdom— and we are about to discuss the biggest pyramid of them all, which was built by Khufu (called Cheops by the Greeks), the son and successor of good King Snefru. Khufu is remembered by the world at large for only one accomplishment; yet the size of the one is so gigantic that it has brought Khufu's name and fame down undiminished through four thousand years. So much has been written about the Great Pyramid of Giza that it is impossible to add any new facts or even approach it from a fresh

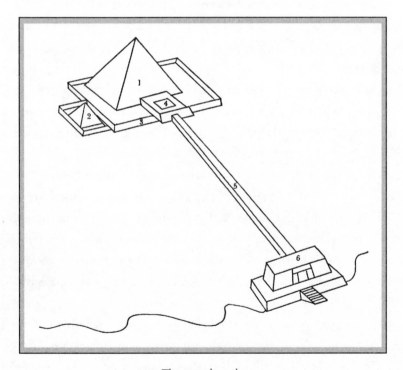

The pyramid complex
(1) pyramid (2) subsidiary pyramid (3) enclosure wall (4) pyramid temple
(5) causeway (6) valley temple

wpoint. Everybody wrote about it—poets, statesmen, tourists, archaeologists, novelists, engineers, fortune-tellers. Even Mark Twain's carefully
cultivated contempt for the Old World deserted him when he stood under the Great Pyramid's immensity of stone.

The pyramid form has a certain austere beauty, and the tawny color
of the stone is capable of bewitching and subtle variations from pale silver to gold as the sunlight changes. But it is not the aesthetic qualities of
the Great Pyramid which have hypnotized so many people. Partly, it is
the size—two and one-half million blocks of stone averaging two and
a half tons each, comprising a structure which covers an area equal to the
combined base areas of the cathedrals of Florence, Milan, St. Peter's,
St. Paul's, and Westminster Abbey. In part the attraction lies in the
atmosphere of mystery and mysticism which has surrounded the pyramids
from the beginning. They were Houses of Eternity even to the Egyptians,
dwellings in a land that was beyond mortal ken. "No one has returned
from there to tell us how they fare." When Greeks supplanted Egyptians,
and Romans conquered Greeks, and the ancient heritage of Egypt was
shadowed by ignorance, the imaginative visitors of classical and later
times added their inventions to swell the mystery. Even in modern times,
when people, one would think, should know better, the Great Pyramid of
Giza has proved a fertile field for fantasy.

The people who do not know better are the pyramid mystics, who
believe that the Great Pyramid is a gigantic prophecy in stone, built by a
group of ancient adepts in magic. Egyptologists sometimes uncharitably
refer to this group as "pyramidiots," but the school continues to flourish
despite scholarly anathemas. I cannot refrain from quoting a few of the
more entertaining blunders of the mystics, which appear in one of the
books they publish with such alarming frequency.

"The Egyptian word Pir-em-us meant to them something of great
vertical height." (No such word; the Egyptian name for pyramid is *mer*.)
"In *The Book of the Dead* the Great Pyramid is called 'The Temple of
Amen.'" (No, it isn't.) "The subterranean temple which is mentioned in
the ancient mystical writings, and whose existence as an initiatory center

scholars long denied, has recently been discovered." (I guess the temple is the Valley Temple of the Second Pyramid, whose function had to do with the mummification of the dead; it was not built underground but was buried by sand and silt.) "The great stone in front of the breast of the Sphinx with its symbolic writings and laws for the initiate has been discovered." (This must be the stela of Thutmose IV, which explains how he acquired the throne, and which is about as mystical as a campaign speech.) "This stone ... would open to the commands of candidates upon the pronunciation of the proper word." (So far it hasn't.) "In adopting the mystical pyramid inch as a unit of measurement, the Egyptians realized that the Anglo-Saxon races [sic] would be the first to recognize the unit of measurement and look upon the messages concealed in the Great Pyramid as intended for them principally."

The last statement is beyond criticism, surely. I have not mentioned the specific prophecies of the Great Pyramid, in which significant dates in world history are marked by bumps or lumps or cracks along the walls of the passages. Petrie wrote, with fine contempt, that he once caught one of the mystics surreptitiously filing down a stone boss in order to make its measurements conform to his theory. Sir William Flinders Petrie can hardly be called a biased witness; indeed, he is sometimes hailed by the pyramidiots as one of their own because his first year's work at Giza was undertaken at the request of a friend of his father's, one of the leading Pyramid mystics of his day. I think Petrie's conclusions, arrived at after a long season of measuring and comparison, are worth quoting:

> The theories as to the size of the pyramid are thus proved entirely impossible. . . . The fantastic theories, however, are still poured out, and the theorists still assert that the facts correspond to their requirements. It is useless to state the real truth of the matter, as it has no effect on those who are subject to this type of hallucination.

There is no way out; the Great Pyramid of Giza was a royal tomb, and nothing else. There is no "lost mystery" about the methods of its construction, which required only unlimited manpower and the simplest of tools. We know how this pyramid and others were built, and we could build another one just like it, using the same methods, if we had any desire to do so—and if we could conscript enough workers. Most of the stone was cut on the spot, or at quarries near Cairo from which it was floated across the river on barges at the time of Inundation, when the water extended to the edge of the desert. From that point the blocks were dragged, possibly on rollers, up the slope to the plateau. The first course of stones was laid in a square, on a site already surveyed and leveled. There is no doubt that the Egyptians knew enough about astronomy and geometry to get their angles straight. They did a beautiful job of laying out the ground plan of the Great Pyramid; the errors of orientation are astoundingly small. But they could have done it with very simple tools and equally basic mathematics.

When the first layer was in place, the second level was added by hauling the stones up a ramp of sand and brickwork. There is still some debate about precisely how these ramps worked; instead of stretching straight out from the pyramid on all four sides, and being raised when the next layer of stones was added, they may have wound round the structure. The subject is too complicated to discuss in detail; just take it from me that some form of ramp was involved. Not magic, not Martian science.

Most of the interior rooms and passages were built while the exterior was in the process of construction; the huge stone sarcophagus in Khufu's pyramid was lowered into the burial chamber before the roofing blocks were put on. Once the structure was finished, the facing of fine white limestone was added as the ramps were moved downward, so that when all was done the slopes of the pyramid presented a smooth, unbroken surface, glistening in the sun and looking from a distance as if they had been neatly frosted. This fine casing material is gone today, which is why the Great Pyramid looks like a giant four-sided staircase; the blocks were a handy source of building stone for later kings and conquerors.

Khufu's Valley Temple exists only as a basalt pavement. His Pyramid Temple has been cleared, but it isn't in much better shape than the Valley

Temple. The pyramid and its temple are the only major monuments of Khufu's we possess, and we actually know very little about the monarch who constructed the largest single monument ever raised to the glory of one individual. Khufu had a bad reputation among the Greeks. Like modern visitors to Giza, they took one look at all that stone and immediately started calculating in terms of man-hours. Their calculations were supported by the ancient dragomen, who told Herodotus that it took 100,000 men twenty years to build the Great Pyramid. Modern estimates are considerably lower. The workmen were divided into "gangs," and it's likely that only one gang of, at most, twenty-five thousand was working at a given time. This figure would include not only the men who dragged and laid the stones but quarrymen and support groups. In any case, it would be unfair to picture Khufu as the maniacal whip-wielding tyrant the Greeks envisioned. Most of the work was carried on during the season of Inundation, when the big blocks of stone could be floated close to the building area. At this time the fields were under water and the peasants were perforce idle.

The work was done not by slaves foreign or domestic, but by Egyptians. They were fed while they were working on the pyramid, and if the crops had been bad they were probably glad to get the work. The upper ranks of the workmen—skilled stonecutters, supervisors, and so forth— were housed by the king in permanent villages near the pyramid. They also had the right to build their own small tombs near that of the god-king, and the human remains found in some of them show that although they engaged in hard manual labor they got some sort of medical attention. They were also fed by the state and supplied with basic necessities.

The Second and Third Pyramids of Giza were built by Khufu's successors, though not in unbroken sequence. The Second Pyramid belongs to Khafre, Khufu's son; it suffers only by comparison to its larger neighbor, and still possesses, at its very tip, several courses of the original white casing stone. Menkaure, who built pyramid number three, died before it was finished; an eloquent, if mute, witness to his premature demise may be seen today on the lower courses of casing stones around the base of his pyramid. These blocks were of red Aswan granite instead of the usual white limestone. The outer faces of the stones were not smoothed off until after they were put in place, and we can still see the exact point at which the ancient workers laid down their tools when word came that the god had joined his fathers. This pyramid is the last of the big Fourth Dynasty tombs, and Menkaure is the last of the big Fourth Dynasty kings. This pyramid is also of interest because it is the only one of the Giza group to have its owner's name inscribed upon it. The hieroglyphic text says that Menkaure died on the twenty-third day of the fourth month; it was discovered in 1968 when workmen cleared some of the rubble from the north face, near the entrance.

The other great tourist attraction at Giza is the Sphinx. Later it became identified with a sun god, Horus of the Horizon, but it was built by Khafre as part of his funerary complex. There are a lot of other sphinxes in Egypt, but this is the biggest. I personally am unmoved by this large and maltreated monster, but the remains of the Valley Temple of the Second Pyramid, near the Sphinx, are decidedly worth attention. The dark granite that lines the walls was brought down the river, five hundred miles, from Aswan, and it is laid with such precision that one can hardly see the lines where the enormous blocks fit together. The stark simplicity of the building's design is almost forbidding in its dignity.

The three great pyramids are not the only tombs at Giza, by a long shot. There are seven smaller queens' pyramids near the big ones, and there are private tombs all over the plateau. But the most intriguing tomb at Giza is not a pyramid or a mastaba. It belonged to Hetepheres, Khufu's mother, and its discovery prompted one of the most romantic theories ever proposed by a staid archaeologist.

THE MISSING QUEEN

The great vizier Hemiun, overseer of all the king's works, favored of the Horus Khufu, was slumbering peacefully one morning when a rude interruption ended his repose. An agitated messenger, pale with alarm and stammering in his haste and terror, dared to intrude himself into the presence of the vizier, greatest in the land under the king. But Hemiun's outrage was forgotten when he heard the news; it was news to make the bravest cower. The sacred tomb of the queen Hetepheres, wife of Snefru and mother of the King of Upper and Lower Egypt himself, had been entered by thieves and robbed of all its treasures. Hemiun omitted the usual morning ceremonies. Within an hour he was in his litter, on his way to the scene of the crime.

The two mighty pyramids of Dahshur soared above the golden sand like young mountains, their smooth slopes glorious in the sun. Hemiun had no eye for their splendor, or for the gallant show of the painted temples before them. His proud face remained impassive (a nobleman does not bare his heart to peasants and other low persons), but his heart must have sunk down to the soles of his sandaled patrician feet. This was worse than he had feared; this was catastrophe. Not only had the queen's fabulous jewels been stolen, but the queen herself was gone. A frenzied search of the surrounding sand produced no royal mummy—not even bones, which at this point Hemiun would have accepted for want of anything better.

The vizier had descended from his litter by this time. He was an imposing figure of a man even without the jeweled collar that half covered his broad chest. The years had added a roll of fat to his middle, but his aquiline features held pride so great and so habitual that it was as much a part of his face as were the bones of his skull. It was pride alone that held him erect; dignity alone that kept him from flinging himself down on the hot sand and howling like a beaten slave. His distress was not solely due to piety. It was caused chiefly by reflections on what was going to happen to him, Hemiun, when the Lord of the Two Lands found out that his mother's holy remains had provided entertainment, if not much nourishment, for the jackals of the desert. As vizier, Hemiun was responsible for the royal tombs, among a hundred other matters. It was no use telling Khufu that he couldn't keep track of everything; if a vizier couldn't keep track of everything, he had no business being vizier. It would have been dangerous enough to face the god-king with the fact that the tomb had been robbed. When Khufu found out that his mother's bones were missing, he would see to it that Hemiun the vizier went to make his peace with the royal lady's spirit.

Hemiun did not feel the hot sun scorching his bare head; he was too busy thinking. He came from an illustrious family, one that was related to the royal house itself, but he had not held the highest appointed post in the land for so many years by virtue of birth alone. He was a shrewd, capable man, and it did not take him long to see the only way out of his peril. Absently he brushed a few grains of sand from the spotless white linen of his kilt and ordered his litter to be fetched. More or less in passing he also ordered the execution of the guards whose negligence had led to the disaster.

As vizier, Hemiun had immediate access to the king. He made no attempt to conceal his agitation when he was admitted to the royal presence; who would not be distressed at discovering that thieves had tried to enter the tomb of the king's mother? It was lucky for Khufu, his vizier insinuated, that his officials were so alert to their duties; not only had the thieves been foiled, but he, Hemiun, had conceived a clever plan to prevent future danger. With His Majesty's concurrence, he would arrange for the queen's reburial in a new and hidden spot, a spot so secret that no one would ever find it (in this he was not far wrong). Naturally, the move must be made at once; the longer the delay, the greater the danger of a repetition of the "attempt." Yes, he knew the king had a hard day ahead of him—reports on a new canal in the Delta, visits from the treasurers, a rebellion in Nubia—he would take care of the whole thing. When the new tomb was ready to be sealed (he recommended that this take place at night, for reasons of security), he would himself notify the king, that he might pay his filial respects. On his way out of the presence chamber Hemiun paused to answer a question. The thieves? Oh, naturally, they were already on their way to the West. He had known that the king would not wish to defile his eyes with the sight of such vileness. . . .

A number of sweating workmen had cause to curse the tomb robbers as they hauled the queen's remaining funerary equipment to the new tomb. Hemiun had chosen a good spot, right beside the passage leading from the king's funerary temple to the still unfinished pyramid at Giza. In months to come the hidden entrance would be trampled over by hundreds of feet.

So, late one night, the king was summoned to approve the vigilance and wisdom of his vizier. Borne high in a gold-inlaid litter upon the brawny arms of slaves, Khufu was carried along the road from Memphis up to the plateau on which his pyramid was being built. By the flickering light of torches he saw the shaft going down into the heart of the rock. If he had entertained any pious hopes of laying a funeral wreath on the maternal bier, he dismissed them at that moment. "How far down does this go?" he demanded. Hemiun did not conceal his pride. A hundred feet below the surface lay the tomb chamber—infinitely more secure than the old tomb, and all accomplished in so short a time!

Khufu nodded gravely. Darkness welled up in the shaft only a few feet below the surface. He could not see the glitter of the golden hieroglyphs upon the stately chair and bed, the gift of his father, Snefru, to Hetepheres, nor could he catch so much as a glimmer of the white sarcophagus. But he knew they were there; it never entered his head that they were not. Again he nodded, pleased and impressed. He must plan a suitable reward for his enterprising vizier.

The king watched as the shaft was filled with stone, and plaster tinted to match the rock of the plateau was spread over the opening. When all was done the king went home to bed; a group of slaves went to the mines of Sinai, or to a farther place; and the vizier probably betook himself to a quiet corner of his villa where he could collapse and get drunk.

The Egyptians did get drunk. They brewed more kinds of beer than anyone up to, if not including, the Bavarians, and when time and finances permitted the excess they drank more of it than was good for them. It is, of course, a flight of fancy to imply that Hemiun celebrated the success of his colossal trick in this fashion, though we would not blame him if he did. However, Hemiun's fine portrait statue is not that of a man who yielded to weakness very often; gazing at the imperious, rather ugly, face, we find ourselves thinking that if any man could have carried off such a risk, this one could have. The stately vizier succeeded beyond his fondest hopes, for the tomb of Queen Hetepheres survived the centuries in safety. Not until A.D. 1925 did any living man dream that such a tomb existed.

The Giza expedition of Harvard University had been working at that site for some years when the leg of a photographer's tripod chipped the plaster covering the tomb and told the excavators that the seemingly solid rock was not what it looked to be. When the shaft was uncovered and the big stone blocks that filled it were seen to be undisturbed, the hopes of the staff of the expedition began to rise. At last the shaft was cleared and the men could descend, rather perilously, to the burial chamber. The sarcophagus was there, its massive lid still in place. This was a significant point, for when tomb robbers went to the trouble of removing one of these lids, whose weight is calculated in tons, they did not bother to put it back when they were through.

At this high moment of anticipation the shaft had to be refilled, for George Reisner, the head of the expedition, was in the United States. Reisner was one of America's finest archaeologists. The accuracy and detail of his excavation reports set new standards for the profession; his work at Giza and in the Sudan produced definitive information on large areas of Egyptian history and archaeology. Much of Reisner's later work was carried on under the threat of eventual blindness. Several operations for cataracts proved unsuccessful, but Reisner never stopped working on his magnum opus, a study of the architectural development of the Egyptian tomb, which is now a basic reference book. With limited sight and increasingly feeble health he continued digging throughout World War II, diving into a tomb when an enemy plane appeared over the pyramids. He died during the war, still in harness; neither blindness nor worldwide conflict kept him from his work.

But in 1925 the shadow of tragedy was still in the future, and Reisner was at the height of his powers. He needed them; for when he hurried back to Giza after receiving a rapturous cablegram from his staff, he found a really meaty problem of excavation awaiting him. The tantalizing, closed sarcophagus was the pièce de résistance, but it was not the only thing in the chamber. The tomb was filled with the tattered remnants of what had once been an elaborate set of mortuary equipment.

Seeing a photograph of the original condition of the tomb chamber, one wonders why the excavators did not simply remove the debris with a shovel. This emergency burial chamber was too small to begin with. A bed canopy, in pieces, and the box that held its curtains had been laid atop the sarcophagus for lack of floor space. Next to it was a chest filled with objects, and a carrying chair on top of a low bed. There were also two large armchairs, boxes, baskets, jars, and so on.

The furniture had been made of wood covered with thin sheets of gold or inlaid with ebony. The wood decayed with the years, crumbling quite literally into dust and allowing the inlay and the gold leaf to collapse to the floor. A number of stone jars, heavy things made of alabaster, had been placed on wooden shelves; when the shelves collapsed, the jars fell into the piles of broken inlay, making confusion complete.

Today the bed, carrying chair, and other furniture of the queen adorn the Cairo Museum, looking just as they looked in the days when the royal lady stood among them. They are often ignored by the modern visitor because of their proximity to the showier and more costly tomb furnishings of Tutankhamon, but by some standards they are as beautiful as anything that notorious king ever owned. The designs, in their austere simplicity, are striking in themselves, and the details are exquisite. The titles of the queen and her husband were inlaid in gold hieroglyphs upon an ebony background. Each hieroglyph is less than an inch high, and is carved in low relief so fine that every feather of the tiny birds and every scale of the little serpents is clearly distinct. They are the most beautiful hieroglyphs ever carved or painted, whether you look at them individually or study the overall decorative effect. The reconstruction of this furniture is a brilliant example of archaeological skill and patience at its best. (The Museum of Fine Arts in Boston possesses superb copies of the objects; don't overlook them if you visit that excellent institution.)

The work of clearing Hetepheres's tomb chamber took months. The position of every tiny fragment had to be recorded, since the way in which it had fallen might provide a clue to the original design. At last the slow, agonizing task was completed and the chamber was empty of everything except the sarcophagus. Two years after Reisner got back from the United States, distinguished visitors and high government officials were lowered down the shaft in basket chairs and crammed themselves into the little room. The great moment had arrived. The heavy sarcophagus lid was prized up. In a hush of anticipation Reisner stooped to peer inside. Then he straightened and faced the distinguished audience.

"Gentlemen," he said wryly, "I regret Queen Hetepheres is not receiving."

Egyptologists become philosophical about such disappointments; Tutankhamon was only too unique. What puzzled Reisner was why the elaborate care and secrecy had been expended on the burial of an empty sarcophagus. It had been used for a burial; certain discolorations on the bottom proved that much, to Reisner's satisfaction. After much cogitation he came up with the story I have related.

This theory has always bothered me, although I appreciate it for its dramatic qualities as much as for its ingenuity. Late at night I worry about Hetepheres, after I have finished worrying about burglars and why the cat hasn't come in. What disturbs me is the fact that there have been other sarcophagi found in place, unopened—and empty. Two of them date to the Third Dynasty, not so distant in time from the heyday of Hetepheres. The cases are not exactly parallel, but yet there remains the incontestable and bewildering common feature of the empty sarcophagi. In recent years several scholars have suggested other explanations for Hetepheres's unusual situation. Most of them are pretty boring, frankly. One at least supports a statement I made some years ago, to the effect that there may have been an unknown magical or cult practice involved; according to this theory, the empty coffins are the ka burials of the individuals. (The ka was an exact duplicate of the person, brought into existence by the gods at his or her birth, and surviving his death. Since it was insubstantial, it wouldn't show up in a coffin.) I don't insist on this theory, though. It is likely that the true stories of the death and subsequent adventures of the lady Hetepheres have yet to be told. Certainly no one would regret more than I the discovery that Reisner's brilliant and picturesque reconstruction is not the correct one.

Khufu, the first king to build a pyramid at Giza, also began the private cemeteries there. Wishing to ensure his numerous progeny and friends a good life in the next world, he laid out a real City of the Dead, close to his pyramid so that his relatives might profit from his superior presence. The houses of the City were huge stone mastabas laid out in neat rows like city blocks. They must have looked attractive when first built, with their glistening sugar white walls and painted offering tablets. Later hoi polloi, ambitious for eternity, spoiled the symmetry by building smaller brick tombs around and between and atop the older mastabas. There were sixty-four tombs near Khufu's pyramid to begin with; one of the largest was built for our old friend, the vizier Hemiun, whose postulated shenanigans with the royal mother's sarcophagus had obviously gone undetected.

One can wander for hours among these tombs, reflecting with gentle melancholy upon the various philosophical considerations that cemeteries should induce. The impression we get of Giza today is not one of neatness but of a bewildering honeycomb of holes and pits and tomb entrances. We can walk into one of these tombs, stand where the family of the dead man stood to pay him the last rites, and see his face and figure on the funeral stela. Here we may sense how other people in other times sought immortality—not the common people, for their lot was a hole in the sand of the desert, where they had, indeed, a better chance of bodily survival than did their wealthier contemporaries. The greatest enemy of the dead in Egypt was not time, nor the natural processes of decay, but the tomb robber, who would not bother with a peasant's grave. Almost all the mastaba tombs were robbed in antiquity, some within a few months of the funeral service and by the very stoneworkers who had built the tomb. The massive pyramids fared no better; the devices used to foil prospective thieves posed no problem to the ingenuity of the ancient crooks. Even the heavy stone portcullises, which were lowered after the burial to block the entrance passages, were not serious obstacles; disdaining subterfuge, the tomb robbers cut through or around them. It was toilsome work, but it paid better than any other profession the robbers could have taken up.

Similar family cemeteries surrounded other royal tombs of the Old Kingdom, at Giza, Dahshur, and elsewhere. And what a family it was. From the inscriptions in these tombs scholars have learned a great deal about the sons and daughters and sisters and cousins and aunts of the Fourth Dynasty rulers. Complex genealogies have been constructed. They read like the outline for a soap opera. An uncle marrying his niece, a queen married to three kings in turn, younger sons succeeding to the throne, hints of dynastic feuds and marital disagreements. Unfortunately, that's all they are—outlines. We will probably never know why Khufu's eldest son did not succeed him (he might have died a natural death) or why his son Djedefre moved his pyramid ten kilometers away (there was plenty of room at Giza) or what happened to Djedefre's eldest son, Baka. What's really confusing is the tendency of royal females to be named after Mum or Grandma. There are three Meresankhs, and at least two Hetephereses.

Speaking of Djedefre, whose pyramid at Abu Roash is a right mess, he may have picked a different site for religious reasons. That's always a safe theory.

Despite a thousand generations of tomb robbers, some precious objects from the Old Kingdom have survived—because they were not precious to the robbers. These are the works of art with which the tombs were furnished: offering tablets and statues and, in later tombs, painted wall reliefs. To the Egyptian, beauty was not its own excuse for being; his art had a very practical purpose, for it served the vital business of survival. Painted and carved reliefs supplied the dead man, magically, with all the objects he might require in the future life, and pictured the activities he hoped to enjoy. The full-length statues and busts were emergency equipment, in case the carefully preserved body did not survive.

Still, an artist may serve a pragmatic aim without losing sight of the beautiful. The Egyptian style of painting looks strange to someone who is accustomed to our notions of perspective; the human form, for instance, is always shown with the head in profile, eyes and shoulders in front view, and the rest of the body in profile again. The Egyptians did not work in this way because they could not draw a face in front view; behind their technique was a concept of the universe that made visual impressions unimportant. They did not care what something looked like, but what it *was* like, and they worked out a way of expressing the essential qualities of objects that satisfied them so thoroughly that they continued to use it for three thousand years. The rules governing painting and sculpture were set early in the game, probably by the end of the Third Dynasty, and are so strict that archaeologists refer to them as the Canon. They were never written out, but they were exemplified in every major work of art the Egyptian artist produced, as the Greek Polyclitus exemplified his own canon in the magnificent male figure called "The Doryphorus."

For a nonspecialist, Egyptian sculpture is easier to enjoy than is Egyptian painting, since it was subjected to none of the radical distortions of two-dimensional art. The sculpture of the Old Kingdom is often quite stunning. Like the architecture, it is dignified, austere, and stately; like the architecture, it creates an unforgettable impression. It was equaled in later periods but never really surpassed; in fact, it was never surpassed in any time or any nation until Phidias of Athens took chisel in hand and showed his pupils how to make the white marble move and breathe.

It is hard to photograph statuary properly, and few of the photographs of Egyptian sculptures do them justice. One must see them to appreciate them fully. A number of museums in various countries managed to acquire magnificent examples during the period before the Egyptian government clamped down on exporting antiquities—the British

Museum and the Metropolitan Museum and the Boston Museum of
Fine Arts in the United States, to mention only a few. Naturally the
greatest collection is in the Cairo Museum. Here sits Khafre, enthroned,
with the protective wings of the divine falcon enfolding his head, facing
eternity with inhuman calm and confidence; nowhere else, perhaps, has
the notion of divine kingship been expressed so concisely in a human
face. Here too are such lesser folks as the noble Rahotep, with his neat
little Clark Gable mustache, and his buxom wife Nefret. These last two
statues are life-size and vividly painted; the eyes are inlaid with obsidian
and rock crystal, and are so alive that the fellahin who first discovered
them ran shrieking from the tomb when sunlight first illuminated the
interested stare of the vizier and his lady.

Egyptologists sometimes play a game called "Pick Your Period." Of
the three broadly defined major periods of Egyptian history, some prefer
the Eighteenth and Nineteenth Dynasties for their luxury, cosmopolitan-
ism, and sophistication. Others vote for the Middle Kingdom because of
its social advances; Egypt then showed the nearest approach to our favorite ideals of democracy and social welfare. But a good-size school of
thought vaunts the triumphs of the Old Kingdom. At this time, they say,
the real bases of Egyptian culture were laid. Later periods used them, al-
tering them only slightly and not always for the better. Old Kingdom
sculpture appeals to the classicist and the purist; and in architecture,
what form could be more simple and more satisfying than the pyramid?
We have already considered the achievements of medical science, and
medicine was not the only profession that had been developed at this
early time. Here is an excerpt from a mortuary document of a Fourth
Dynasty official who was establishing the endowment of his tomb in the
proper legal form:

> *Whatsoever mortuary priest of the endowment shall institute legal proceedings
> against his fellow, and he shall make a writ of his claim against the mortuary
> priest, by which he forfeits the portion in his possession; the lands, people and
> everything shall be taken from him which I gave to him for making mortuary*

offerings to me therewith. It shall be conveyed back to him because of not in-stituting proceedings before the officials concerning the lands, people and ev-erything which I conveyed to the mortuary priests.

I don't know what a lawyer might think of this document, but to me it has all the sophistication and legalistic detail that we could expect to find in a modern will. In its way, it testifies to the complexity of the soci-ety of which it was a product just as vividly, if less beautifully, than does the wonderful Fourth Dynasty sculpture.

CHILDREN OF RE

Sun gods are popular in polytheistic cultures, for the solar orb is one of the most conspicuous of natural objects. Its effects are equally con-spicuous and very important to primitive peoples; before the discovery of fire the sun furnished the sole source of both heat and light, and its dawning banished the dangers and demons of darkness. It could also wither crops and blast humans with deadly heat; obviously it was a power to be conciliated. The Egyptian sun god, most commonly known as Re, was always an important deity. But during the Fifth Dynasty something happened to give him even greater preeminence, so that he became Top God of Egypt.

Unfortunately we have only the scantiest scraps of evidence on which to base the theory that a religious coup d'état took place, and almost no knowledge of how it came about. We know that at this time the title "Son of Re" became a standard part of the royal titulary, and that the kings of the Fifth Dynasty erected huge sun temples more impressive than their tombs. And we have a popular tale that gives an allegorical ver-sion of the triumphs of Re. So let us consider the story of King Khufu and the Magicians.

Once upon a time it happened that the great king Khufu found him-self suffering from a painful royal disease: boredom. So he summoned his sons and commanded that they entertain him, each with a tale of wonder or of magic. The first tale is lost; it dealt with events during the reign of Djoser of the early Third Dynasty.

The second story was told by Prince Khafre, who informed his father that the events he would narrate took place under Nebka, another Third Dynasty king. Khafre's was a moral tale about an adulterous wife who was married to a magician—not the easiest type to deceive. When he found out about his wife's duplicity, the magician fashioned a crocodile out of wax and threw it into the river as his wife's lover came to bathe. Immediately it became a real crocodile and seized the lover. The magician went to the king and invited him to come down to the river to behold a marvel. He summoned the crocodile, which terrified king and courtiers with its ferocity. But when the magician took it in his hand, it turned back into a waxen image. Then the magician told the king the whole story, and the monarch ordered that the unfaithful wife be slain.

The next son related a wonder that had occurred under Snefru, Khufu's father. One day Snefru too became bored with life; he wandered through all the palace in search of amusement and found none. So he sent for the priest and magician Djadjaemankh, and asked him to make a suggestion. Said the sage: "Let Your Majesty go to the royal lake: equip a boat with all the beautiful girls of the palace. The heart of Your Majesty will be entertained watching them row up and down." The king liked the idea and refined it further by ordering that the young ladies be attired only in nets of mesh.

For a space the heart of His Majesty was happy as the maidens rowed up and down. But then the leader of the damsels dropped a pretty ornament into the water, and in her distress she stopped rowing. The king demanded the reason and the girl told him. "Give her another one," said Snefru impatiently; but the girl refused, with a proverb—I want my pot down to its bottom—which meant, "I want my own ornament, not another like it."

Faced with feminine stubbornness, the king threw up his hands and again summoned the magician. Djadjaemankh pronounced an incanta-

tion, which folded the lake back like a sandwich, half the water upon the
other half. Upon the exposed bottom lay the ornament, which the magician returned to its owner. He then put the water back in its place and the
rowing continued, to the pleasure of the king.

When it came to the turn of Prince Djedefhor to tell a story, he said:
"We have been hearing tales of past times, in which it is hard to tell truth
from fiction; but, sire, I must tell you that you have in your own kingdom
a great magician who is the equal of all those you have heard about."

In great excitement the king sent his son to fetch the venerable sage,
whose name was Djedi. The meeting of prince and wise man is charm-
ingly told; the sage greeted the royal youth with courteous words of
praise, and the prince helped him to his feet and gave him his arm to
assist him to the waiting boat, for Djedi was 110 years old.

When Djedi arrived at the palace, the king asked him to perform his
famous trick of putting back a head that had been cut off. The sage was
willing, but when the king ordered a prisoner to be brought out, Djedi
protested: "No, not a man, O sovereign, my lord; for this is forbidden."
So the guards decapitated a goose, and Djedi repaired it, to the admiration of all beholders.

After these magical divertissements, the tale gets down to essentials.
The king asked about a particular magical secret and Djedi informed
him that it would be brought to him by the eldest of three children who
were not yet born. The secret is only a device to introduce the children;
for, Djedi tells the astounded king, all three of them would one day be
kings of Egypt. "They are at this time in the womb of a wife of a priest
of Re, but their father is none other than the sun god himself."

The scene switches to the birth of the divine children, who are delivered by the great goddesses of Egypt disguised as dancer-musicians. As
the children come forth, the goddesses address them with speeches involving puns on their names; this leaves no doubt that the kings in question are really Fifth Dynasty rulers.

Obviously this story was not composed during the reign of Khufu; it
was a pretty piece of propaganda commissioned by a Fifth Dynasty king

to give mystical sanction to his dynasty. Why the new dynasty should need such support is a mystery, for it seems to be distantly related to the royal family of the Fourth Dynasty. Perhaps the "religious coup d'état" was really a political usurpation, by a lesser branch of the Khufu-Khafre family. Speculation—but that's the stuff of which much of Egyptian history is made.

But what a wealth of information we can infer from such sources as these regarding social customs, attitudes, and ethics! From the composite tale of Khufu and the Magicians we can begin to sense something that is almost impossible to get except by indirection—the moral attitudes of a long-dead culture. We are accustomed to state our views on ethical and spiritual matters in long tomes and in verbose speeches; we express them, and analyze them, and criticize them. The Egyptians did write books of wisdom literature, but for the most part these consist of advice to aspiring young men, and one is never certain that the smooth-tongued precepts are really sincere. It is in the actions, the daily responses, of human beings that we can see the ethical sense at work; and in the tales of Khufu there are several interesting points. The maiden who dropped her ornament was only a concubine, but when she spoiled the god-king's pleasure, he did not order her thrown to the crocodiles; the patience with which he humored her unreasonable demands evidently did not strike the Egyptians as unusual, or worthy of comment. (It is interesting to note that the amiable monarch was none other than good King Snefru, whose reputation for benevolence may be well deserved.) The tale of the unfaithful wife reminds us of themes from Boccaccio and Chaucer, but there is no mockery of the cuckolded husband in Egypt. It is in the story of Djedi that the attractive qualities of the Egyptian conscience are most clearly demonstrated—the reverence paid the wise old man by king and prince, and, most significant of all, Djedi's swift response to the king's command that he use a criminal for his experiment—"Not a man, O sovereign, my lord!" Men were the cattle of the god, and not subject to the whims of even a king.

We are far from the subjects that are ordinarily thought of as the proper study of archaeologists—pottery and tombs, mummies and hieroglyphs. Yet material objects are only the naked bones of history; the ideas, and ideals, of a people are the flesh and blood of their culture, which animate the dry details and give them meaning. When we study the past we try to see the ethics, the doubts, and the hopes that moved men's minds, as well as the products of their hands. And as we tend to identify ourselves just a bit with the people we study, we like to find signs that our remote ancestors cherished to some extent the same notions that we have accepted as universal moral values. One of the reasons why the ancient Egyptians have interested so many people is that they are a rather amiable set of human beings. We are seldom shocked by their activities, as we are by the cold-blooded ferocity of the Assyrians or the sickening brutality of the Aztecs. We sometimes think of the Egyptians as being preoccupied with death, yet actually the converse is true. They enjoyed life so much that they took every means possible to continue its pleasures after that change which men call dying.

The pyramids of the Fourth Dynasty represent the greatest effort ever made by any people to insure survival through material means. The kings of the Fifth Dynasty were less fortunate, or less prosperous; they lavished much of their substance on their imposing sun temples, which survive today, when they survive at all, only as crumbling foundations hidden in the sand. Several of them, known only by inscriptions in the private tombs of officials who served in them, are still missing. The end of the dynasty saw the end of the sun temples. Why? Speculation is still rife.

Fifth Dynasty pyramids were not built of stone throughout, but of rubble and sand held together by stone facings and covered with the usual handsome white limestone. Today these tombs no longer hold even the pyramid form; they are mounds of gravel that look like natural hills upon the great plateaus of Sakkara and of Abusir. The rubble of the super-structure of the pyramid of Unis, last king of the Fifth Dynasty, stands close by the towering steps of Djoser's pyramid—the great beginning and the degeneration of a noble architectural form.

However, Unis's tomb is visited by most tourists to Sakkara because it is the earliest known pyramid to be inscribed with the so-called Pyramid Texts. The white walls of the burial chamber and antechamber are completely covered with incised hieroglyphs painted a pale blue. The ceiling is star inlaid, and the total effect is quite lovely.

The Pyramid Texts are very ancient. The language is archaic, and the religious beliefs which are described are confused and contradictory, suggesting an accumulation of generations of changing dogma. The Egyptians were broad-minded, and the idea of logical exclusiveness never troubled them. In the same body of texts the dead king is described as occupying all of several Afterworlds. He may (rather beautifully) "become one with the imperishable stars," the pole stars which, in this latitude, never set; he may become a ba, a human-headed bird that flits from tree to tomb; he might journey to the Land of the West or inhabit a lovely paradise called the Fields of Yaru, located in the northeastern heavens, where the grain grew taller than earthly grain and the dreadful ferryman "Turnface" waited to carry the souls of the just to their reward.

In later times these texts, and the magical protection they provided, were taken over, in altered form, by the humbler folk, who had them painted inside their wooden coffins. In this stage they are called the Coffin Texts. During the New Kingdom period the texts were written on papyrus scrolls and were changed even more. Today these later texts are often lumped together under the general name of *The Book of the Dead*, but in ancient times there were several different collections, such as *The Book of Coming Forth by Day*, referring to the emergence of the soul from the tomb.

The Pyramid Texts are often described as "religious" in nature, yet their primary function was not the affirmation of a faith or a belief. Like the pyramids, they were designed to serve the end of survival. The pyramid protected the body of the dead king, and the texts assured his soul of continued life—life as a god, as a ruler of gods, or even as a humble rower in the boat of the gods—but life, at any cost and in any role. In the strictest sense, the Pyramid Texts are magical rather than religious. "What I tell you three times is true," said the Bellman; and, like much of Lewis

Carroll, this is more than just a solemn absurdity. It is actually a good expression of one of the basic principles of magic (and those other manipulative activities, advertising and politics), in which the Word, spoken or written, can affect actuality. If saying a thing three times makes it true, then saying it more than three times makes it even truer—neither Madison Avenue nor the necromancer's textbooks worries about comparative degrees of absolutes. Modern political campaigns have made deliberate, cynical use of this principle, whose success depends to some extent on the gullibility of the hearer.

Repetition is important, but the Word itself has great significance. Primitive peoples know the import of a man's name, and they guard their own with care lest an enemy learn it and use it against its owner. Incantations and "spells" are elements of most magical formulae. The Egyptians, who were known to later ages as great magicians, used written words to produce the real thing in their mortuary activities. In case the regular offerings made to the dead by their posterity were neglected, lists of food and drink could make good the lack. There is a constant harping on the word *living* in all the funerary texts; the dead man lives, he is living, he lives forever and ever. By inscribing the texts that describe the future life, or lives, of the soul in the very chamber where the mummy lay, the magical significance of the Word was made stronger and the dead man had further assurance of immortality.

It was logical enough that, while considering other means of ensuring life everlasting, the Egyptians should have paid attention to the preservation of the body itself. The air and the soil of Egypt are in themselves excellent preservatives, and it may have been the sight of the naturally mummified bodies of the more ancient dead, baked into leather by the heated sand, that gave the early dynastic Egyptians the idea of helping the process along by artificial means. So we have the development of mummification, and the production of that typically Egyptian object, the mummy, which is inseparably connected with Egypt in the minds of most people, despite the fact that mummies are found in other areas and other periods. When I was studying Egyptology, some of my more distant acquaintances thought it the height of humor to chortle, "So, you're studying to be a mummy"—a remark that failed to amuse me even at the first occurrence.

The best description of the process of mummification comes from those helpful Greeks, Herodotus and Diodorus. According to the former, there were three methods, which differed in elaboration and in price. In the cheapest type, the intestines were cleaned out by means of a purge and then the body was placed in natron, a compound of sodium carbonate and sodium bicarbonate. The application of natron was the penultimate process in all three types of embalming. In the second type the corpse was first given an oil of cedar enema; the oil dissolved the stomach and intestines. Modern authorities question the word *cedar*, claiming that the substance in question came from a juniper or other coniferous tree; and there is some doubt as to how this "oil" was employed.

The fanciest, and most expensive, method of mummification employed during the New Kingdom involved the removal of the internal organs, except for the heart and kidneys. The brain was removed through the nostrils and the viscera through an incision made in the lower abdo-

The mummy and its equipment, and the ba

men. The internal organs were cleaned and treated, and then placed in four containers called "canopic jars," which were, in turn, placed in a square canopic box. The empty body cavity was cleaned and anointed, and then the corpse was covered with natron, as in the other two methods. The abdomen was filled with linen packing, or with sawdust. Once dehydration was complete, the body was washed and treated with oil or precious ointments, and, finally, the wrappings were applied.

The wrappings were of fine linen, torn into strips and wound around limbs and body; sometimes even the fingers and toes were separately wound. The cloth padded out the shriveled body, which had suffered from the desiccating procedures of embalmment. Occasionally, additional pads of linen were inserted to fill out sunken areas, or the external contours of the body, such as a woman's breasts, might be modeled in plaster.

After the mummy was wrapped and placed in the coffin, another ceremony might be performed, consisting of the pouring of a liquid preparation of resin or pitch over the wrappings and coffin. This may have been a kind of anointing, or it may have been intended to preserve the body. Ironically enough, it had the reverse effect. In certain cases the pitch fused the tissues or produced a chemical reaction in which the flesh was consumed.

Yet the greatest threat to the dead man's hope of immortality in the flesh was not putrefaction, but the tomb robber. Mummies were often destroyed by thieves in their search for the jeweled ornaments with which the bodies were adorned. The Egyptians of the Old Kingdom developed a way of dealing with this terrible possibility: they carved statues of themselves, which were placed in the tomb and which could, if necessary, assume the vital functions. No man was entirely obliterated if anything of himself remained—his likeness, or even his name carved on stone.

The kings of the Fifth Dynasty were the first monarchs, so far as we know, to add the carved Pyramid Texts to their varied forms of insurance of life everlasting. This, and the rise of the cult of Re, are the most interesting features of the dynasty. The beautiful painting and sculpture of the preceding dynasty continued during the Fifth, and some of the private tombs of the period are handsomely designed and decorated. The most striking of these tombs is that of the great noble Ti, at Sakkara, which has two great columned halls, a large storechamber, and a portico fine enough for a villa. The interior has some stunning bas-reliefs, which show the daily activities of the nobility with grace and humor. Birds and animals are depicted with particular elegance; there is a scene of hippopotami wallowing around in the marsh, which is my special favorite. It is hard to imagine a hippopotamus as being charming, but these little animals are just that.

The Sixth Dynasty began with a king we know as Teti and gathered steam under his son, the competent and powerful Pepi I. Externally, the picture has the same unity and solidarity that we saw under the mighty monarchs of the Fourth Dynasty. Pepi's officials paid him proper homage, carving his picture on the walls of their tombs and bragging about royal favors received. But there is a difference. The tombs of the nobles no longer huddled around the pyramid of their royal master; they were built in the capitals of the provinces, or nomes, which their owners eventually

Hippopotami and crocodile

ruled as semi-independent princes. We might compare the situation, superficially, to the Feudal Age of Western culture. When a strong king
held the throne of Egypt he could control his ambitious underlings. But
when a weak monarch wore the Red and White Crowns—then woe to
the throne of Horus!

The most interesting of the local princes were the lords of Elephantine, an island located at the region of modern Aswan. Here ended the land
of Egypt and here began Nubia; here also was the first of six cataracts,
which interrupted navigation to the south. The granite quarries at Aswan
are now a tourist spectacle; they contain the skeleton form of what would
have been the tallest obelisk ever erected, if the great spire had ever been
cut from its rocky bed. Aswan granite was highly prized for statues and for
building; it was brought by barge all the way downriver to Memphis.

The island of Elephantine is in the middle of the river, but the tombs
of the men who ruled this frontier post were cut into the western desert
cliffs. They look to the south, to Nubia, as the fortresses of the Lords
of the Welsh Marches faced the direction from which danger would come.
Nubia had long been a source of interest to the adventurous, or greedy,
Egyptians. There were expeditions to the area as early as the First Dynasty. The A-group people disappeared during that period and were replaced in Lower Nubia (remember, that's the northern part) by what may
be signs of Egyptian settlement. These lasted no longer than the Fifth
Dynasty, if they were there at all, and the next settlements in the area
belonged to a culture called the C-group. What about the B-group? Nobody believes in it anymore. To put it in more pedantic terms, the scanty
materials once assigned to this culture do not represent a "homogeneous
phase."

The C-group people (I do wish someone would give them a more
descriptive name) were tough customers, but Egypt wanted gold, and
Nubia had a lot of it; and Elephantine was the "Door of the South." Beyond that door lay other countries which had even more to offer than did
Nubia. From the farther Sudan came ebony, ivory, gold, ostrich feathers;
somewhere to the south was the mysterious, half-legendary land of Punt,

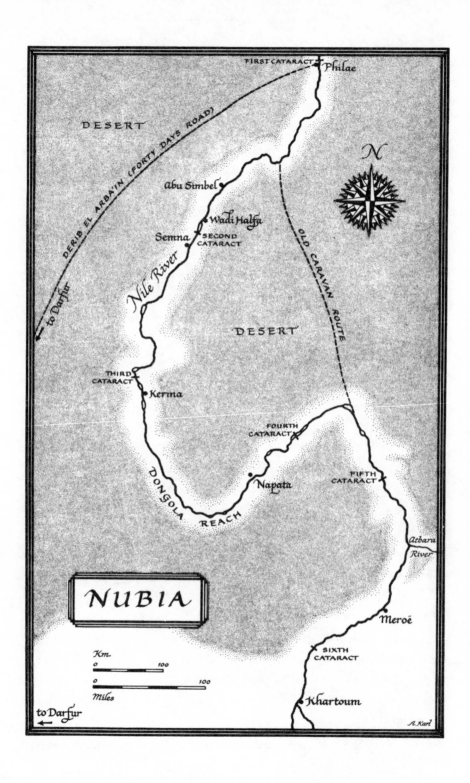

FIRST CATARACT — Philae

DESERT

DERIB EL ARBA'IN (FORTY DAYS ROAD)

N

Abu Simbel

Wadi Halfa

Semna SECOND
CATARACT

Nile River

to Darfur

DESERT

OLD CARAVAN ROUTE

THIRD
CATARACT

Kerma

DONGOLA REACH

FOURTH
CATARACT

Napata

FIFTH
CATARACT

Atbara
River

NUBIA

Meroë

Km.
0   100

0   100
Miles

SIXTH
CATARACT

to Darfur

Khartoum

A. Karl

God's Land, which supplied myrrh and spices and other precious things.

The first of the great barons of the Door of the South was named Uni, whose career began under Teti and continued under Pepi I and his son Mernere. One of Uni's duties was to oversee the working of the granite quarries, but his primary function was to protect the southern boundaries and to keep the region peaceful so that trade could be carried on without hindrance. So well did he accomplish this that he was able to quarry the granite for the royal sarcophagus with "only one warship"! The boast speaks volumes about the dangers of working in that area.

When Uni passed on to his reward he was laid to rest in the tomb he had excavated high in the cliffs, where he left a biographical inscription that does his deeds only justice. He was succeeded by another man called Harkhuf, whose name is even better known. Harkhuf and his colleagues were the first African explorers; two of his associates died far from home, among strange and barbaric peoples, carrying out the king's commands. It is with obvious pride that each adds, after his conventional princely title, the words "Caravan Conductor, who brings the products of the countries to his lord." After lives of danger and adventure, they came home to die—or were brought back from the distant lands where they had been murdered—and were buried in the tombs above Aswan. On the walls of their tombs these explorers inscribed the record of their deeds, and as we read them we have the feeling that they were not driven into the Unknown by duty alone. They went "because it was there," in the words of a modern representative of the courageous fellowship of which the lords of Elephantine were such notable members.

Harkhuf began exploring when he was only a boy, accompanying his father on a trip to the distant land of Yam. On the second trip he commanded his own men. These trips took seven or eight months and were major expeditions. After Harkhuf's third trip, Mernere, the reigning king, died and was succeeded by his young half-brother, Pepi II, who was a child of only six or seven. Harkhuf was confirmed in his post by the little king and his advisers, and went again to the south. His next trip to Yam produced one of the most delightful documents that has come down to us from ancient times. Harkhuf was so proud of it that he had it copied on the walls of his tomb. The original, doubtless written on papyrus, was a letter from the king. Harkhuf had brought back all sorts of rich loot from the gold-bearing south, but it was not gold that produced the excited letter from the six-year-old ruler.

"You have said, in your report," wrote Pepi, "that you have brought a dwarf from the land of the horizon dwellers. . . . Come northward at once to the Court! Hasten and bring with you this dwarf, alive, sound and well! When he comes down with you into the ship, appoint trustworthy people to be beside him on every side of the ship so that he won't fall into the water. When he sleeps at night, appoint trustworthy people who shall sleep beside him in his tent. Inspect ten times a night! For my Majesty desires to see this dwarf more than the products of Sinai and Punt!"

This was the high point of Harkhuf's life, although we never learn exactly what royal reward was given him for the gift the king prized so highly.

Harkhuf was not the only noble to venture his life in inner Africa. Another governor of the south, named Sebni, tells of his trip upriver on a more tragic errand. His father had been killed by the wild tribes of the Second Cataract area. When Sebni got the news he gathered his men and marched south, on vengeance bound. He dealt with the killers, collected his father's body, and brought it back to Elephantine. He was met at the border by messengers of the king, who had sent his own corps of embalmers, priests, and mourners, equipped with all the necessities for burial. When he had paid his last respects to his father, Sebni went north to thank the king—and to deliver the goods his father had collected. Personal sorrow had not made him forget his duty.

Other names deserve mention—Eneenkhet, the naval commander, slain by the Bedouin on the shores of the Red Sea; Pepinakht, the prince of Elephantine, who rescued the commander's body and brought it back to Egypt. Men like Pepinakht did not risk their necks for the sake of a beau geste. If a man's body was destroyed, if he was not laid to rest with the proper ceremonies and grave goods, he died a second and final time.

Throughout Egyptian history those who served abroad, as soldiers or merchants or emissaries, came home to die when they could.

The adventures of Harkhuf bring to mind another of the varied subjects which are the concern of the Egyptologist. Remember the nebulous knowledge we have of the predynastic period; it would seem that at this point in history, with the aid of inscriptional material, we ought to be able to solve all our problems. We know a great deal about the lords of Elephantine—their names, their business, the products they sought, and even where they were going. To the land of Yam.

Therein lies the rub. Where on earth is the land of Yam? Or, more precisely, where was it? Some archaeologists like to play with words; they produce long articles about the derivations and meanings and pronunciation of Egyptian nouns. Others like numbers; from them we get thick volumes on such subjects as chronology or Egyptian science. Then there are the people who prefer maps. Most of us number map addicts among our acquaintances; they can pass an evening quite contentedly with no more vivacious volume than an atlas. If they were Egyptologists, they would probably be arguing about Yam.

The details of mileage and distance so dear to modern travelers did not interest Harkhuf and his friends, and there was no reason why they should specify the location of the countries they visited when everybody who would read their autobiographies knew quite well where they had been. The divine gods certainly knew, and it is likely that all the literate inhabitants of Elephantine did too. The only figure given by Harkhuf is the length of time a trip to and from Yam took—about seven months. Since we do not know how long he stayed there, nor how fast he traveled, nor even in what direction he went (except that it was generally "south"), this figure is obviously not much help. But do not delude yourselves. Egyptologists have tried to use it, as they use every scrap of evidence they can get their hands on. Harkhuf gives the Egyptian names of the areas through which he passed on his way to Yam; but since the location of these places is also uncertain, this piece of information is equally indecisive.

Most Egyptologists have assumed that Yam lies on the Nile, but

Harkhuf never actually says so. One interesting omission in his story may provide a clue—Harkhuf does not mention the use of boats. Since the Nile is more or less navigable up to the Third Cataract, it is strange that he did not go at least part of the way by water.

If we study our map, we can see other reasons which make this location of Yam questionable. As early as the First Dynasty the kings of Egypt had made excursions into this very region. By the Sixth Dynasty the area must have been traversed many times by Egyptian troops and traders; a journey there could not have been the momentous and arduous enterprise that Harkhuf implies. Nor could it have taken seven months, unless he went by way of Timbuktu.

The most daring suggestion to date came from A. J. Arkell, an authority on the Sudan and its archaeology. He gives Harkhuf credit for real enterprise, for he would locate Yam in the region of modern Darfur, which is far to the west of the Nile at about the latitude of the Sixth Cataract. There is an old caravan route leading from the Nile, near Elephantine, to the Darfur region, which has been used at least since medieval times. Arkell thinks it was used much earlier, and that Harkhuf was one of the pioneers of the route. Today it is an agonizing journey through arid regions, which would appall most travelers. Yet it is still being made by camel and donkey caravans. Arkell pointed out that the region was less arid in ancient times, and added that even today the trip could be made with three hundred donkeys, a hundred carrying goods for trade, a hundred carrying forage, and a hundred carrying water. Harkhuf had three hundred donkeys on at least one of his trips.

Arkell's most ingenious bits of reasoning concern the names of the areas through which Harkhuf passed on his way to Yam. He has identified some of them with modern tribes who live between Darfur and the Nile, though he does not claim that these people are necessarily living today where they did in ancient times. Another point is that the ancient caravan route was probably the most famous route by which ivory came into Egypt from the south. And Harkhuf says, in one section, "I set forth upon the Ivory Road."

Arkell's theory is not accepted by most scholars, but I like it. Since the location of Yam is one of those subjects that worries me almost as much as the problem of Hetepheres, I had hoped, a few years back, that we might find some clues during the extensive survey of Nubia that accompanied the construction of the second Aswan Dam. The news of the dam prompted a flurry of activity in Lower Nubia, whose sites would be threatened by rising water. The temple of Abu Simbel, built by Ramses II, was the most publicized of the endangered temples; a truly monumental project cut it free of the rock in which it had been built and raised it high atop the cliffs, to a new position. But the publicity given Abu Simbel overshadowed a far more impressive accomplishment—the wholehearted, worldwide response to an appeal by UNESCO for aid in saving the less spectacular Nubian remains. Over twenty nations, from Argentina to Yugoslavia, sent teams to work in Nubia. There was a certain amount of bickering, naturally. But as an example of what can be accomplished when people turn their energies to preserving instead of destroying, the Nubian campaign was an inspiration. Many smaller temples were dismantled and moved, dozens of cemeteries, town sites, temples, and churches were excavated and recorded.

However, they didn't really settle the location of Yam.

The little boy who wrote with such rapture about a dwarf to play with could not have been much of an administrator at first. The country was controlled by Pepi II's mother and her brother Djau, prince of Thinis. But the fiction of divine rule was maintained; the bronzed explorer-counts of Elephantine, and the proud princes of other nomes, reported to their child-king and received his orders with becoming humility.

Prince Djau was not a wicked uncle. He administered the kingdom ably and cherished his small nephew with such care that Pepi II reached his majority and lived on ... and on ... and on! He ruled for over ninety years, the longest reign attributed to a king of Egypt. Hence he must have reached the century mark, or near it, before he died.

Pepi might have said, with far more truth than Louis XV, "After me, the deluge." For when he died, the whole vigorous, complex, coherent structure of the united kingdom of Egypt fell in ruins, and a time of anarchy ensued. We have noted the beginning of the trend; a strong ruler cannot permit equally strong subordinates, and even at the beginning of Pepi's reign his barons had taken unto themselves a degree of independence that contrasted ironically with the lip service paid to the power of the god-king. During the years of Pepi's young manhood, the central power was in good hands. But for the last thirty or forty years of his reign, the hands grew more and more palsied with age.

This is, of course, an oversimplification. Many other factors might have contributed to the decline of the dynasty—a series of low Niles, resulting in drought and famine, for example. The dire results of natural disasters are sometimes unrecorded and underestimated, but they have certainly played a role throughout history. Plagues such as the Black Death decimated Europe during the Middle Ages; it is likely that equivalent epidemics occurred in ancient times, although we seldom find them recorded.

The last kings of the Sixth Dynasty are little known. One of them was a woman; any man, including Manetho, could tell you that this was a bad sign. If it were not for a reference to this lady, whose Greek name was Nitokris, in the Turin Papyrus, I would be inclined to suspect her of being as apocryphal as are the stories the Greeks collected about her. "She was the noblest and loveliest of the women of her time, of fair complexion, the builder of the Third Pyramid," said Manetho romantically. Herodotus adds a melodramatic story, which tells how she avenged the murder of her brother by inviting the villains to a banquet and then flooding the dining room; she followed up her watery revenge by committing suicide.

Nitokris (Egyptian Neitkrety) was not the builder of the Third Pyramid; this particular monument at Giza was the tomb of Menkaure. However, there is another structure at the same site, which may have some bearing on the problem. It is a mastaba, but of such huge proportions that it is sometimes called the Fourth Pyramid; and it was built by a woman. Unfortunately for Manetho, this woman belongs to the Fourth Dynasty instead of the Sixth, and her name was Khentkaus. It would take a wild leap of the imagination to derive the Greek form Nitokris from this Egyptian name. One of Khentkaus's titles is unique, not to mention confusing. "The mother of the king of Upper and Lower Egypt, the king of Upper and Lower Egypt." Did this mean she was the mother of two kings, or that she was a king and the mother of a king? Opinion leans toward the first interpretation, but the size of her mortuary monument indicates her importance.

We must also consider another Fourth Dynasty queen named Hetepheres II, granddaughter of the lady of the same name whose empty sarcophagus was found by Reisner. The second Hetepheres built a tomb for her daughter, in which the color of the original reliefs has been preserved to a remarkable degree; here Hetepheres II is shown with her hair painted yellow and crossed by fine red lines.

Egyptologists, who are just as imaginative as the next man, had a wonderful time with the redheaded queen Hetepheres. Since blondes are fairly uncommon in Egypt, they proposed that Hetepheres or one of her ancestors came from the Libyan people of north Africa, who lived not far from the Delta in the western desert. The legends of Nitokris might represent a composite from a lot of different sources: a real Sixth Dynasty queen of that name, the "pyramid-builder" Khentkaus of the Fourth Dynasty, and the redheaded Hetepheres, whose memory had survived in the "fair complexion" description of Manetho.

Nitokris may be a compound, but the Titian-haired queen is no longer fact. A friend of mine once mentioned the Hetepheres II story to an anthropologist acquaintance and was taken aback when the latter gentleman exploded. There were, he said, no fair-haired Libyans in north Africa. Yes, he knew that Egyptologists had been talking about them for years—everyone he met told him the story of Hetepheres, and he contradicted it every time; but a good story seemed to have better survival value than the truth. (There is some justice in this claim.) Of late, Egyptologists have had to discard the redhead for other reasons. Several Fourth Dynasty queens are depicted wearing headdresses of the same shape as the wig or hair of Hetepheres. The color has, in all the other cases, disappeared, but it seems more probable that what Hetepheres had on her head was a yellow wig or kerchief. The red lines? They are the practice lines of the artist, known from hundreds of other examples, which were never erased. So much for romance.

Three

THE GOOD SHEPHERD

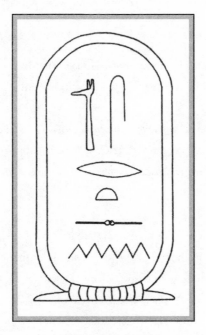

Cartouche of Senusert

DESPAIR AND DELIVERANCE

When we look back over the first six dynasties we look across ten centuries of history. It is hard to avoid the symbol of the pyramid, which towers above the desert as the culture of the Pyramid Age towered above the mud huts of prehistoric Egypt. However much we may frown upon autocracy, we cannot see the collapse of a civilization as impressive as that of Egypt under the Old Kingdom without regret—regret not only for the artistic and intellectual enterprises that came to an end, but for the suffering social chaos always brings to the people who live through it.

> *The land spins around like a potter's wheel; poor men have become rich and he who could not afford sandals is wealthy; but he who never slept on so much as a plank now owns a bed; he who never wove for himself possesses fine linen.*

To the Egyptian, the breakdown of *maat*, the divine order, would have been bad enough. But the trouble went beyond that.

> *I show you the son as a foe, the brother as an enemy, and a man killing his own father. The wild beasts of the desert will drink at the rivers of Egypt and be at their ease. Men will seize weapons of warfare, and the land will live in chaos.*

These quotations come from two great laments composed by scribes named Ipuwer and Neferti. Like the Old Testament prophets, and in similar language, these men came before the king and cried woe upon the land of Egypt. At least that is the premise of both compositions. It must be borne in mind, however, that these are literary texts, and that their authors had an ax to grind. By contrasting the wretchedness of earlier times with the reestablishment of the cosmic order, the kings responsible for the latter gained in prestige. And, in fact, one of the two compositions ends with a "prophecy" about a king from the south who will restore order and subdue the enemies of Egypt.

Some of the archaeological evidence suggests that things weren't all that bad for everybody. As the court at Memphis lost power, the local princes gained it, and a strong prince could make life a lot easier for his subjects, providing security and perhaps organizing food distribution. People were still building nice tombs for themselves and furnishing them with a variety of objects.

I personally view with suspicion most attempts to characterize a national "ethos" or spirit—if such a thing can be said to exist at all. Yet the written documents from the First Intermediate Period and early Middle Kingdom differ profoundly from the inscriptions of the stable eras that preceded it. The disillusionment of the prophetic texts is echoed in other documents. One of the most curious texts of the period is a long poem in which a man debates with his soul the problem of suicide. Life has become unbearable; "the slings and arrows of outrageous fortune" have overwhelmed the poet, and only death seems sweet. At first his soul seeks to dissuade him, pointing out, as does the prince of Denmark, that death may hold terrors greater than any evil of life. But at the end, the arguments of the misanthrope prevail; his soul agrees to accompany him wherever he may go, even into the shadows. Death, then, is one solution to the suffering and disillusionment of the time of troubles. Here, expressed with the concise eloquence of true poetry, is another:

> *The gods who lived formerly rested in their pyramids; the glorified dead also, buried in their pyramids, and they who built houses, Their places are no more.*
>
> *I have heard the words of Imhotep and Hordedef, whose sayings are so famous; What of their places now? Their walls are broken apart and their places are no more, As though they had never been.*
>
> *Therefore make holiday without wearying of it. Lo, no one can take his goods with him. Lo, no one who departs returns again.*

See how the terrifying conclusion builds up—the vanity of temporal power is as futile as the vanity of intellectual accomplishment; not even their wisdom can save the famous sages of the past from oblivion. The conclusion? Eat, drink, and be merry, since you can't take it with you.

The minstrels who entertained the nobleman at his feasts sang this song; some of the listeners inscribed the words upon the walls of their tombs, where they became a statement of belief. Some of the nobles copied another harper's song, which expresses a different approach to life and death.

I have heard those songs that are in the ancient tombs, and what they tell praising life on earth and belittling the region of the dead. Why do they do so, concerning the land of eternity, the just and the fair, which has no terrors? Wrangling is its abhorrence; no man there girds himself against his fellow. It is a land against which none can rebel. All our kinsfolk rest within it, since the earliest day of time; the offspring of millions are come hither, every one. For none may tarry in the land of Egypt, none there is who has not passed yonder.

The span of earthly things is as a dream; but a fair welcome is given him who has reached the West.

Either of these lovely songs would strike a strange note in a noble's tomb of the Old Kingdom, which vigorously expressed the material and naive expectations of the life to come. In the Fourth Dynasty the individual boasts of his deeds and his promotions. "I was greatly praised on account of it; never had the like been done by any noble before me." The biographical inscriptions of the First Intermediate Period still brag about great deeds. "I rescued my city," says one nobleman pointedly, "from the terrors of the royal house." (Well, really!—as Khufu might have said.) But there is a new emphasis in the texts of this period, an almost anxious affirmation of other deeds and other accomplishments, which contrasts sharply with the pride in advancement or in wealth.

I gave bread to the hungry, water to the thirsty, and clothing to the naked. I buried the aged. I was a father to the orphan, a husband to the widow. I did no wrongdoing against the people; it is what the god hates. I have rendered justice, which the king desired.

This is a composite, from many inscriptions, of claims to virtue that characterize this period. It is superfluous and needlessly cynical to point out that some of the men who made these claims may have been sinners of the deepest dye. What is significant is the fact that the claims were made, and had to be made. The quest for immortality must be almost as old as man himself. Even the ape-faced Neanderthal hunters buried their dead with the tools they would need in another life and with food to supply them on that longest of journeys. As society became more complex and life more pleasant and desirable, the human animal sought ever more means to ensure a continuance of pleasure: elaborate tombs, magical supplies of food and comforts, complex methods of preserving the body, gold and jewels and boasts of high office. But he could never be sure. He could never know for certain that his gold was the proper medium of exchange in Paradise. The upheaval of the First Intermediate Period gave the doubts of the Egyptian greater poignancy. So during this time, along with cynicism and hedonism, we see an attempt to substitute other values for the ones that had proved inadequate—values which, being invisible and intangible, were not susceptible to decay.

There are vague references to a judgment of the dead as early as the Pyramid Texts, but we do not get a clear picture of the concept until after the collapse of the Old Kingdom. The judge is Re, the sun god; and the creature that stands before the bar of justice is the human soul. "Your fault will be expelled and your guilt will be expunged, by the weighing of the scales on the day of reckoning characters; and it will be permitted that you join with those who are in the sun-bark." The image of the scales of justice requires no commentary. In the balances were weighed the sins and the virtues of the dead man, and only good deeds could insure eternal life.

The questions asked by the men of this troubled age so far in the past are not unique to their times, nor peculiar to their culture. They are the universal questions asked by all men who have ever pondered the tragedy of life and the mystery of death. Never before nor after, perhaps, until the Hebrew prophets began their long debate with God, did men express the questions so clearly nor with such eloquence as did the Egyptians of the First Intermediate Period and Middle Kingdom.

For two generations after the end of the Sixth Dynasty we know very little about actual events. The clouds of dust that arose from the collapse of that mighty edifice, the Old Kingdom, obscure events and people.

Manetho lists a Seventh and an Eighth Dynasty, but they could only have lasted for about a quarter of a century, and the ephemeral "kings" have left almost no contemporary records. The names and titles of local princes appear instead, in the tombs and in the quarries.

Around 2160 B.C. the clouds thin out a bit, in one area at least. That area was the Fayum, the great oasis-lake just south of the Delta. Here, in the city of Herakleopolis, a powerful family gained control under a prince named Akhtoy (aka Khety). Akhtoy's successors retained his name, and the only way we can tell one from another is by means of their alternative appellations. (As I mentioned, kings had several different names.) Manetho gives them two dynasties, the Ninth and Tenth. Of the first dozen or so of these Herakleopolitan kings we know very little, but by the middle of the Tenth Dynasty we are on firmer ground. The third king of this dynasty, Wahkare Akhtoy III, was a good ruler, and he felt himself qualified to give advice to his son, who would succeed him on the throne. *Instructions for King Merikare* is the title of the text, one of the best known of all Egyptian literary works. It is one of a general type of which the Egyptians were very fond; we call it "wisdom literature," and it consists of helpful hints to youth from an older, more worldly-wise individual.

Akhtoy was a king, so his precepts are intended for a youth who will hold the responsibilities of the highest office. There are none of the prosaic comments upon manners, which amuse us in some of the other teachings, written for and by commoners. "If you are one of those sitting at the table of one greater than yourself, take what he gives when it is set before you. Speak only after he has addressed you; this will be very pleasing to his heart."

So runs the advice of Ptahhotep, a Fifth Dynasty vizier. The Merikare text contains no such trivia. Akhtoy begins with some sound precepts as to character: "Be not evil; kindness is good. Be a craftsman in speech, for the tongue is a sword to a man and speech is stronger than fighting." After some weighty comments on statecraft and the handling of officials, the royal author rises to genuine heights of feeling and expression when he speaks of the judging of the heart in the West, the land of the dead.

> The council that judges the deficient—you know that they are not lenient on that day of judging the miserable. A man survives after death, and his deeds are placed beside him as his treasures. Existence yonder is for eternity and he who reaches it without wrongdoing shall exist there like a god, stepping out freely like the Lords of Eternity. More acceptable is the character of one upright of heart than the [sacrificial] ox of the evildoer.

Unfortunately for Merikare, his father was a better poet than he was a politician. The older king does mention the domestic situation, warning his son about the wretched Asiatics of the north and assuring him that "it is well with the Southern Region." That statement comes into the category of Famous Last Words. We cannot blame the king, because he was unable to predict the future, but he might have remembered the past. Once before there had come a conqueror, stepping with long strides down the Nile to unify the Two Lands. He had come from the south.

This is one of those cases which almost lead us to suspect that history can repeat itself. For three millennia the kingdom of the Nile would exist, its unity broken from time to time by internal strife and by foreign invasion. And from the beginning, even with Menes the Unifier, the force of renewed cohesion would come from the south. Why? We do not know. In fact, if we were trying to predict from which area the conqueror would originate, we would in most cases choose the north. The success of Upper Egypt at the beginning of the dynasties, under Menes, is inexplicable if the north was really more sophisticated, more highly developed. The same is true of the situation after the first great breakdown at the end of the Old Kingdom. Herakleopolis during the Tenth Dynasty was the most effective of all the city-states of the divided country, and she seemed well on the way to leading the reunification. In art and in military power she was ahead of her contemporaries; the literature she produced is of high quality. Yet—once again—the conqueror came from the south.

Four hundred and fifty miles south of Memphis the frowning cliffs retreat from the river edge, leaving a broad and fruitful plain. At the end of the Old Kingdom there were a few small settlements in this plain. The villagers worshiped Montu, a war god—a suggestive choice, in view of what followed. There may also have been a temple—a small and unimpressive one—to a petty local godling, Amon, a form of the fertility god Min. From these scrappy beginnings came a phenomenon: Thebes of the Hundred Gates and her patron god, Amon-Re.

The rise of Thebes (modern-day Luxor) can be traced back to about 2250 B.C., at which time a lady named Ikui in one of the villages of the Theban plain had the happy fortune to be blessed with a son whom she called Intef. He was a prince and a count, and his immediate descendants held the same titles.

A century or so after the birth of Intef, son of Ikui, the insidious air of the southland inflamed the ambitions of one of his descendants. The Theban princes had not been sitting supinely in their local capital while the Herakleopolitans expanded their influence; they had been engaging in a little expansion too, and they eventually extended their control as far south as the First Cataract. Count Intef's successor, Mentuhotep I, declared his independence of the kings of Herakleopolis and assumed the royal titles, but it was not until the reign of his younger son that the rivalry flared into bloody conflict. Wahankh Intef II drove the Herakleopolitans north and captured Abydos. A stela describing his prowess, from Wahankh's tomb at Thebes, is mentioned in a Twentieth-Dynasty papyrus that records the results of an inspection of the royal tombs. Depredations among the tombs had grown increasingly bold, and the investigating committee reported that Intef's pyramid, which must have been a small affair of brick, had been "removed"—a pleasantly nonjudgmental verb—but that the stela was still in place, and that "the figure of the king stands on this stela with his hound named Behek between his feet." Three thousand years after the inspection, in A.D. 1860, Auguste Mariette, then chief inspector of antiquities, found the lower part of the stela still intact. He left it there (one can almost hear Petrie's remarks on this negligence), and the inevitable happened. When Mariette's successor, Gaston Maspero, ran across the stela again in 1882, it was in fragments. The pieces were finally collected and brought to the Cairo Museum. The king was a true lover of caninity; he had not one but five of his favorite hounds shown on his stela so that they could enter the western paradise with him.

Truce or stalemate followed the first stage of the war. Then a new man came to the throne of the southern city. His name was also Mentuhotep, and he was the greatest warrior of his warlike line. We give him the number II, though such designations were never used by the Egyptians. (It's easier to keep track of these fellows by such means than by trying to remember their distinctive throne names, which are often annoyingly similar and which were sometimes changed in midreign.) Within twenty years Mentuhotep II had conquered the rest of Egypt. His opposite number in Herakleopolis was Merikare, who probably found his father's philosophy small comfort in defeat.

We would certainly like to have a contemporary account of this war, but none has been found. There is indirect evidence of a unique kind bearing on the last great battle, the siege of Herakleopolis. This evidence was discovered by H. E. Winlock, working at Deir el Bahri for the Metropolitan Museum of New York.

Deir el Bahri is part of the great west Theban necropolis area, which includes such marvels as the Valley of the Kings, a large group of nobles' tombs of the New Kingdom, and the huge mortuary temples of the Ramseses. At Deir el Bahri itself is the beautiful temple of Queen Hatshepsut, arguably the finest and most graceful piece of architecture in all of Egypt. There was an earlier temple at the same site, built by the conquering Mentuhotep. Winlock deserves the credit for the excavation of this temple. It was in very poor condition, but it must have been an impressive sight when it was built. A walled avenue of approach led from the green cultivated land to a huge shield-shaped court in front of a pillared temple which was surmounted by a small pyramid, or maybe it was a moundlike mastaba—so little is left of it that Egyptologists don't agree as to which. The king excavated his tomb under this monument, and he buried his family in other tombs nearby. Winlock found some twenty-odd graves in the temple itself, including the burial place of Mentuhotep's chief queen.

But the most interesting tomb of all was not that of a courtier or royal lady. Located in a place of honor, near the tomb of the king himself, this grave contained a mass burial of sixty soldiers, with their weapons beside them. They were commoners; we do not even know their names. From the nature of their injuries, Winlock deduced that they had been slain in an attack on a castle or fortified place. Some had died at once. Others, wounded by the defenders on the walls, had been left behind when their comrades retreated before an assault of the besieged garrison. The assault being temporarily successful, the wounded men were "picked up by their bushy hair" and clubbed to death by the defenders. Their bodies lay upon the field long enough to be mutilated by carrion birds; then a final attack on the castle gave victory to their comrades, who took up the battered bodies of the slain and brought them back to Thebes for burial.

It is a grim and surprisingly vivid picture to have been re-created from a group of unidentified mummies. But the most interesting feature is that Mentuhotep honored these Unknown Soldiers by burying them near his own tomb, in a proximity usually reserved for royalty or for high nobles. No less a battle than the final siege of the enemy capital, says Winlock, could have merited such favor. I like his deduction, not only because it is reasonable, but because it is so romantic. However, some scholars believe the men were killed during a battle outside Egypt, for Mentuhotep led campaigns in Nubia and against the Libyans, reestablishing trade routes and expanding Egyptian control. If the Unknown Soldiers did die at Herakleopolis, one can only wonder at the scant numbers—only sixty men lost their lives in the decisive battle of a great war! These men might have been selected from the slain because of unusual bravery, but war was a less efficient killer in ancient times than it is today.

These men went into battle unprotected except for the bushy hair Winlock mentions. The carefully cultivated mop atop their skulls might have been some help against clubs or maces, which were often of no harder substance than wood. Egyptian soldiers of this period also used axes and daggers. The boomerangs which have been found were probably used for hunting rather than war; we have both right- and left-handed models, and one which was tested performed exactly as a boomerang is supposed to perform. The most common weapon was the simple bow, with arrows tipped with flint or ebony; so unsophisticated in the art of war were the pre-Empire Egyptians that they did not usually use even copper arrowheads. The ones they used could kill a man just as dead as a metal point could; one of the slain soldiers had been hit in the back by an arrow that stood out eight inches in front of his body.

We know of the equipment of soldiers of this period from two sources—the burials of the veterans, and the models of soldier body-guards found in tombs. The most attractive example of the latter comes from Assiut and consists of two companies of some forty men each. The men of one group are painted red-brown, the standard body color for Egyptian men, and they carry tall spears and shields painted with various insignias. The other company is black—Nubian auxiliaries, evidently— and its weapon is the bow, which is carried in one hand, with a fistful of arrows in the other. The individual figures are relatively crude, but the craftsman has caught the martial bearing and determined stride of the fighting man; Count Mesehti of Assiut could have started his journey through the unknown dangers of the Afterworld feeling secure, with such soldiers to protect him. They are lovely warriors, and they are now in the Cairo Museum; if I thought I could burgle that admirable institution with impunity, I would certainly load them onto my truck.

This is the time of tomb models. Americans are fortunate in that they do not have to go to Cairo to see some of the best, which come from the Eleventh Dynasty Theban tomb of the Chancellor Meketre. The Metropolitan Museum, which conducted the excavations, was allowed to keep most of them. They reproduce, in faithful miniature, the estate of a wealthy nobleman. The estate was almost a small village, containing numerous shops or workhouses in which various specialized activities were carried on. Life was good, at least for the wealthy. In the Met models one can see the little serfs and craftsmen working away, some in the brewery-bakery (bread and beer went through the same initial process of fermentation), some in the butcher shop, where kicking cattle are given the coup de grâce, others in the stable and the weaver's shop. A nobleman had to have a regular fleet of boats, so the tomb models included reproductions of several types, including the last bark of all—the barge of the dead upon which, gilded and stiff with resinous bandages, the mummy of the noble lord made pilgrimage to Abydos, the home of Osiris. The journey may have been purely symbolic, but with the model in his tomb the noble could claim that he had performed this useful ritual act.

So skillfully made are these little models that we view them with the delight we would feel for elaborate toys. Of course they were not toys to their owners. The model symbolized the actuality, and the presence of the miniatures in the tomb assured its owner that the real thing would be supplied him in the next world. The models are equivalents of the paintings on the walls of the tomb or the written lists of offerings.

We have a good deal of Eleventh Dynasty tomb material, but the greatest tomb of them all was empty. The alabaster sarcophagus of Mentuhotep was found in his burial chamber under his temple, but the crafty thieves of ancient Thebes had found it long before. Nor was Mentuhotep's mummy among the royal bodies reburied by the priests of the late period. Presumably it was destroyed by the thieves.

Mentuhotep ruled for some fifty years, and his son was a middle-aged man when he came to the throne. The records of this king are records of peace; the old struggle with Herakleopolis was evidently finished. He was succeeded by another Mentuhotep, number four by modern reckoning. The most interesting fact about this king, who is known to Egyptologists by his Horus name of Nebtawi, is not how he gained the throne, but how he lost it.

The inscriptions of the Wadi el Hammamat quarries begin in the Old Kingdom. The quarries lie along the shortest route from the Nile to the Red Sea; it leaves the river at the great eastward bend just below Thebes, and many of the expeditions that followed the route, on their way to the sea or in search of fine stone, left inscriptions there. King Nebtawi sent an expedition to Hammamat to get stone for his sarcophagus, and the commander of the troop had a long inscription carved on the rock, which told of a marvel that there befell them. A gazelle, great with young, came bounding across the desert and stopped to deliver upon the very stone that had been selected for the lid of the sarcophagus. The gratified gentlemen of the expedition repaid the gazelle by cutting her throat. The inscription does not mention what became of the baby gazelles.

The name of Nebtawi's commander was Amenemhat. He accomplished his task efficiently, bringing back his force without losing so much as an ass. What intrigues us about the man, though, is not his talent as a servant of the king, but the fact that he did not remain a servant long. Within a few years after his return he finished the job he had begun by putting the king's body inside the sarcophagus whose construction he had supervised, and then taking the throne of Egypt for himself.

BINDER OF THE TWO LANDS

Let us admit that there is no evidence that Amenemhat shoved the old king over the threshold of eternity. He was not of royal birth, but he was qualified for kingship by talent if not by blood. He was regarded as the founder of the Twelfth Dynasty, and he sired a long line of Amenemhats and Senuserts, who restored the glory of Egypt under the later Middle Kingdom.

One of the first acts of the new ruler was to move his capital northward. Menes had done the same thing, perhaps for the same reason: it was easier to control the princes of the Delta and northern Egypt from there. The Twelfth Dynasty capital was not at Memphis, although this city continued to be important; it was near the road into the Fayum, and was called It-tawi, "Binder of the Two Lands."

Amenemhat's first job was restoring proper order in Egypt. The independent princelings needed more than the years of the Eleventh Dynasty to teach them their places. It did not take Amenemhat long to regulate internal affairs to his satisfaction, and then he could turn his mind to other things. One project he began was the official conquest of Nubia. Another was the construction of the "Walls of the Ruler," a fortress designed to protect the northeast frontier from incursions by Asiatics. He also started a new series of pyramids, which are poor objects indeed compared to the splendors of Giza. They cluster around the capital of It-tawi, at three cemeteries now known as Lisht, Hawara, and Lahun, and at the site of Dahshur, near Snefru's big pyramids. Amenemhat I's pyramid was of limestone. His quarries were not in the hills of Cairo, but in the older monuments of Giza and Sakkara. The pyramid is badly ruined, so we can see that the internal blocks include sculptured stones from the valley temples of Khufu and Khafre, among other sources. Some archaeologists have suggested that this pyramid be dismantled; as it stands it is not much to look at, and if we could get at the core blocks, all from Old Kingdom temples and tombs, we might learn a great deal.

Amenemhat had time to finish his pyramid and temples, but he had no time to spare. Perhaps he had a premonition of what was to come, for during his last years of rule he apparently made his son, Senusert I, co-regent. This joint kingship was a practical procedure, but it has confused chronology considerably. Each king dated events by his own years of reign, and only rarely, when we have an inscription that gives simultaneous year dates for both kings, can we be sure how long the coregency lasted, or even whether a coregency existed at all. You will not be surprised to hear that "the coregency question" is a popular subject for debate among Egyptologists, not only in the Middle Kingdom but later. Some scholars don't believe in any coregencies; others see them all over the place.

Thirty years after he had seized power, Amenemhat sent his son off on a campaign to "chastise" (a favorite Egyptian word) the Libyans of the western desert. While the younger king was gone, disaster struck. Possibly it was planned to take advantage of the absence of the younger, more virile ruler; Amenemhat was getting old. It is unlikely that a conspiracy aimed at his life could have been formed without his knowledge during his palmier days. Entering the royal bedchamber in the dead of night, the conspirators fell upon the king as he lay helpless and half-asleep. Although he fought for his life, hand to hand against the grim shadows in the night, he succumbed at last to the daggers of his foes. But treachery had not infested the entire court. Certain loyalists sent swift messengers to Senusert, now sole king of Egypt. He had already accomplished the purpose of the campaign and was on his way home. The news reached him in the evening as he made camp somewhere in the desert. Swearing the messenger to silence, the young king waited until dark had fallen and then set out with all speed for It-tawi. He reached the royal residence so soon and so unexpectedly that he was able to nip the conspiracy in the bud and ascend his throne without further difficulty. Undoubtedly his prompt and decisive action had saved the day for the royal house.

This story is known to us not from historical documents, but from two literary texts. The one that tells of the assassination is called *The Teaching of Amenemhat*, and purports to be a series of admonitions from the king to his son. There is bitterness in Amenemhat's words; he gave to the beggar and nourished the orphan, but those whom he trusted rose against him and those to whom he gave his hand came by night to murder him. "Do not fill your heart with a brother," he concludes. "Know not a friend, nor make intimates for yourself. When you sleep, guard your heart yourself, for a man has no adherents on the day of evil."

It may seem somewhat startling that this discourse is written in the first person, by the murdered king, and it has led some scholars to believe that Amenemhat was not killed by the conspirators, but lived on to write his admonitions. However, poetic license allows a voice from the tomb even in our own literature. The death of the king by assassination fits in with the second half of the story, for it is unlikely that if Amenemhat had died peacefully in his bed his son would have received the news with such alarm, or hurried away from his army to take possession of the throne unless that throne had been threatened.

The dramatic night march of Senusert is told in one of the most famous of all Egyptian literary works, *The Story of Sinuhe*. Sir Alan Gardiner, the doyen of Egyptian philology, considered this a tale that should rank as a world classic, and his opinion was shared by Rudyard Kipling, who was himself no slouch at writing good stories.

At the beginning of the tale we find Sinuhe, overseer of the king in the land of the Asiatics, taking his ease near the royal tent as the army made camp on its way back from the war with the Libyans. He saw the messengers from It-tawi arrive, and heard them speak to Senusert. The results were electric. "My heart pounded," Sinuhe admits. "My arms went limp, trembling fell upon all my limbs."

Such bodily enfeeblement might be due to shock—very proper when hearing of the death of one's king. But Sinuhe's next move makes us wonder: "In leaps and bounds, I sought a hiding place; I put myself between two bushes in order to separate myself from the road."

Having made a good start, Sinuhe did not stop; he crossed the Nile and kept right on going, through the Walls of the Ruler which marked the eastern boundary of Egypt, and out into the wilderness of Sinai.

The rest of the story is wonderful fun to read, but we will have to pass over it briefly because it has no bearing on political events. Sinuhe rose to great eminence among the "Asiatics"; at last he settled down somewhere in Syria and took himself a wife or two. But although he was honored in his adopted country, his heart increasingly yearned for home. And, with the pleasing harmony found only in fairy tales, the all-knowing king of Egypt got wind of his old servant's heimweh. He sent messengers to invite Sinuhe back to Egypt.

The king's letter is marvelously tactful, but it asks a question to which we ourselves would like to know the answer. "What have you done, that action should be taken against you? You have not blasphemed, you have not spoken against the council of nobles. . . ."

Whatever their cause, Sinuhe's apprehensions were removed by the letter. To return to his home was no small thing, but his greatest reason for rejoicing was the prospect of laying his bones within the blessed soil of Egypt. He was so moved when at last he was brought face-to-face with the majesty of the king that he was on the verge of collapsing, and could not speak. The king received him kindly and sought to relieve the tension by summoning the royal children and the queen, whom Sinuhe had once served.

"Here is Sinuhe," said royalty affably, "returned as an Asiatic, a true son of the Bedouin." The queen shrieked aloud, and the royal children exclaimed, with one voice: "Is it really he?"

This is a real Egyptian happy ending, but we cannot help wondering what brought it all about. What did Sinuhe overhear at the royal camp to send him scampering for sanctuary, as far from Egypt as his legs could carry him? We may be excused for suspecting that he was involved in the conspiracy himself. There are too many protestations of innocence, from Sinuhe and from the king, for him to be wholly guiltless. If so, the magnanimity of the king is admirable. Even though he had been ruling in peace for many years, he could have no motive except mercy for granting the heart's desire of an old enemy.

While Sinuhe was swashbuckling around among the Asiatics, his king was carrying on the traditions established by Amenemhat I. He built his pyramid near that of his father and pushed the borders of Egypt farther south, furthering the process which was to end with Lower Nubia as an Egyptian province. Under him and his successors the country enjoyed peace and prosperity. Another Amenemhat and another Senusert held the throne for fifty years, during which time all was well.

All the kings of this dynasty were competent rulers. But with Senusert number three, the Twelfth Dynasty reached its peak. The first kings of the Twelfth Dynasty had sent troops into Lower Nubia as far as the Second Cataract, but it remained for Senusert III to put the country under organized military occupation. He was, in later times, regarded as the patron saint of the whole region—by the Egyptians. The natives of Nubia may have had another opinion of him.

At this time there lived in the region south of Egypt the aforementioned C peoples. They had entered Lower Nubia during the time of the weakness of Egypt between the Old and Middle Kingdoms. Though primitive by Egyptian standards, they were not barbarians. They made good pottery, raised cattle, and buried their dead in stone tombs circular in shape and with a chapel for offerings on one side.

These were the people whom the kings of the Twelfth Dynasty encountered as they pushed south. The Egyptians were not received with shouts of joy. Before the Aswan dam drowned Lower Nubia travelers heading south along the Nile from Aswan could see the ruins of great buildings located at strategic spots beside the river, all the way to the Third Cataract. They were the remains of the forts built by the Egyptians to hold the river route to the gold lands of the eastern desert. Fourteen of these fortified towns were built during the Middle Kingdom. In the heavy walls and the strategic location of each we see recognition of an enemy of no mean quality; the forts were close enough so that they could reinforce one another in case of an attack.

Fortunately, before the waters of Lake Nasser covered them, the forts were extensively studied by scholars. It does not take too much imagination to reconstruct them, or to imagine the life of an Egyptian outpost garrison two millennia before Christ. The heaviest fortifications were on the land side. The Egyptians held the river, and the forts could be supplied and relieved by water. A low wall and ditch served as the outer ring of defense; then came a forewall with bastions, inside which was a narrow passageway. The innermost wall was very high and thick, built of mud brick strengthened with timber insertions, and supported by towerlike projections at intervals. A narrow street ran around the inside of the wall. Within the defenses was the garrison town itself, with a big house for the commandant and barracks for the soldiers. There were also storehouses and a treasury, plus a small temple. Most of the forts up to the Wadi Halfa region of the Second Cataract were built by Senusert III's predecessors. He built eight more in the fifty miles—as the crow flies—which lie south of Wadi Halfa. Senusert III fixed his boundary by formal decree at the most southerly of these forts, Semna.

After Semna, the Nile runs through a district called the "Belly of the Rocks," where the difficulties of navigation are immense. Rocks and shoals threaten the boats, and the river runs almost at right angles to the prevailing northwesterly winds. There is an easier stretch after this, and then another series of cataracts—the Third—after which the battered boats come out onto a stretch of river known as the Dongola Reach, which is safe for navigation. At the head of this smooth stretch, just beyond the fanged rocks of the Third Cataract, stands an amazing structure. The modern name for it is the Western Deffufa.

We are now at the site known as Kerma, which Reisner excavated in the early 1920s. It is 150 miles south of the Twelfth Dynasty frontier at Semna—150 miles in a straight line, much farther if one follows the bends of the river. But if Reisner was right, the Egyptians were here during the Middle Kingdom. They built the great mound called the Western Deffufa, which looks less like a man-made structure than a peculiar wind-carved formation in a desert region.

I remember reading about Reisner's work when I was a student, and I remember too that his conclusions were generally accepted. He thought that Kerma was the provincial capital of an Egyptian governor of the far south. Several generations of such governors controlled the area during the Middle Kingdom, died there, and were buried where they died. If Reisner's theory is correct, Senusert III was indeed a mighty conqueror.

What are the actual physical remains upon which Reisner based his ideas? It is difficult to know the precise functions of the Western Deffufa. The top part, which contained the buildings or rooms, has been worn away by erosion; the lower section is simply a gigantic brick platform. A group of rooms on a lower level survived, and the litter found in these rooms included scraps of imported Egyptian articles and also local products such as ostrich eggshells, rock crystal, and copper oxide.

East of this mound is another ruin called the Eastern Deffufa, beside which is a large cemetery. The bigger tombs consist of a central chamber, where the body of the deceased was laid upon a bed, and a long corridor running through the mound past the central chamber. In the corridor of each of the largest tombs Reisner found the bodies of several hundred people, most of them women and children. They had been buried alive. Some lay with their faces hidden in their hands or protected by a bent arm; one poor girl had crawled under the bed on which her dead lord lay, thus prolonging the agony of death by suffocation.

In one of these big multiple graves Reisner found an object which was of primary importance for his theory. This was the statue of an Egyptian lady who was the wife of a Twelfth Dynasty prince of Assiut named Hapdjefa. The lower part of a life-size statue of the prince himself was found in the same grave-mound. This, said Reisner, must mean that the chieftain for whom this court of the dead was assembled was none other than Hapdjefa himself. Hence the theory of the Egyptian governors of the south, buried in the land they had ruled, with the bodies of their Nubian harem around them. This was "going native" with a vengeance.

Let's look at the rest of the evidence that bears on the situation. There is a tomb of this same Hapdjefa at Assiut, in Egypt. Some scholars assert that he was never buried in it, but it is a nice tomb—as tombs go—with a particularly elaborate set of mortuary contracts inscribed on its walls. The titles of Hapdjefa do not include any epithet which would indicate he was a governor of Nubia. Last of all, I should mention Reisner's statement that the statues of the Egyptian prince and his lady were carved from native Nubian rock; they were not, then, imported objects.

Well, there it is, such as it is—the evidence. What can we do with it?

A. J. Arkell, whose work in the Sudan I have mentioned before, was one of the first to disagree with Reisner. The burial mounds differ from standard Nubian funerary practice only in the magnitude of their size. Since only great chiefs could have squandered so many slaves in death, Kerma must have been the capital of Cush (also spelled Kush), a powerful Nubian kingdom after the Middle Kingdom. Kerma was a trading post during the Middle Kingdom, but the Egyptians did not have political or military control over the region.

The big stumbling block in the way of this interpretation is Reisner's claim that the significant statues were carved of native stone. But we can get around the difficulty, if we want to, by suggesting that Reisner was mistaken (he was sometimes). The turning-home of the Egyptians as the time of death approached, which we see illustrated in *The Story of Sinuhe*, is a strong psychological point against the burial of Hapdjefa in Nubia. Equally formidable as an objection to the theory of Egyptian political control so far south is the long, unfortified stretch of river between Kerma and the frontier fort of Semna. It is hard to believe that a strategist of the caliber of Senusert III would build a military establishment so far from potential reinforcements.

The international excavations in Nubia before the completion of the dam contributed a great deal of information about the history of that region, and there is no doubt (in my mind, at least) that earlier theories were influenced by the no-doubt unconscious snobbery of Egyptologists about "inferior" cultures. It now seems clear that Kerma was the capital of an increasingly potent Cushite kingdom, whose rulers, as we shall see, were to pose a continual threat to Egypt. The impressive Deffufa was the base of a Cushite temple or palace, not an Egyptian-run trading post. Other Egyptian articles have been found at Kerma; they could have been acquired in trade, or in Cushite raids into Lower Nubia or Egypt itself.

Senusert III led several military expeditions to the south, so we may presume that the C peoples continued to give him trouble. He "pacified" the region so energetically that there was peace for the rest of the dynasty. But when the inevitable end came in Egypt, it was marked by fire and fury in Nubia. All the forts of the Second Cataract area were burned.

Senusert III's greatest military exploits were in Nubia, but he led at least one expedition into a part of Palestine. The Egyptians of the Middle Kingdom probably did not have a military empire in Syria, as they did in Nubia, but contacts increased during the Twelfth Dynasty. Excavations in the Syrian cities of antiquity have turned up a goodly number of imported Egyptian objects, so Egypt must have carried on considerable trade with the east.

It is no wonder the Greeks admired Senusert, whom they called Seso-stris. He had settled Nubia, ventured into the rich lands of the east, and quenched the ambitions of the noble families of Egypt—their tombs at the provincial capitals disappear during his reign. Toward the end of his life he associated his son with him on the throne, as his ancestors had done, and when he died, after thirty-eight years of unceasing activity, he sought a well-deserved rest in his pyramid at Dahshur.

Senusert's pyramid was built of mud brick. A casing of fine white limestone hid the deficiencies of the construction for a time, but when the outer stone was removed the brick collapsed into ruin. Shortly before this time the kings had abandoned the traditional northern entrance to their tombs; that was as good as drawing a map for the ubiquitous tomb rob-bers. The entrance to Senusert III's pyramid was far to the west of the structure, but as a subterfuge it was not very successful. When the French archaeologist Jacques de Morgan entered the pyramid in 1894, he found that he had been anticipated. The body of the king was no longer in the huge red sarcophagus. But de Morgan proved once again that careful ex-cavation can turn up material which the tomb robbers missed. In a gal-lery under the northwest corner of the pyramid he found a collection of wonderful jewelry which had belonged to princesses of the royal family. De Morgan seems to have had a sixth sense for gold; it was he who found the second great cache of Middle Kingdom jewels near the pyramid of Amenemhat II, also at Dahshur.

Both collections included collars and bracelets, pectorals, crowns and rings that had belonged to the daughters and wives of the Twelfth Dynasty kings. The pectorals consist of inlaid gold plates cut out into elaborate de-signs, with cartouches of the kings flanked by hawks and supported by little kneeling gods. The workmanship is superb; sometimes there are as many as three or four hundred separate bits of semiprecious stone in each of these small masterpieces, each bit cut to fit within a space outlined by fine gold wire. The effect is that of cloisonné enamel. The colors are rather bright—red-orange of carnelian, deep lapis blue, turquoise. The pectorals were worn on the breast, suspended from necklaces of large beads.

The prettiest of all the pieces of Twelfth Dynasty jewelry is a crown made of strands of fine gold wire, starred at irregular intervals with tiny five-petaled turquoise flowers with carnelian centers. The wire was caught here and there by cross-shaped pieces of gold, and the effect of the dainty flowers against the shining black hair of the princess must have been lovely.

Most of this jewelry is in the Cairo Museum. However, another such hoard, from the pyramid of Senusert II at Lahun, was found by Petrie in 1914, and this magnificent example of the ancient jeweler's art is now in the possession of the Metropolitan Museum. Except for the crown I have described, which is a uniquely lovely thing, the Met's jewelry is the equal of anything in the Cairo collection. It belonged to a lady named Sit-Hathor-Iunet.

When archaeologists find anything as valuable as this jewelry, they like to deal with it personally. But when the news of the find reached Petrie, he was in a quandary; he had strained himself and was physically unable to do the job. This was not a question of going down into the tomb and lifting up a box neatly packed with pieces of jewelry. The box had decayed, as had the thread on which the beads and separate elements were strung, and the resulting mess looked like the burial chamber of Hetepheres on a miniature scale. Petrie's standards demanded that each individual bead be cleared and recorded on the spot; otherwise, all hope of restringing the necklaces and bracelets in something like their original order would be lost. Petrie's assistant at that time was Guy Brunton, who, like most of his students, was to become a prominent Egyptologist in his own right. Brunton spent a solid week in that tomb, curled up on the bare floor of the corridor at night to guard against thieves, and digging beads out of petrified mud by day, until the find was cleared and recorded.

Once the jewelry was restored, it was obvious that Petrie had made a superb discovery. The Cairo Museum was a lot more relaxed about releasing objects in those days, and they already had a magnificent collection of Twelfth Dynasty jewelry, thanks to de Morgan. Petrie was allowed to keep what he found. He had been excavating under the auspices of the

British School of Archaeology, which was composed of individual members as well as institutions such as museums and universities. Up to this time the discoveries that the Cairo Museum relinquished had been divided among the members in proportion to the amount of their contributions, but it was obvious that the jewelry was too valuable and too important to be included in the usual seasonal division. Petrie decided to offer it to the member who (or which) would pay the most for it, the proceeds, of course, going to the School's excavation fund. Being a loyal Englishman, he offered it first to British museums but was chagrined to discover that none of them could, or would, take advantage of the proposition. Finally he had to expand the offer overseas, and the rich Americans got into the picture. Thanks to the generosity of private donors and the solvency of its funds, the Metropolitan Museum was able to acquire Sit-Hathor-Iunet's jewels.

Senusert III's son was another Amenemhat, the third in number. He too was well known to the Greeks, but his achievements were in the arts of peace rather than war.

The capital of Egypt at this time was, as we have said, It-tawi near the entrance to the Fayum. The Fayum might be called a large oasis; it is a depression in the desert which, in prehistoric times, was filled by the Nile to produce a large lake. In shape the depression is strikingly leaflike; the narrow stem is the connection with the Nile valley, which leads to the river through an opening in the western cliffs. Early in the Middle Kingdom an anonymous genius conceived the idea of controlling this great mass of water for the benefit of the irrigation system, which was always a matter of interest to kings and people alike; the whole internal prosperity of the nation depended on it. The unknown genius need not have been the king, although court fiction credited him with every talent. The king does deserve credit for seeing the value of the suggestion. Great regulators for controlling inflow and outflow were built, and an immense wall was begun inside the Fayum to hold back the lake and reclaim land for cultivation.

Amenemhat III was not the initiator of this great labor, but he did more than any other king before him; his wall was probably about twenty-seven miles long and opened some seventeen thousand acres to cultivation. In a country such as Egypt, where every square foot of irrigated land is worth a fortune, these new acres were a great addition to the country's agricultural potential. One cannot help comparing this monumental public works system with the Fourth Dynasty undertaking which was its equivalent in extent and in labor, if in nothing else—the Great Pyramid of Giza. Not that the Senuserts and the Amenemhats were altruists. The reclaimed land was not distributed to the humble peasants but was kept by the crown. Hence we may see the Great Pyramid and the dam as examples of ostentation versus practicality, rather than exploitation versus charity.

Many buildings sprang up on the new lands of the Fayum—temples, palaces, towns. They have vanished today into the soil that gave them birth, but we know about one structure in some detail. It was still standing in Greek times, and as a world-famous tourist sight was visited and described by both Strabo and Herodotus. The building was known as the Labyrinth, which gives some indication of its size and complexity. Today only a mass of limestone and granite chips, covering the surface of the ground for hundreds of square yards, shows where this wonder of antiquity once stood. But Strabo tells us that the ceilings of the chambers each consisted of a single stone, and that the passages were walled with monolithic slabs. Herodotus says the Labyrinth contained twelve walled courts and no fewer than three thousand rooms. The historian himself saw the fifteen hundred rooms that were aboveground—he says—but he had to take the word of the priests as to the existence of the corresponding fifteen hundred underground chambers, since they were burial places, and sacred.

We know enough to discount about 50 percent of what any Egyptian told Herodotus. He was a marvelously receptive audience for a good story, whether he believed it or not, and the ancestors of the dragomen must have fought over who was to guide the Greek; if they resembled their descendants, they liked appreciation almost as much as they did baksheesh. Yet Herodotus is not a bad source when he is describing things he actually saw. Such a construction was perfectly possible for the Egyptians of this period. They worked massive blocks for the pyramids and carved sarcophagi and even burial chambers out of one gigantic square of stone. So we need not doubt the word of the Greeks—in this case. A modern archaeologist has calculated the size of the Labyrinth as 305 meters long by 244 meters wide—big enough to contain the enormous temples of Luxor and Karnak.

The resources and effort which the Old Kingdom monarchs had put into their tombs the Twelfth Dynasty kings used elsewhere; their pyramids were unimpressive. Amenemhat III's pyramid was near the Labyrinth, at a site called Hawara. The Labyrinth, then, may have been in part a mortuary temple. The Hawara pyramid is a labyrinth on a small scale. Built of mud brick like that of Senusert III, its interior is fantastic; nowhere during the Middle Kingdom did a royal architect so challenge the ingenuity of the tomb robbers. The entrance was on the south, opening onto a flight of stairs leading down to a vestibule. There was no visible way out of this little chamber; the hidden exit was in the roof, of all places, where one of the slabs slid back to reveal another room. The passage leading from the second room was completely filled by huge blocks of stone. One group of thieves had laboriously chiseled a tunnel through these blocks, thus falling for one of the oldest of all practical jokes. This passage was a blind. The real one led to another chamber, which had all the appearance of a dead end. A hidden sliding door led to a second dead-end chamber; from this a trapdoor opened onto a passage that led not into the burial chamber, but past one side of it. Two false burial shafts descended from the floor of the passage (one can almost work up some pity for the thieves, chipping their way through all the extraneous stone provided for their befuddlement and uttering fulsome curses in ancient Egyptian). The far side of the same passage was filled in with stone, in order to suggest that something important lay beyond. The real entrance to the burial chamber was concealed in the middle of the passage. If a thief actually did get this far, he found himself staring in dismay at a burial chamber which was hollowed out of a single block of stone and was roofed with a gigantic stone slab that weighed forty-five tons. This stone had sealed the chamber after the royal mummy had been placed within.

It is hard to believe, but thieves did penetrate into the burial chamber. They took everything they could carry away and then set fire to the remainder, including the king's body. Their annoyance is understandable.

When Petrie investigated this pyramid in 1880 he had as much trouble as the robbers. He found the burial chamber by digging right into the pyramid and then realized that he would have to import some expert masons to chisel through the roof block. The masons came, but the tunnel through which they had to pass was dug through sand and kept caving in. Petrie, typically, regarded the possibility of being buried alive as one of those occupational hazards an archaeologist has to put up with, but he was sufficiently aware of the foibles of lesser human beings to know that the masons would have quit on the spot if they had known how dangerous the sand tunnel was. So while the experts from Cairo were employed, Petrie spent his nights in the tunnel, shoring up the worst spots and repairing what had fallen in during the previous twenty-four hours. Finally the masons finished and Petrie wriggled, head down, through the hole. The chamber was full of water; Petrie cleared the floor by pushing chips of stones and small objects onto a hoe with his feet. When the chamber was cleared, the eminent archaeologist found the original entrance by traversing the passages in reverse, from the burial chamber out. They were filled with mud, and there was just room for him to slide, stripped and prostrate, through the traps and complications, in absolute darkness and miasmatic air, and in slime up to his ears. From this perilous and repellent trip Petrie gained nothing except the knowledge of the location of the entrance. He never dreamed of questioning that it was worth it.

We have, from time to time, talked about methods in archaeology. Here, in Petrie's exploit, is a method that is not for the faint of heart. Let us quickly add that few Egyptologists of today have to undergo discomforts even remotely like those Petrie and his contemporaries had to endure. But the spirit that animated the pioneers is, and must be, an integral part of the archaeologist's character. He may never have to hang by one hand from the edge of a cliff in order to copy an isolated inscription, or slither through the boggy bowels of a pyramid. But he should be ready to do so if the necessity ever arises; his is the responsibility, and his the expert eye. And if he is willing to relinquish to another the glory of being the first to gaze upon a new page out of the past, he lacks the spirit of adventure that is part of the quest for knowledge.

Amenemhat III built another pyramid at Dahshur, though he was probably buried in the labyrinthian structure at Hawara. Once again we find this strange and as yet unexplained phenomenon of two tombs, which appeared at the very beginning of the dynasties. I doubt we have yet found the complete explanation for such lavishness, but the theories keep coming.

Amenemhat III is the last of the great Twelfth Dynasty kings. The end of the dynasty is lost in obscurity, and the impact of its collapse put an end to stable government for two centuries. A period of upheaval, which we call the Second Intermediate Period, followed the fall of the Middle Kingdom, as the First Intermediate Period followed the Old Kingdom. We may talk glibly about the failure of centralized government as a cause of the anarchy, but the more basic question—what caused the centralized government to fail—is still unanswerable.

Superficially, the broad sequence of events at the end of the Old Kingdom is paralleled by what happened after the fall of the Middle Kingdom. There is even a repetition of that most ominous of all portents, the appearance of a woman on the throne of Horus. The Twelfth Dynasty lady, Sobekneferu, was apparently the last of her line; if there had been an eligible male around, he would probably have married her and taken over the throne. What is surprising is that no ineligible male (speaking from the legitimist point of view) came to carry out this procedure. We might learn a great deal, not only about the rules of inheritance in Egypt, but about the causes of the fall of the Middle Kingdom, if we knew more about this lady. It is assumed she was the sister of the last Amenemhat (number four in our reckoning). Statues (headless, unfortunately) of the lady show her in an unusual combination of male and female clothing. She must be considered a reigning queen, since one object gives her the full royal titulary. Her tomb has disappeared, unless it is one of the two disintegrated pyramids between Dahshur and Lisht, at Mazghuna. Both these pyramids were explored by—guess who? Petrie. But he found no identifying marks. There is never enough money for excavation, and one of the obvious methods of pyramid identification has never been tried at Mazghuna—the excavation of the tombs around the pyramid. It would be illuminating to find the tomb of Queen-King Sobekneferu's vizier with a long account of his career and hers. It is more likely, however, that these pyramids date from the Thirteenth Dynasty.

What were the accomplishments of the Middle Kingdom, as compared with the Old? In one sense they were not as profound or as dramatic. The men of this second great period may have climbed as high as did their ancestors, but they did not have to start so far down on the ladder. Writing, monumental building, a state religion, a philosophy of kingship and the social order, and many other basic elements of civilization were defined in the Old Kingdom and reused by its successor. But there are changes. One of the most striking is the alteration in the face of kingship, as it appears in the statues. Look at the portrait of Senusert III—the deep lines from nose to mouth, the unsmiling, somber set of the mouth, the heavy furrows in the brow. The face of Khafre, of the Fourth Dynasty, is truly the face of a god; the features show supreme confidence, in himself and in the universe. The faces of the Middle Kingdom rulers show the weight of grave responsibility, if nothing more tragic.

We may see in these faces, and in the contrast between egocentric pyramid and public irrigation works, a sign of a change in the notion of the role of the king. Is he now the shepherd of his people rather than a remote godling; the primus inter pares of a feudal state rather than a being unique in his divinity? That would be imposing modern viewpoints that would have made no sense to the Egyptian of the Middle Kingdom. At best, any conclusion is affected by the old temptation to see the bright side (from our angle) of the people we have selected as the object of our study. Even so, there is some truth in the claim that this period developed a stronger sense of social and moral responsibility than had formerly existed. Nowhere is this claim supported more strongly than in the literary works of the period. Let us examine just one more story, in order to nail down the point.

The Tale of the Eloquent Peasant must have been the special bane of little Egyptian schoolboys. It was copied extensively and used as a school exercise; its style is so confoundedly literary and artificial that a translation cannot be read by a non-Egyptologist without pages of commentary explaining the figures of speech. Some of these, let us add, are not precisely clear even to an Egyptologist.

A peasant of the Fayum is on his way to market with a train of donkeys when he encounters a petty official belonging to the household of Rensi, the great steward of the king. This petty official, whose name is Thutinakht, covets the peasant's property and concocts a dastardly plan; he spreads linen across the path, forcing the peasant to lead his donkeys along the edge of the field. One of the small sad animals succumbs to temptation and snatches a bite of grain, whereupon Thutinakht confiscates the whole caravan and drives the protesting peasant away. After several days of fruitless appeal to the unscrupulous official, the desperate peasant seeks out the grand steward. He addresses this mighty man in a speech so eloquent and so poignant that the steward is loath to relinquish the pleasure of listening to him speak. So he makes no answer to the plea. The peasant, who can certainly count persistence among his character traits, returns again and again to the seemingly indifferent steward and addresses him in no fewer than eight fine speeches. In the meantime the steward has reported the peasant's plight, and his eloquence, to the king, who orders that a copy be made of each beautiful word. He also orders that the peasant's family be fed while the orations are being delivered—a nice touch, which we might not have expected from a tyrant. The story has a happy ending and even a touch of poetic justice: the peasant gets his property back and is further enriched by the goods of the greedy official who robbed him.

In the course of his travail, the peasant makes use of every device to sway his impassive audience—threats, pleas, exhortations, flattery. Among his arguments is an appeal to a more solemn matter: justice for the sake of justice. "Righteousness descends with the doer thereof into the tomb, and he is remembered because of it." The argument of the peasant, and the events of the tale, pronounce the same conclusion—justice is the same for rich and poor alike. It is a conclusion that may startle us, coming at this time and this place; perhaps in no other culture did the monarch enjoy such absolute power as in ancient Egypt, where dogma proclaimed him a veritable god. But we have seen hints of this ideal in other texts and in other areas of life, so we can understand why some scholars venture to use the word *democratic* about certain aspects of this particular period.

Even Paradise begins to lower its barriers, for the prerogatives of immortality have been usurped by the nonroyal dead. Here a peculiar twist is given to our notion of equality; all men were equal, because every man was a king. The Pyramid Texts of the Old Kingdom had assured the ruler of life everlasting; the Coffin Texts of Middle Kingdom commoners endow them with a similar privilege. The soul of the dead man must face a judgment, but the judge is no longer Re, as in earlier times. He is now Osiris, ruler of the kingdom of the dead. Since the deceased was also Osiris, imitating the status of the dead king, this presents a picture that may be confusing to modern eyes—Osiris the deceased being judged by Osiris the god. But it did not bother the Egyptians. Very few inconsistencies bothered them.

Of course when we talk about commoners we are really talking about the nobles, petty and otherwise, and about the craftsman and tradesman class. Real commoners—peasants—had no coffins to write texts upon and no tombs to put the coffins in; all they had was a hole in the sand and a few pots containing food. Even so, Paradise was democratized in the sense that any man who could afford to have a coffin painted could be Osiris. The name of the god became a sort of epithet, applied to the deceased—the Osiris Hapdjefa, prince and count, or the Osiris Sanakht, carpenter. The Hereafter was becoming a capitalist society.

Four

THE FIGHT FOR FREEDOM

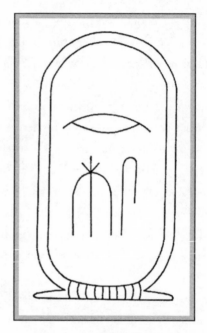

Cartouche of Ahmose

INVASION

There was a king of ours whose name was Tutimaois, in whose reign it came to pass, I know not why, that God was displeased with us, and there came unexpectedly men of obscure birth out of the eastern parts, who had boldness enough to make an expedition into our country, and easily subdued it by force without a battle. And when they had overpowered our rulers, they afterward savagely burnt down our cities and razed the temples of the gods, and used all the inhabitants in a cruelly hostile manner, for they slew some and led the children and wives of others into slavery. . . . All this nation was styled Hyksos, that is, Shepherd Kings; for "hyk" in the sacred language denotes a king, and "sos" in the vulgar tongue signifies a shepherd.

This is one of the few surviving quotations from Manetho; it was copied by Josephus, for reasons of his own. I may have given the impression that Manetho is not to be trusted, and, in fact, I don't think he is. (Neither is Josephus.) Three statements in the account given above are partially correct. Egypt was invaded by people who took over part of the country, the invaders came from "eastern parts," and some of them—not all—were styled Hyksos.

Obviously, the fact that we are able to sneer at Manetho means that we have other sources of information. Contemporary inscriptional evidence, mostly isolated monuments and scarabs, is spotty. The Turin Papyrus or King List, one of the basic chronological sources, is also spotty. In fact, it's in pieces. People have been trying to put it back together for years. Certain Egyptian texts mention the great humiliation inflicted by the Hyksos—whom they call "Aamu," or "Asiatics"—but all of them were written long after the event. The Egyptians suffered from a sort of official amnesia with regard to unpleasant facts; one has the feeling that the conquest would never have been mentioned at all if there had been a reasonable way of glorifying a king for liberating his country without referring to what he was liberating it from.

Manetho's etymology, among other matters, is inaccurate. The word *Hyksos* does not mean "Shepherd Kings"; it is derived from two Egyptian words that mean "Rulers of Foreign Countries." It seems to have been a title and was applied not to the invaders as a group, but to their rulers; however, for the sake of convenience, we will refer to the whole lot by that name. The foreign countries were probably the lands of southwest Asia. Asiatics were always seeping down into Egypt; they came as immigrants, traders, and, in later periods, slaves, and some seem to have settled down quite peacefully in various parts of the Delta. During the period of internal weakness after the Old Kingdom, greater numbers of immigrants entered the country, just as the Hyksos seem to have done after the fall of the Middle Kingdom. There was considerable restlessness in Asia during this period, and great movements of tribes and ethnic groups. New faces and names appear in other areas of the Near East, and it may be that the Hyksos were part of the wide Völkerwanderung, which originated, perhaps, in the steppes of the Caucasus and picked up additional components as it wandered.

The conquest was not so bloody nor so destructive as the melodramatic Egyptian writers claimed. The Hyksos rulers became Egyptianized, using the hieroglyphic writing, assuming the Egyptian royal titulary, and worshiping the old gods. They particularly honored Set, the enemy of Osiris. This may be explained by Set's resemblance to one of their own gods. It was not the affront to Egyptian sensibilities that one might think, for as we have said elsewhere, Set was a perfectly good god in his own time and place, and that place was the northeast Delta, where the Hyksos entered Egypt.

One little mystery about the Hyksos has been cleared up in recent years. We knew the name of their capital, Avaris, from Egyptian records. But where was Avaris? The favored contender was Tanis, the site that became the capital under the late dynasties. However, an Austrian expedition under Manfred Bietak has established, beyond doubt, that the modern Tell el Dab'a is the right place. Working under the difficult conditions that prevail in the Delta area, Beitak found several layers of occupation, with characteristic non-Egyptian pottery.

The major contributions of the Hyksos to Egyptian life were in the realm of warfare. They probably introduced the horse and chariot and the compound bow. As yet we cannot add much more to our picture of the mysterious people called the Hyksos, except for one small fact. Some of these people had Semitic names.

Asiatics—men of Semitic speech—in ancient Egypt; here biblical scholars pricked up their ears. The connection of the Hebrews with Egypt has been the subject of long and wearisome discussion among historians. There is no Egyptian reference to Moses, nor to Joseph; no text contains even a faint echo of the long captivity or the Exodus. Israel is mentioned only once, in a list of conquered territories. It is no wonder that the theories about the Hebrews in Egypt vary considerably. One school of thought would place the Exodus in the fifteenth century B.C., another in the thirteenth; a third version contends that there was no single, large exodus of enslaved peoples, but a series of small exodi, so to speak, which were coalesced by Jewish tradition and historians into a single event. More on this later; what we are concerned with now is how the Hyksos can be fitted into the story.

If we suppose that it was during this period that Joseph was brought down into Egypt by the slavers to whom his wicked brothers had sold him, we find it easier to understand the speed with which he, a slave, rose to power. He was a man of Semitic speech and customs serving a king from the same sort of ethnic background. If this sounds plausible, let us not forget that the ancients were not so conscious as we about the ties of "blood and birth"; social distinctions were very important, and a slave was a slave wherever he came from. We can hardly envision the Egyptianized Hyksos king taking a slave to his bosom just because the fellow came from his hometown. Still and all, it may be more likely that Joseph could have overcome the handicap of his servitude under a non-Egyptian ruling class. The position he came to hold was equivalent to that of vizier, the highest nonhereditary post in the land and the most powerful under the king. The people who made up the Hyksos consisted of many different tribes and ethnic groups. One of these groups, say some biblical scholars, could have been the Hebrews. Later, when an Egyptian royal family expelled the Hyksos, the men and groups which had been favored by the invaders would have been in disrepute, and so new kings might indeed be called "kings who knew not Joseph." So, the advocates of this theory claim, the servitude of the Hebrews began.

It all makes perfect sense, but so do the plots of good historical novels.

At first the Hyksos occupation was limited to the Delta region, at whose eastern end the Asiatics had entered Egypt. The Thirteenth

Dynasty continued to rule most of Egypt, except for an area near Xois, whose princes belong to Manetho's Fourteenth Dynasty. Then, about 1675 B.C., a new impetus, perhaps in the form of a more energetic Asiatic prince, prompted further Hyksos expansion, which ended in the conquest of a larger part of Egypt. Manetho called the second period the Fifteenth Dynasty, and its rulers he termed the "Great Hyksos." He lists six of them, and they ruled for over a century. Each is given the title "Ruler of Foreign Countries" in one of the Egyptian king lists, which makes the etymology of Manetho's "Hyksos" certain. Their power extended at least through Middle Egypt. A Sixteenth Dynasty, centered in Thebes, was probably contemporaneous with the Fifteenth; the Seventeenth Theban Dynasty also overlapped with the end of the Fifteenth.

The next to last Hyksos king was named Apopi (Apophis). During his reign a well-known pattern repeated itself. There must have been a peculiar quality in the air of the southland, centering around the city of Thebes, which rendered the men of the south disinclined to share power. As at the end of the First Time of Troubles, the standard of rebellion was raised in Thebes.

> Now it happened that King Sekenenre was ruler of the southern city [Thebes]. The chieftain Apophis was in Avaris, and the whole land was tributary to him. Now a messenger of King Apophis reached the prince of the southern city, saying: "King Apophis sends to you, saying: 'The hippopotamus pool which is in Thebes must be done away with. For they permit me no sleep by day or by night; and the noise of them is in my ears!'" Then the prince of the southern city was struck dumb, for he did not know how to answer the messenger of King Apophis.

The end of this particular text is missing, but the intent of the preposterous message is obvious. Apophis, three hundred miles from Thebes and the bellowing hippopotami, was trying to pick a fight. He succeeded— or someone succeeded, for it is quite possible that the ambitious princes of Thebes actually began hostilities.

The Seventeenth Dynasty began with a king named Rahotep. He was followed by three Intefs, who are given the numbers VI, VII, and VIII, since they were preceded by other Intefs who didn't rate the kingly title. If you find this confusing, just wait. The next to last king of this dynasty was Senakhtenre or Sekenenre, also known as Taa (the Brave). Or, according to some scholars, he-they were two people, Sekenenre II being the son of Senakhtenre, aka Sekenenre I. I refuse to take a stand on this matter. Let us get back to the interesting part.

Our Sekenenre died a violent death; his mummy is a ghastly sight, with several gaping holes still visible in the skull, and the face contorted in a frightful grimace of pain. The wounds were inflicted in battle, by an ax or a club. The first, on the jaw, would have been sufficient to send the warrior-king reeling to the ground; his adversary finished him off with at least four crashing blows that split his skull wide open. The king's death threw his men into confusion and probably lost that particular battle for Thebes; for several days the royal corpse lay untended where it had fallen. At last it was recovered and given a proper, if hasty, burial. The dead and withered face still seems to hold the emotions that were the last to animate the dying brain—fury and pain and the knowledge of defeat.

Not all Egyptologists agree on this version of the tragedy—and tragedy it was, for Sekenenre the king, if not for Thebes. Certainly the king died violently, they say, but these were troubled times; perhaps Sekenenre fell to the assassin rather than in battle. But this theory is fairly unconvincing. The ferocity of the wounds, the nature of the weapons, the evidence of the beginning of decomposition in the body tissues—all this, added to the folktale about the hippopotami, suggests that Sekenenre fell on the field of battle with the ax of a Hyksos warrior in his skull, after he had decided to answer the insulting demand of Apophis with war instead of words. Folktales may contain a true fact buried among yards of embroidery, and popular memory would long preserve the name of the first prince of Thebes to take up arms against the barbarians.

LIBERATION

With the last ruler of the Seventeenth Dynasty we reach the point the Egyptians did not mind talking about, and so we have a historical text. King Kamose, who may or may not have been the son of Sekenenre, took up the battle standard the latter's dead hand had dropped. Two great stelae gave Kamose's account of the war. One of the texts survived in a hieratic copy, which broke off right in the middle of a battle; it was believed by some to be a fictitious literary exercise until fragments of the original stela were found. Twenty years later, excavations at Karnak turned up a second stela that reported Kamose's successful campaigns and described his triumphant return to Thebes. The discovery caused quite a stir, for this kind of luck does not occur very often in archaeology.

The text begins with the king meeting with his council and holding forth with great passion upon the ignominy of his position:

> *What use is this strength of mine, when one prince is in Avaris and another in Cush, so that I sit here associated with an Asiatic and a Nubian, each in possession of his slice of this Egypt and I cannot pass by him as far as Memphis!*

In texts like these the council members are depicted as timid souls so that their caution may cause the king's impetuous bravery to shine more strongly. Kamose's council tried to soothe the king by pointing out that their part of the country was peaceful and prosperous. Why start trouble?

Naturally this excellent advice falls on deaf ears, and Kamose goes forth to battle. When the first text breaks off, the war is going well; Kamose's advance has been unopposed. Something is missing between the end of one stela and the beginning of the second, for when the sequel starts, Kamose is already approaching the enemy capital, the heavily fortified city of Avaris in the Delta. The Hyksos king had prudently shut himself up in the fortress, and none of Kamose's taunts and insults could induce him to come out and fight. He was the same Apophis who had sent Sekenenre the Brave that outrageous message about the hippopotami, and he may have suspected that Kamose's antagonism had a personal as well as a patriotic cause. Kamose devastated the fields and villages around the capital and got so close to the enemy palace that he was able to see the women of the harem looking down from the roof at him and his army. He sent more threatening messages to Apophis via these ladies, but nothing, it seemed, could shame the Hyksos king into taking action. Before long, Kamose found out why.

One day Egyptian soldiers captured a messenger heading south from the besieged city. The dispatch he carried was an urgent appeal for aid to the prince of Cush, or Nubia. The terms of the letter made it clear that the Asiatic and the Nubian were in cahoots; Apophis volunteered to keep Kamose busy until the Cushite army could arrive, whereupon the allies would crush Kamose and divide Egypt between them. The Hyksos king may thus be the first diplomat in history to use an ancient device—how ancient we did not know until this text was deciphered—for he says that Kamose is planning to attack Cush too: "Help me now, or you'll be next."

Kamose arranged that the ingenious appeal would never reach Cush, but it doesn't seem that he was too worried about the Cushite kingdom, perhaps because he had made sure his southern boundary was safe before he took on the Hyksos. Still, he was not in sufficient strength to attack so formidable a fortress as Avaris; he went back to Thebes, where he was met by cheering crowds. He had won the battle, but it was not given to him to win the war. We do not know what cut the courageous prince of Thebes off in his prime; a Hyksos weapon, in some later and unrecorded battle, or one of the diseases to which the ancients were prey? We can be pretty sure that if Kamose had lived he would have taken another crack at Avaris. It was left to his successor, possibly his younger brother, Ahmose, to complete the work he had begun, though a period of at least ten years ensued before Ahmose led his armies northward. He may have been a mere child when Kamose died, his mother serving as regent until he reached his majority.

The later campaigns are recorded by two soldiers who fought under King Ahmose in the concluding years of the War of Liberation. These men were not historians or scribes; in evaluating their stories we must allow for the normal amount of exaggeration in the case of a man who is recounting his exploits for the admiration of posterity and the consideration of the immortal gods. (Like the Greeks, the Egyptians could consider their deities omniscient in theory but quite capable, in practice, of being befooled by a clever man.) Even so, we have the feeling that our two soldiers did not boast extravagantly. There is an air of verisimilitude about their naive claims that is conspicuously lacking in some of the later accounts of military prowess; and while a man might swindle the gods and lie to his descendants it would not be easy to pull the wool over the eyes of a warrior-king like Ahmose. He rewarded the two soldiers liberally for valor, and under succeeding kings they rose to high military rank.

Just to keep the record straight, let us deal with the confusion of names. Both the soldiers were named after the king—Ahmose—and both came from the same town, El Kab. For the sake of clarity we call one of them Ahmose, son of Ebana, and the other Ahmose Pen-Nekhbet. Ahmose son of Ebana was a sailor, later rising to a rank equivalent to that of admiral; the other Ahmose served in the infantry and became a general. Both made a career of the service and saw fighting under the successors of Ahmose the king. Ahmose Pen-Nekhbet—General Ahmose—must have been the younger of the two, for his service under King Ahmose was limited to a campaign in a single Palestinian town. But the other Ahmose was with his king through the whole campaign, and it is from his tomb inscriptions that we learn of King Ahmose's final success in clearing the land of the Hyksos.

Ahmose the Admiral was a marine rather than a sailor; he speaks of fighting on land and in the water. In his first fight he was so young that he had not yet taken a wife. His father had served under Sekenenre, and it is odd that there is no mention of Kamose, who certainly used the royal marines. Possibly Ahmose the future admiral was too young to go to war immediately after his father died. He soon proved himself; he married and was transferred to the northern fleet, the post of danger—for the king was about to carry out Kamose's unfinished plan and lay siege to the yet unconquered Hyksos capital. Several battles were required to take the city; in one of them Ahmose the Admiral won himself a hand—an unattractive old Egyptian custom, which is meant to be taken literally; the hand was removed from the body of the dead foe. In later battle reliefs we see great heaps of amputated hands being piled up before the stately figure of pharaoh, and presumably they were used as a tally of the dead as well as a proof of personal valor.

Avaris finally fell; instead of hands, Ahmose the Admiral took a few live bodies, which he was allowed to keep as slaves. Avaris was the last Hyksos stronghold in Egypt, but King Ahmose was not content with driving them out of the country. He wanted to break their power permanently and ensure that they could never return to shame Egypt again. He chased the fleeing Hyksos host to Sharuhen in Palestine, and there fought another great battle, after a siege which, according to Admiral Ahmose, lasted for six long years.

The battle of Sharuhen ended the peril from the north, and excavations at Tell el Dab'a indicated that Ahmose leveled the Hyksos structures before rebuilding the city.

There was still danger from the south—from the Cushite kingdom, which had been allied with the Hyksos. It may be that Kamose had begun the reconquest of Cush, which had been under Egyptian control during the Middle Kingdom; Ahmose finished the job, at least as far as the second cataract. Ahmose the Admiral accompanied his king and "made a great slaughter" among the Nubians. He was well served in those days, for he had taken a total of ten slaves.

The enemies of the south were not crushed in one campaign. Again and again they rose in rebellion. The leader of the last revolt under King

Ahmose is specifically named; he was called Teti-en, which we might translate, if we are feeling romantic, as Teti the Handsome. He must have been a particularly annoying opponent, for the Egyptians ordinarily designated their enemies only by opprobrious epithets—That Fallen One, or That Enemy. The magical import is clear; the name was a part of a man's identity, and to deny him his name was to destroy him in part. Perhaps Admiral Ahmose had a sneaking admiration for "that fallen one, Teti-en," who was eventually slain by the king. We can spare him a little sympathy too; he was a rebel only because he failed. If he had succeeded, he would have become a liberator, like King Ahmose and General George Washington.

The Hyksos were gone—but not forgotten. They left a mark on the mind of Egypt that would never wholly disappear, and a seed in the body politic that would bear strange fruit in future years. Whether she liked it or not, Egypt was now a military power. Not as yet had the army become the sharp, professional tool it would become a few generations later; but it had gained a lot of practice and several new weapons. The horse may have been known before the Hyksos, but records from that period are the first mention of its use in war; and what an appalling weapon the chariot must have been, with its pounding, snorting steeds, thundering down on a group of unarmored foot soldiers! Each chariot held two men, the warrior and the driver, who also shielded his companion with the long heavy body shield. The compound bow, perhaps another Hyksos contribution, was considerably more powerful than the old simple bow, which the Egyptians had always used.

The Hyksos added a more important and less tangible factor to Egyptian life. "The wretched Asiatic" was no longer a figure of contemptuous fun. No more could the Egyptian feel secure in his green "island," isolated by sea and sand. The walls had been breached, and never again would Egypt feel the complete superiority she had enjoyed under the Old and Middle Kingdoms.

At least, this is how some scholars interpret the situation. Psychoanalysis of a whole nation is a tricky business, especially when all the members of that nation have been dust for millennia. And it is very hard to find visible signs of a persecution complex during the brilliant centuries that are to follow. Materially the height of Egyptian culture is yet to come. Spiritually and intellectually—that is another question, and a rather complex one.

Ahmose is considered the founder of the Eighteenth Dynasty, which begins the New Kingdom (formerly called the Empire) period. He was laid to rest among his ancestors in the Seventeenth Dynasty cemetery at Thebes, of which very little remains. Almost nothing of Ahmose has survived except his mummy, which was found in a great secret cache of royal mummies in the late nineteenth century A.D. It is now in the Luxor Museum.

One of the striking things about the new Theban family of kings is the unusual importance of their women. Ahmose was especially devoted to his womenfolk; not only did he honor his wife and his mother, but he took time out of his many wars to think nostalgically about his grandmother. A stela from Abydos shows Ahmose and his queen sitting in conversation in the great audience chamber; they are speaking of ways in which they may honor the dead. "I have remembered the mother of my mother and the mother of my father," says the king reflectively, "the great king's wife and king's mother, Tetisheri." Although she already has a tomb and a tomb chapel, Ahmose decides to build her a bigger and better one, "because he so greatly loved her, beyond everything."

There is a little statue of her in the British Museum, which shows a slender body and a delicate, wistful face framed by the queen's vulture crown. Unfortunately, it seems to be a fake.

Here's an example of revisionism, if you like, and I must admit it cut me to the quick. I love that little statue. The evidence is incontrovertible, however, not so much on stylistic grounds as on the brutal fact that chemical analysis of some of the paint proved it is not ancient. I still cling to the hope that the statue we have is a copy of a lost original. At one time there was a base almost identical to the base of Tetisheri's statue in the French Institute in Cairo. It has vanished, who knows where, so it can't be inspected, but there is a possibility—nothing stronger—that the French base belonged to the original statue of Tetisheri, which was copied by a particularly talented forger.

As should be painfully apparent to the reader, the genealogies of the period are still being debated. Tetisheri's royal husband may have been the first Taa, aka Senakhtenre, if there were two of them. If there was only one . . . Never mind. Tetisheri survived him, whoever he was; she lived to see her daughter Ahhotep marry her full brother, Sekenenre Taa. Her granddaughter, Ahmose-Nefertari, also married her brother, Ahmose. (The period certainly has a plethora of Ahmoses; I have mentioned only a few of them.) Ahmose's queen was a great lady; in later times she and her son were worshipped as patrons of the workmen's village of Deir el Medina.

Tetisheri was the ancestress of this line of queens. Several of them were found in the cache of royal mummies discovered in the nineteenth century, and Tetisheri may have been one of those that are not identified. It's hard to tell what a mummy may have looked like in life, but the remains of the royal women of this period have one outstanding characteristic—a pronounced overbite. It was probably not for beauty or charm that they were remembered so long and honored so highly. Was it for their importance in the inheritance of the throne? The notion of inheritance through the female isn't accepted nowadays. Perhaps the quality that distinguished the queens and princesses of the early Eighteenth Dynasty was that elusive thing called personality; in the next chapter we will see what happened when Tetisheri's great-great-granddaughter decided to exert her share of the family character.

These women were the wives of kings and of soldiers; the fragile Tetisheri, while still a young woman, may have seen the mutilated body of her son borne home from the battlefield, and watched from a window of the palace as her grandson(s) marched out to war in their turn. Maybe she egged them on, as did the equally fragile and bloody-minded ladies of the Confederacy. According to a stela found at Karnak, the queen Ahhotep, wife of Sekenenre the Brave, upon one occasion had to rally the troops and put an end to rebellion. This is one of the most tantalizing references in Egyptian history; and we know nothing more about it. Historical novelists, take note.

Ahmose's son bore a name which the Eighteenth Dynasty was to make famous—Amenhotep. Like the similar dynastic name of the Middle Kingdom, Amenemhat, it honored the patron god of Thebes. But unlike the Twelfth Dynasty kings, the new rulers did not move their capital to the north. From this time dates the rise of Thebes, whose monuments still awe the visitor.

Ahmose left his son a united Egypt, free for the first time in centuries of foreign interlopers. He also left to him, and to us, his two soldier-namesakes from El Kab. We are grateful for the legacy, since the tomb inscriptions of these men have given us much useful information. General Ahmose and Admiral Ahmose served, in all, six kings of Egypt. Both fought in Nubia under Amenhotep I, in the campaign that regained all the territory formerly held by the Twelfth Dynasty, and perhaps more. "I fought incredibly," says the admiral modestly. He also rushed the king back to Egypt upon the news of a threatened invasion by the Libyans, a distance of two hundred miles in two days. We can say little more about Amenhotep I; he fought in Nubia, he probably fought in Asia, he built monuments. Then he died.

His successor is a more interesting character, if for no other reason than because he was the father of one of the most fabulous personalities who ever sat upon the throne of Egypt. He was a man of no mean accomplishments in his own right—Thutmose, the first to bear the second famous name of the Eighteenth Dynasty. Apparently he was not related by blood to Amenhotep I. We don't know why he was selected to wear the Double Crown. One of his wives, Mutnefret, was a king's daughter, the other—named Ahmes—was not. At least she doesn't claim that title. So if Amenhotep I died childless, which seems to have been the case, whose daughter was Mutnefret? (This may give you some idea of why there are so many arguments about Egyptian royal genealogies.)

"From the Horns of the Earth to the Marshes of Asia"—such were the boundaries of the empire Thutmose I gained for Egypt. The Asian marshes are the swamps of the Euphrates. It is a grandiose claim, but we have abundant evidence for its accuracy. The tomb autobiographies of the two gentlemen from El Kab describe their valor in the Asiatic wars, and Thutmose I's stela on the banks of the Euphrates was found by his grandson when he came that way. The Horns of the Earth, then, must lie to the south. How far south we cannot be sure. The former boundary at the Second Cataract was passed, and the site of Kerma as well. An inscription of Thutmose I was found even farther south, near the Fifth Cataract. But there are no striking topographic features in this region that could be called horns, if this term means tall hills. Some scholars think Thutmose I got down as far as the site of Meroe, beyond the junction of the Nile with its first tributary, the Atbara. Admiral Ahmose commanded the flotilla that sailed upstream to—wherever it was in Nubia—and acted with his usual amazing bravery. The king's military exploits in the south were substantial enough to warrant the creation of a great new bureaucratic office, comparable in importance to the vizierate. The prince, or king's son, of Cush was thereafter the right hand of the king in the region south of Elephantine.

It was a goodly territory, from the far cataracts of the Nile to the Euphrates. The tribute began to pour into Thebes. Thutmose used it to beautify the city and to honor the gods, and also to provide for his good name in the Hereafter. His royal architect, Ineni, is one of the officials who left rich tombs filled with inscriptions boasting of their own prestige. Ineni tells of his work in the great Amon temple at Karnak, and in the desolate valley where Thutmose had ordered his tomb to be built.

The pyramids were impressive and enduring, but it had become evident that they had certain drawbacks as true Houses of Eternity. Thutmose I decided to sacrifice publicity for safety. His tomb was dug out of the rock in a remote valley, far from the river, richly equipped within, but completely hidden from sight. "I supervised the excavation of His Majesty's tomb," says Ineni. "I was alone, no one seeing, no one hearing."

Obviously the aristocratic official did not wield pick and shovel him-

self, but he was responsible for all the arrangements. He chose a spot some
seven miles from the river, on the West Bank; it is now known as the Valley
of the Kings. How secret the operation really was is open to doubt. There
is no indication that the king had all his workmen executed when the tomb
was finished, as some bloodthirsty writers have suggested. Skilled artisans
were too valuable to be tossed away. The fact that all the royal tombs in the
valley—with one famous exception—were completely stripped of their
valuables in antiquity is a good indication that some of the workmen survived. Once the exact location of a tomb was known, it was as good as
robbed; the hidden passages and massive barriers bothered the thieves no
more than did the similar devices in the pyramids—and small wonder,
when we remember the magnitude of their eventual reward.

The king was laid to rest in the tomb which he had built with such
high hopes of secrecy. Needless to say, there is some debate as to which
one it was. The tombs in the Valley of the Kings are numbered, not in the
order of their construction, but following an arbitrary modern system.
KV38 was once believed to have been Thutmose I's original burial place.
However, some scholars claim it was a reburial, since its plan seems to be
later in date than that of Thutmose I's grandson. To be continued in the
next chapter.

At the end of his life, Thutmose I could view his accomplishments
with pride, and the future with few misgivings. His principal wives had
borne him several children, one of whom was a daughter named Hatshepsut. By marrying her to her half-brother, Thutmose II, the old king had
settled the question of the succession and given Egypt a new Horus to
take his place on the throne. The empire was stable; the Two Lands were
at peace, prosperous, healthy. If any man could give up his last breath
with the consciousness of leaving all his affairs in order, Thutmose I was
that man. He had no way of knowing that the next few years would see
a strange phenomenon, unparalleled in all the fifteen centuries of history
that had gone before.

Five

THE WOMAN
WHO WAS KING

Cartouche of Hatshepsut

HATSHEPSUT THE QUEEN

Hatshepsut and Cleopatra; Zenobia; Catherine of Russia; Elizabeth the Great.

History records the names of many famous women and many famous queens, but the women in the brief list above share one attribute in addition to their royalty and their fame. Born into one sex, they carried out the traditional duties of the other. Further—all of them succeeded, at least temporarily, in the difficult and conventionally masculine task of directing the affairs of a great nation.

Hatshepsut of Egypt heads the list because (except for the short-reigned and little known Sobekneferu of the Twelfth Dynasty) she is the earliest of that impressive group. She merits the highest place for another reason. In her assumption of the throne she cast off the trailing skirts of a woman and put on the kilt and crown of a king, and she carried it off for twenty years.

She was beautiful, of course; all great queens are beautiful. The statues we have of her do not give much of a clue to her actual appearance. One of them shows a small, rather gentle face, with a pointed chin and a broad forehead; but the sculptured body of a queen of Egypt was always as slim and graceful as that of a goddess, just as a king's body had to be the ideal of masculine beauty. Since she was an Egyptian, we can assume that Hatshepsut was slim and fine-boned, with small hands and feet; she must have been dark, with black hair and the black eyes of most Egyptian women. If, in middle age, she acquired a double chin and the harsh-lined face of royal responsibility, we need not take official cognizance of such a disillusioning idea.

From earliest childhood she had been taught the duties of the high position she would one day fill. She was the daughter of a king of Egypt and his chief royal wife; inevitably as sunrise, she would be queen of Egypt in her turn. The king? He would be her husband—her half-brother, named Thutmose after his father and hers. Thutmose II's mother was a noble lady, one of the official wives of the king, but not the chief wife, who had borne Hatshepsut.

There is an impression among archaeologists that Thutmose II was not the man his father had been. In part the idea stems from the description of his mummy as that of a "diseased" man who died young; in part from the contrast of his two minor campaigns with the warlike prowess of his father; and perhaps in part from the mere fact that he was married to Hatshepsut, whose personality overshadowed stronger men than her young husband.

The picture may be unfair to Thutmose II. The mummy in question may not be his, and it may not be diseased. Opinions as to the length of his reign differ, and if he only occupied the throne for a few years he would not have had time to do much. Still, the impressive figure of his wife towers above him and all he did.

Thutmose II died. Whatever his potentialities, this is just about the most important statement of fact we can make about him. He left, with regard to the problem of the succession, a domestic situation similar to the one which had prevailed after his father's death. His chief wife, Hatshepsut, had borne no sons, only a daughter, Nefrure. By a woman of lowly birth, a palace concubine named Isis, Thutmose II had sired one son. The situation and its solution were not unusual. The child, Thutmose III, would, in due course, expect to marry his little half-sister, Nefrure. Upon his father's demise, the toddler became the Horus, Lord of the Two Lands, Beloved of the Two Ladies, Menkheperre, Thutmose III.

They were heavy titles for a small boy, and the weight of the Red and White Crowns was a burden no infant could assume. Again, the situation had precedent, but in this case the mother of the king was no fit person to assume the regency. A commoner to administer the affairs of the Two Lands? That was against tradition, particularly when Egypt had so fitting a regent available in the person of the Great Royal Wife Hatshepsut, Wife of the God, Daughter of the former King and his Great Wife.

So far, the affair had been conducted in a perfectly respectable and dignified fashion, consistent with tradition and—as the Egyptians might have said—"in keeping with *maat*," the universal order of justice and correctness. Hatshepsut was now dowager queen and regent of Egypt, as we would say; the Egyptians had no equivalent titles, and Hatshepsut simply retained the ones she had used when her husband was living.

Then, a few years after the little king had climbed the high stairs to the throne, the universal order received a shock that rocked it to its foundations.

Came forth the king of the gods, Amon-Re, from his temple, saying: "Welcome, my sweet daughter, my favorite, the King of Upper and Lower

Egypt, Maatkare Hatshepsut. Thou art the king, taking possession of the Two Lands."

THE KING OF UPPER AND LOWER EGYPT

The Egyptians were tolerant people, and they were seldom troubled by inconsistencies. But here was an astounding event, so unusual that the very structure of the language rebelled against it. The word we translate from the hieroglyphs as *queen* literally means "king's wife." There are a number of words that refer to the king; the most common was originally the title of the king of Upper Egypt only, but when it appears alone it is translated as *king*. The king was also called "sovereign" or "His Majesty." His titles included "King of Upper and Lower Egypt" and "Lord of the Two Lands." During the first years of the Eighteenth Dynasty we find the famous word *pharaoh* as a title of the king. (It comes from two Egyptian words meaning "great house," and originally referred to the palace.)

The point is that all these titles were masculine. Egyptian has two genders, the feminine ending being a *t*; and there were no words for a reigning monarch that were feminine in gender. The bewildered scribes were forced to some strange expedients in order to deal with Her Majesty, King

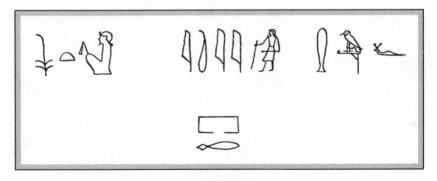

Titles of the Egyptian king
Above, left to right: king; sovereign; his majesty
Below: pharaoh

Hatshepsut. They usually employed the feminine pronoun, but now and then, in the middle of one of the long, flattering texts that they could have written in their sleep, they would forget, and a *he* or *his* might creep in. Sometimes they added the feminine ending to the word for *lord* or *majesty*. But they still had to face such grotesque descriptions as "the (female) Horus."

Hatshepsut's statues and reliefs show her in both roles: as a woman, wearing female dress and the queen's crown, and as a king, in a man's kilt (and body!) wearing the king's crown and the artificial beard. The dichotomy carries over into other spheres: two tombs, one in a remote valley where other queens' tombs were located, and the other in the Valley of the Kings; two sarcophagi, one for a queen and one for a king.

Can her seizure of the kingship be regarded as an usurpation? Strictly speaking, no. Thutmose III was not deposed. He kept his titles and appears on various monuments with his coruler; but when the two are shown together there is no question as to which is number one, and the fact that she is there at all, in a king's crown and body, could be seen as usurpation of a sort.

Whatever the strength of her will and personality, Hatshepsut must have had the support of powerful forces in the state to hang on to power as long as she did. We have not yet tried to explain how she succeeded in this fantastic coup, which seized the throne of Horus for a woman; and in fact it is very hard to understand how she did succeed. She must have had that indefinable quality that is called "charisma"; it blazes at us now over a gulf of four thousand years, and we can imagine what the impact must have been firsthand. But personality alone is not enough to explain a phenomenon such as Hatshepsut. She must have had the help of powerful supporters.

The most influential of Hatshepsut's adherents was a man named Hapuseneb, who was, early in her reign, both vizier and High Priest of Amon. One is tempted to see in this man the power behind the throne, the Cardinal Richelieu of the reign. It is hard to vizualize Hatshepsut in the role of Louis XIII; her husband, Thutmose II, might have fit the part better. But certainly a woman in her position needed all the help she could get, and Hapuseneb represented a lot of help. An interesting, and as yet unexplained, point is that a number of Thutmose I's favored officials transferred their allegiance to Hatshepsut when she assumed joint reign with her nephew—Ineni the architect and Ahmose Pen-Nekhbet, the old soldier from El Kab, among others. Another of her officials had the unusual name "Nehsi," which means "the Nubian."

The most intriguing of her supporters was a man named Senenmut (formerly read Senmut). He was a parvenu, an upstart, a nobody; he was not even particularly good-looking. His long aquiline nose and flexible, rather cynical mouth were distinctive rather than handsome. Who and what he was originally we do not know; he appears among the servants of the queen even before she proclaimed herself king—possibly before her husband, Thutmose II, died. From that time on, Senenmut's meteoric rise

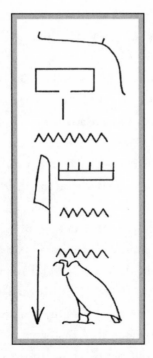

Senenmut's name (below) and
title, steward of Amon

to power parallels that of Hatshepsut. He held over twenty different titles, and he was singled out by the queen as was no other official.

Hatshepsut bolstered her position with propaganda as well as with
picked allies. The propaganda was based on two major pieces of evidence,
both of which are totally fictitious. One of them claimed that she had
been chosen by her father as his successor and raised to the throne by his
own hand. The other proposed the magnificent notion that she was the
physical daughter of Amon-Re, the god.

There was nothing new about this idea; other kings were called "son
of Amon" and "son of Re," and the queenly title "God's Wife," which is
first held by the mother of King Ahmose, certainly applies to the god
Amon, the patron of the Seventeenth and Eighteenth Theban Dynasties.
Hatshepsut's reliefs depict in some detail the process by which she became the daughter of the god. They are the earliest of this type of scene
to survive, although the fiction must have been current earlier.

On the walls of the temple of Deir el Bahri we see the god on his way
to visit the queen and God's Wife Ahmose, Hatshepsut's mother. "He
[Amon] made his form like the majesty of this husband, the king
Aakheperure [Thutmose I]. He found her [Queen Ahmose] as she slept, in
the beauty of the palace. She awoke at the fragrance of the god, which she
smelled in the presence of His Majesty. He went to her immediately."

At this point Breasted, who first translated these inscriptions, primly
breaks into Latin, but the sense is clear without any translation at all.
Afterward, Amon made a little speech to the delighted queen: "Hatshepsut shall be the name of this my daughter, whom I have placed in your
body. She shall exercise the excellent kingship in this whole land."

Successive scenes show the matters, physical and religious, that have
to do with the birth of the divine child. Khnum, the creator of men, is
instructed by Amon to fashion the baby and its ka, or double, on his
divine potter's wheel. Both the little figures are unquestionably male—
another of the unconscious slips of the confused artist, who probably
copied the whole series from more ancient reliefs, now destroyed. Then
the queen is shown holding the newborn infant and attended by the

traditional goddesses of birth and midwifery. There are other scenes, most of them badly broken.

Except for the little error of the male babies, this sequence makes an impressive story. How impressed anyone actually was is open to question. Whatever the combination of propaganda and power, Hatshepsut succeeded not only in gaining the throne but in holding it for more than twenty years. Under her reign the land prospered. She built magnificently all over Egypt and Nubia, particularly at the Temple of Amon at Karnak, where one of her huge obelisks, the largest to be quarried in Egypt up to that time, still towers into the sky. These tall, four-sided spires were usually erected in pairs near the gateway, or pylon, of a temple. The obelisk form suggests majesty and ambition, and the ancient Egyptians were not the only ones to appreciate these qualities. The Washington Monument is an obelisk, and many of the biggest Egyptian obelisks were carried off by foreign conquerors to augment the grandeur of their native capitals, from London to Constantinople. The second obelisk of this pair of Hatshepsut's collapsed in antiquity. When they were first erected, both monuments were ornamented with fine gold. The inscriptions on the sides and base of the obelisk state that the queen measured out the precious metal by the bushel, like sacks of grain.

From this, and from other evidences, we can be fairly sure that the female king's acccession did not interrupt the flow of wealth into Egypt. There are some references to military campaigns, in Nubia and Syria, but I am inclined to take them with a grain of salt. The scenes on her surviving monuments do not show her leading the charge or bashing captives on the head. They feature religious activities and, in one case, an economic triumph—a trading mission to the distant, almost fabled, land of Punt.

No one knows exactly where Punt lay; the latest guesses put it somewhere on the Somali coast. The products of this country included goods highly coveted by the luxury-loving Egyptians—apes and ivory, gold and spices—and dwarfs, like the one Harkhuf brought to his king during the Old Kingdom.

The scenes showing Hatshepsut's expedition to Punt, which was organized and led by Nehsi the Nubian, occupy more of the wall space at the Deir el Bahri temple. The great ships are shown setting out, with sailors hanging like monkeys from the rigging. When they finally reached Punt they were greeted by the astounded natives, including the wife of the chief—an enormously fat woman accompanied by a very small donkey, presumably her means of transportation. (The Egyptians undoubtedly thought this was very funny; even in so solemn a venture as the Punt expedition, they could not resist poking fun at inferiors.) After a successful trading mission the ships returned, bringing not only gold and ivory, but also a collection of myrrh trees, zealously tended on the long journey, to adorn the terraces of the temple of Amon and the queen.

All this energy—the expedition, the obelisks, and other undertakings—were carried out to the glory of Amon. "Her Majesty did this because she loved her father Amon so much, more than all other gods. . . . I have done this from a loving heart for my father Amon." It looks as if Hatshepsut were trying to propitiate someone—the god or the priests or both.

We have mentioned the great obstacle of her sex, and the sullen weight of tradition, which Hatshepsut had to overcome in her quest for power. But we have not yet discussed another handicap, which makes her success truly inexplicable. All the time Hatshepsut was wielding the scepter so energetically, there was another king of Egypt in the background. He was to be one of the greatest and most forceful kings who ever ruled Egypt, a conqueror who, in breadth of vision and martial prowess, may legitimately be compared with the great Alexander. To be sure, Thutmose III was only a child when Hatshepsut squeezed herself onto his throne. But she ruled for over twenty years; long before the end, the boy would have become a man and begun to show the stubbornness and intelligence that are so conspicuous in his character later on.

She didn't ignore him altogether. He appears with her in a number of scenes—behind her. To what tasks did Hatshepsut set the future warrior? She let him burn incense before Amon when her Punt expedition returned in triumph.

This image would make a good subject for historical drama. The queen, brilliant in her gorgeous regalia and robe of sheer pleated linen; conspicuously near her, the no-less-gorgeous figure of that upstart Senenmut, loaded with the ornaments of gold and precious stones with which the queen's bounty had provided him; above all, the towering statue of the god, wreathed in blue, sweet-smelling smoke. And behind them, obscure and unnoticed, the slender figure of the boy-king—he must have been in his early teens by then—smoldering with suppressed fury and aquiver with thwarted ambition, his sullen black eyes glowering at the intricate shape of the Red and White Crowns upon the head of his aunt—those crowns which should have been his alone.

Hatshepsut and her allies were at the height of their power, unchallenged. Trade flourished, great building works gave employment to the people, there was no lack of food. The large professional armies of the later empire, who turned to looting and violence when foreign conquests failed, had yet to be formed. The great campaigns of Thutmose I lay years in the past. And if there were men who chafed at the boredom of peace, and yearned to continue the imperial designs of the queen's father, no doubt there were men—and women—who cherished the peaceful years and found happiness in the simple activities of family and crops. The life of the peasant was hard, but it was life; and almost any kind of existence was preferable to dying far from home and being buried at a distance from the gods and temples of Egypt.

Many of the common people, and all of the artisans and craftsmen, were busy with Hatshepsut's main interest, the construction and restoration of temples and monuments. She was, she claims, the first ruler to restore the damage which had been done by the Hyksos to many of the sanctuaries of the gods, and her own building works were numerous. In the thick of it all was Senenmut, who held the offices of overseer of works at Karnak and at Deir el Bahri. Ancient Egyptian had no word for *architect*; we cannot be certain that the overseer of works designed the monuments whose construction he supervised. He certainly approved the plans, and since no other candidate is known, we may as well give Senenmut credit for the marvel of Deir el Bahri: the most beautiful temple in Egypt, and one of the finest of all ancient buildings.

Deir el Bahri lies across the Nile from modern Luxor. In its bay is the temple that Hatshepsut built for her mortuary cult and for the glory of Amon and other gods. The external design is dramatically simple; in form and in mood it echoes the strong, severe shape of the cliffs that rise behind it. The temple consists of rows of pillared colonnades on three levels, which are reached by long sloping ramps. A wing at right angles to the lowest level has fluted circular columns, which irresistibly suggest Greece rather than Egypt. The first impression of this noble building is, somehow, non-Egyptian, although the basic inspiration for its design was drawn from the earlier Eleventh Dynasty temple of Mentuhotep II nearby. But Senenmut was not an imitator. His design is as superior to the older building as the Parthenon is superior to the graceless, stubby old temple at Corinth. The implied comparison with the Parthenon is not inappropriate, for both structures—the Parthenon and the temple of Deir el Bahri—have one major triumph in common: the observer is instantly struck with a sense of harmony in the proportions. No dimension could be altered without damaging the whole. The graceful colonnade of the Egyptian temple show that the Greeks were not the first to comprehend this particular architectural form.

The architect of Deir el Bahri also made full use of the terrain and of the peculiarly brilliant Egyptian climate. The overhanging cliffs do not diminish the handiwork of man but support and frame it, and the contrast of strong shadow and sharp sunlight is deliberately made a part of the design.

Though this temple, which was named Djeser-djeseru ("holiest of holy places") in Egyptian, was dedicated to Amon and other gods, its primary function was to serve the funerary cult of the king Hatshepsut. Her first tomb, when she was still queen, was high in the cliffs of the western desert. Howard Carter found it in 1916, or, to be more accurate, he followed a group of would-be robbers who had found the tomb first and were busy at work inside when Carter arrived. Since the only access was via a rope from the clifftop above, Carter had the fellows right where he wanted them. He threatened to cut the rope and leave them stranded unless they came out with their hands up. Being sensible men, they did. Anyhow, they had wasted their time; the tomb was empty except for a handsome but unwieldy sarcophagus.

Presumably work on this tomb stopped when Hatshepsut proclaimed herself king. Her second tomb is one of the most extraordinary in the Valley of the Kings. It may have been the one Ineni constructed for his master—opinions differ on this. If it was, Hatshepsut, who liked to emphasize her relationship to her father, decided to have herself buried with him and began enlarging it. The seven-hundred-foot-long corridor wriggles around, but its general direction is in a line toward the temple at Deir el Bahri. Perhaps the original intention had been to drive the corridors straight under the mountain ridge so that the burial chamber would lie directly below the temple. The poor quality of the rock and the sheer dimensions of the tomb may have frustrated this intent; working in those airless lightless depths must have taken a toll on the workers. Few modern excavators have had the gumption to follow in their footsteps. One was Howard Carter, who got, for his pains, only the two sarcophagi from the burial chamber. One was Hatshepsut's; the other, originally made for her, had been reinscribed for Thutmose I. He wasn't there, and neither was she.

It is believed by some that Thutmose was removed by his grandson from the contaminating presence of Hatshepsut and reinstalled in another tomb in the Valley of the Kings—number 38, which contains fragmentary objects inscribed with his name. Formerly scholars thought KV38 was Ineni's tomb, so to speak, the original sepulchre of Thutmose I. The revisionists base their theory on the fact that KV38 is simpler in plan than Thutmose III's tomb, so it must be earlier in date. Maybe they're right, although I am always skeptical of dating based on typological sequence. But if Thutmose I originally occupied KV38, then Hatshepsut moved him to KV20 and then Thutmose III put him back in KV38.

Anyhow, Hatshepsut's father wasn't in KV38 either. Tomb robbers had gotten to him, as they did to most of the other royals. One of the mummies from the royal cache was thought to be his, but of Hatshepsut the only certain trace is a mummified spleen, from the same cache. People are still looking for her, most recently in the tomb of her nurse, which contained two female mummies. One of them may be Hatshepsut's. Another potential candidate is an unidentified mummy found in the tomb of Amenhotep II, along with the bodies of other monarchs rescued from their desecrated sepulchres. The techniques of mummification suit the period, and the investigators described the body as that of an "elderly woman." (I take leave to resent the adjective; the lady was probably between thirty-five and forty-five when she died.) This same mummy has been identified as Queen Tiye, wife of Amenhotep III, and as Nefertiti.

Or it could be somebody else.

There was a tomb under the sanctuary of the temple of Djeser-djeseru. It was the tomb of the commoner, Senenmut, and his image still remains in the "holiest of holy places."

Deir el Bahri has changed a lot since I first visited it in the 1960s; some would say not for the better. A Polish expedition has carried out extensive restorations. Greatly as this has added to the preservation and appearance of the temple, the retaining wall at the back, designed to prevent rockfalls, cannot be said to be an architectural success. One critic has compared the effect to a modern parking garage.

Though the dedicated Poles have opened up areas that were not accessible all those years ago, one part of the temple is no longer open to visitors. I will never forget my sight of it. Supervision of the sites was laxer in those days, and as I strolled, musing, I must have mentioned the name of Senmut (as we used to call him). One of the unavoidable guides pounced, nodding eagerly and making imperative gestures. "Senmut! Senmut!" he exclaimed and led me back into the shadows of the inner rooms. The darkness thickened, and the floor was rough and hazardous. I stumbled over a loose stone and wondered what the devil I was doing alone in the dark with a strange gentleman. Then the gentleman, for indeed he was, stopped and lit a pitiful little stub of candle. There was an open doorway to the left, leading into a small windowless room. The doors that had once closed it in had long since vanished. I squatted (I could do it then) and saw, by flickering candlelight, the small carved figure of a man, in the space that would have been hidden by the opened door. He knelt in the graceful Egyptian position of worship, with hands uplifted; and above him was the name that he dared to intrude into a shrine reserved for divinity: SENENMUT, STEWARD OF AMON.

The small carving is rather rough, and the conventionalized profile probably bears no resemblance to its supposed model. It is impossible to explain why the sight of it should have left such an unforgettable impression. Outside the temple the brazen sun blistered down out of a hard, hot sky; but the corridor beside the little storeroom was black and breathless, just as it must have been on that vanished day when Senenmut the Overseer of Works supervised by lamplight the insurance of his survival among the gods. Was it done with the approval of the queen, or did he risk her divine anger in his anxiety for life everlasting in her company?

Senenmut's tomb under the temple has been described as another piece of matchless impudence; only members of the royal family could hope for such a favor. Some archaeologists have suggested that Hatshepsut found out about her favorite's presumption and dismissed him from favor (possibly from life), but it is fantastic to assume that he could carry out a project as large as this without Hatshepsut's knowledge; she was a woman of great energy and undoubtedly visited her mortuary temple often while it was abuilding. As for the images of Senenmut at Deir el Bahri—over sixty of them—they were signs of extraordinary privilege, granted by royal permission, according to a contemporary inscription. The tomb was disfigured later, but there is no way of knowing why or by whom. It was meant to have truly royal proportions; the corridors are over a hundred yards long as they stand.

The steward of Amon's gamble for eternity did not pay off. He never occupied his gorgeous tomb; we do not know where his bones were laid to rest, if they found rest at all. He had another tomb, more suited to his official rank, on the slopes of a hill not far from Deir el Bahri. Perhaps

Senenmut was buried here. His magnificent sarcophagus certainly was; it is strikingly similar to Hatshepsut's sarcophagus and was probably made at the same time. (Is there no limit to this man's ambition? asked the scandalized nobility.)

Senenmut may have been a "man on the make"—one of the most successful of all time—but he did not lack finer feelings. He caused his mother and father to be reburied near him so that they might share his good fortune in the West. In proximity to his tomb are several other burials that may be connected with him. He may have been a lover of music, for one of these burials is that of a minstrel, with the singer's harp laid in the coffin. His pets were buried too—a pet ape and a little mare, enclosed in coffins and provided with food and water to last them until they reached the West.

Was he the queen's lover? Serious historians might come back with another question: Who cares? The answer has no bearing on the important events of Hatshepsut's reign—foreign policy, trade, political developments. But history is not only sterile events, it is people, and we are, most of us, gossips at heart. So let's gossip.

I don't know the answer to my question, and neither does anybody else. In official documents Senenmut is never shown as having more intimate relations with the queen than any other courtier. That doesn't prove anything one way or the other, since the standardized formulae and conventional depictions of royalty would not allow for such deviations. His prominence, his high titles, and that interesting tomb at Deir el Bahri are the only evidences of unusual status.

Unofficial documents suggest that Senenmut's contemporaries were not above a little gossip. The most interesting is a graffito—a sketch—in a cave near Deir el Bahri, which may have been dashed off in an idle hour by one of the men working on the temple. It shows two people in an intimate position. One of them is unquestionably female, the other unmistakeably male. Sketches like this are not altogether uncommon; the depiction of explicit sexual relations was not allowed by the puritanical, formal art canon, but in their private lives Egyptians were no more prim and proper than anyone else. In this particular case, some scholars have suggested that the couple are meant to be Hatshepsut and her chief architect. The female figure wears (only) a headdress with long lappets that fall over her shoulders. The male figure appears to be wearing a close-fitting cap. Is the headdress the nemes of royalty? Is the cap the type worn by certain officials?

Even if the answer to both questions is yes, even if the graffito can be dated to Hatshepsut's reign, it proves only that people were smirking and gossiping about the queen and her overseer of works. In fact, we haven't the faintest idea how such a liaison would have been regarded. Maybe everybody knew and nobody cared. Egyptians kings were allowed all the wives and concubines they wanted. Egyptian queens probably were not encouraged to stray, for the simple reason that a king likes to be sure he is the father of his heir. But Hatshepsut was a reigning king.

To an aficionado of detective stories, no fictitious crime holds the fascination of the many unsolved mysteries with which history abounds. Did the little dauphin die in prison, or was the child who perished a substitute? Was Richard III really the murderer of his nephews in the Tower? Did Leicester push his wife down the staircase at Kenilworth, in the overweening hope of marrying Elizabeth the Queen? Whose gold hired the cutthroats who stabbed Cesare Borgia's brother and threw his body into the Tiber? To these delightfully ghoulish questions we might add another, with equally dark implications: How did Hatshepsut meet her end?

We have a lot of material about the other mysteries of history (at least it seems quite a bit to an archaeologist), enough for a strong presumption in most cases, if not a certainty. But an inquest on the death of Hatshepsut would be a brief affair. We know that she disappeared from the scene and that her nephew, Thutmose III, became sole king of Egypt. But the lack of information only whets our curiosity. Was it Hatshepsut's death that gave Thutmose sole power? Or, as some have recently suggested, did she retire, voluntarily or otherwise? If she did die, was it of natural causes? What part did Senenmut the Steward of Amon play in the last days and years of her reign?

There was no one to replace her. Her daughter, Nefrure, was her only child. What little we know about this princess provides more questions than answers. One of Senenmut's titles was that of tutor to the princess, and several statues show them in a close if conventional embrace. Some scholars believe she married young Thutmose III. If so, she did not last long. Did she die a natural death, and if so, when?

It's no wonder that historical novelists and some historians (including me) have interpreted this morass of nonevidence in dramatic terms. The new king was careful to ensure that Hatshepsut would die the second and final death, by obliterating her name and her carved image from every spot he could get at. One of the places that echoed to the blows of sledge-hammers smashing stone was the temple at Deir el Bahri. The Metropolitan Museum Expedition, working at that site, found the pieces of dozens of statues of Hatshepsut dumped into a quarry near the temple, and fragments of others were strewn over a wide area. Hatshepsut's titles and portraits were erased from the walls of the temple. The great obelisks at Karnak were not overthrown, but Thutmose III ordered them sheathed in masonry, which would cover up the female king's name and her proud inscriptions.

Hatshepsut's kingly sarcophagus was left intact, but Senenmut's, the mate to hers, was literally broken to bits. Over twelve hundred fragments of it were found, scattered broadside over the ground near his tomb, and these pieces represented only about half of the original sarcophagus. Of the mummy that lay within it, there is no trace. Thutmose even sent his agents after the little images behind the doors of Djeser-djeseru. Luckily for us, the human tools erred. They had no strong feelings one way or the other about Senenmut, and in the heat of the day it was pleasant to snatch a nap in a secluded spot where the overseer could not see. Many of the hidden figures escaped their notice, and it is these that we would see today if we could venture into the recesses of the great temple.

We have been talking all this time about people, and quite rightly, because Hatshepsut and her successor are figures that cannot be ignored.

But there were other elements involved in the struggle for power; they certainly affected Hatshepsut's seizure of the throne, and they were, perhaps, connected with her downfall. Hatshepsut's devotion to Amon, and the position of her ally Hapuseneb as high priest of Amon, suggest that this mighty spiritual power supported her. But Thutmose III also honored Amon; and how he honored Amon! After he assumed full power, he caused to be circulated a curious and suggestive story.

As a youth, or "nestling," he had served in the temple of Amon as a minor priest. One day came the occasion of a great festival of the god, in which the shrine was carried in procession through the north colonnaded hall of the Karnak temple. The reigning king (who is not named) made the offering, while the young priest stood humbly in his place, unnoticed. Then, to the amazement of all beholders, the shrine that held the god began to wander about, as if in search of something. It made an unexpected circuit of the hall and finally stopped before the gaping young priest. When that worthy prostrated himself, the god raised him up and led him to the "Station of the King." "Thereafter the god opened for me [Thutmose speaking] the doors of heaven, and I flew to heaven as a divine hawk that I might see his mysterious form."

And so on. The god Re himself crowned Thutmose, his titulary was fixed, and he was seated at the right hand of Re.

The last part of this tale, one need hardly say, is a fine example of poetical fiction-making. But the first part is significant—and perhaps no less fictitious. It is hard to believe that such an event really happened at the time Thutmose says (or implies) that it did. He can hardly have been more than a toddler when his father died, too young to have even a minor temple position; and if the unnamed "king" of the inscription was Hatshepsut in her prime, I, for one, would not like to have been one of the priests who guided the movements of the god under her critical eye. All ruling kings blandly claimed the favor of the god, and Hatshepsut was assiduous in honoring Amon—with good reason, since according to her version that divine spirit had fathered her. What we see in these tales is an attempt to use the symbol of the god as a polite substitute for the political support of the priesthoods. There are only two possible explanations for Thutmose's story. Either it is pure fiction, like Hatshepsut's divine birth, or the event took place at a later date and may have been the signal for a coup d'état. This implies a political shift, or split, in the priesthood itself.

Hapuseneb, the politician-priest who had supported Hatshepsut's claim, was not the man who led the transfer of allegiance to the rising sun of Thutmose. Hapuseneb is significantly absent after Thutmose assumes power; in fact, his memory was bitterly persecuted. If Amon decided to switch to Thutmose, the oracle who voiced the god's decision was another man.

But why switch at all? The Egyptians never heard of the adage about the horses and the middle of the stream, but no people were ever more satisfied with the status quo. Was the queen getting old? Then Thutmose would succeed to the throne in any case (in theory he already held it, and had for more than twenty years). Why rush things in an undignified and violent manner? A plausible answer is that the cannier of the priests knew quite well that nobody who had been popular with Hatshepsut was going to be a bosom companion of her nephew's. It would be good policy to assure the coming king of one's loyalty before allegiance became a necessity.

Conspiracies have been formed for less logical reasons, but in this case there may have been a stronger motive. Let us anticipate a trifle and look at Thutmose's first official act as king de facto. Within a few months of assuming power, Thutmose had left Egypt. He was on his way to Syria, where a powerful confederation of local princes was threatening the supremacy of Egypt, established in that area by Thutmose I.

We have no records of disaffection or of rebellion under Hatshepsut, but it would be naive to suppose that there were none just because she did not choose to mention them. We know, from later cases, that the "pacified" territories of Syria did not stay pacified very long without a display of force from Egypt. The last major campaigns before those of Thutmose III had been those of his grandfather, some thirty years earlier.

Although Hatshepsut's reign appears to have been peaceful and prosperous, we can be fairly sure that by the end of her time the local princes of northern Syria were getting ideas. No matter how benevolent its control, a conqueror will be resented by the conquered, especially by those who want power for themselves.

Thutmose III marched, not for exercise, but to face a confederation of rebels. It is tempting to suppose that it was the news of this confederation, reaching Egypt, that brought l'affaire Hatshepsut to its crisis. It has been suggested that Hatshepsut did carry out a few minor military campaigns. I find the evidence for this idea unconvincing, and I am equally unpersuaded by the argument that Thutmose III led Egyptian armies abroad during her reign. I can't imagine how Hatshepsut would dare let her gifted nephew become a military hero, or win the allegiance of the army. The overwhelming impression of her reign is one of peace, commerce, and trade, especially in contrast to the reigns of her father and her successor.

So, in detective story tradition, we might ask who profited most by war, after the king himself? The beneficiary of Thutmose's generosity is clear—the god Amon and the priesthood of the god. The young king's sudden favor in the eyes of the god might have been due to the fact that he had succeeded in convincing a significant part of the priesthood that Amon would wax fat with gold if he were allowed to run things in Egypt. One can, in fancy, see the meeting, in some dark cell in the temple of Amon; the young man, eyes alight above the magnificent Thutmosid nose which so eloquently supported his claim to kingship, leaning forward and gesturing in the eagerness of his discourse; the group of priests in their immaculate white linen robes, faces impassive at first—and then, wordlessly, a nod of agreement here, a slow and thoughtful scratching of a shaven chin there.

This is historical fictionalizing, of course. There is a difference between a theory and a possibility; neither should contradict known data, but an honest theory ought to have some little something in the way of proof behind it. Unless new facts come to light, there never can be a theory about Hatshepsut's fall because there is no evidence of any kind. You can see why Egyptologists occasionally turn to fictionalizing for lack of anything more solid. As a feeble justification for my own predilections in that direction, I can only add that I'm not the only one.

There were other reigning queens in ancient Egypt; some of them even assumed the king's titles. But none ruled for a generation without opposition, and none held the throne during the adulthood of a man like Thutmose III. They have come down to us as equals, each unique in his or her own sphere. None of his successors tried to tarnish Thutmose's glory, and his designs on Hatshepsut's name and fame were foiled by the leveling forces of time and by the brilliance of modern scholarship. The masonry with which he encased her mighty obelisks collapsed, and archaeologists put the pieces of her shattered statues back together. They stand today in the museums of Cairo and New York, and on the terraces of her temple.

THE HATSHEPSUT PROBLEM

Scholarly feuds are a lot of fun for laymen, and even for the scholarly world itself, with the possible exception of the combatants. The spectacle of two dignified and learned gentlemen belaboring one another over a misplaced verb form or a piece of broken pottery, with adjectives which should be restricted to political debates, is inherently ridiculous and consequently entertaining. In point of fact there is nothing more absurd about the subjects of "Gelehrtenduelle" than about the causes of many wars, when one considers the stakes involved; but the tragedy of warfare, which removes any possibility of humor unless it be of a macabre variety, is missing in the academic battles. They rarely descend to violence, except that of a verbal nature.

One of the most hard-fought skirmishes on the battlefields of academe was waged around the turn of the last century on the Hatshepsut question. Let not the unwary reader be misled as to the nature of the question. The problem in Egyptological minds was not why Hatshepsut did what she did, or how she got away with it; it was basically a problem of what happened, and when. The historical sequence which I have given above is now the accepted view, but it was not arrived at without a good deal of Sturm und Drang. I mention it primarily because it is a good example of how illogical a scholar can be when he becomes enamoured of a theory. Besides, there's a funny story connected with it.

The protagonists in the battle were Kurt Sethe on the one hand and Edouard Naville on the other. Sethe was one of the best Egyptologists Germany ever produced, which is saying a good deal. In appearance Sethe was the popular stereotype of a scholar—small in size and solemn of manner, though capable of deep and genuine warmth toward his close friends. The Swiss Naville was Sethe's antithesis, being a big, burly man with a jovial personality. Beneath the joviality, however, was a stubbornness which his opponents might reasonably have termed "bullheadedness." When the solemn German and the bullheaded Swiss met in conflict, they met head-on.

Sethe's interpretation of the facts was based on the assumption that when King A's name is erased from an inscription and replaced by the name of King B then King B must have followed King A. This sounds reasonable. But when Sethe applied the rule to the succession of the Thutmosid kings, he came up with the following sequence:

1. Thutmose I
2. Thutmose III
3. Thutmose III and Hatshepsut ruling jointly
4. Thutmose III ruling alone after having deposed Hatshepsut.
5. Thutmose I and Thutmose II as corulers, having displaced Thutmose III by a coup d'état
6. Thutmose II ruling alone after the death of Thutmose I
7. Hatshepsut and Thutmose III again—coup d'état.
8. Thutmose III alone after the death of Hatshepsut

Obviously this proposal had its difficulties. Naville fell upon them with cries of contempt. So heated did the debate become that in 1902, when Sethe and Naville were both camped out at Luxor for the winter season, they were not on speaking terms with each other. Then a domestic catastrophe befell the Naville camp—the kitchen, complete with cook, collapsed into a tomb pit—and Madame Naville was for calling the whole thing off. Sethe, hearing of the trouble and of Madame Naville's laments, gallantly offered his hospitality, on one condition—the name of Hatshepsut was not to be mentioned. For several weeks the two deadly rivals lived in amity, enjoying many discussions on Egyptological matters—all matters except one. When the Naville establishment was restored to order, the Navilles moved out and the status quo was reestablished. Naville and Sethe stopped speaking.

Despite the criticism of other scholars, Sethe stuck doggedly to his theory. It's an absurd scenario, really, and it is hard to understand how Sethe could have overlooked the obvious fallacy. When Thutmose III hacked out Hatshepsut's name from her monuments, he put in its place not only his own name, but the names of his father and grandfather. Thus we derive the chronological sequence we have used in our chapter, the simplest and most logical.

Such examples of filial piety are not too common in Egypt. Ordinarily the kings who proclaimed this virtue in loud voices went around scratching out everybody's name so they could put up their own. Thutmose III wasn't the only king to demonstrate filial piety, though, and—who knows?—he may not have appreciated Hatshepsut's implicit preemption of Thutmose I. She did make rather a point of the relationship.

THE OTHER HATSHEPSUT PROBLEM

Yes, there is another one, and it has more far-reaching implications than Sethe's little error. I regret having to report that recent research has thrown

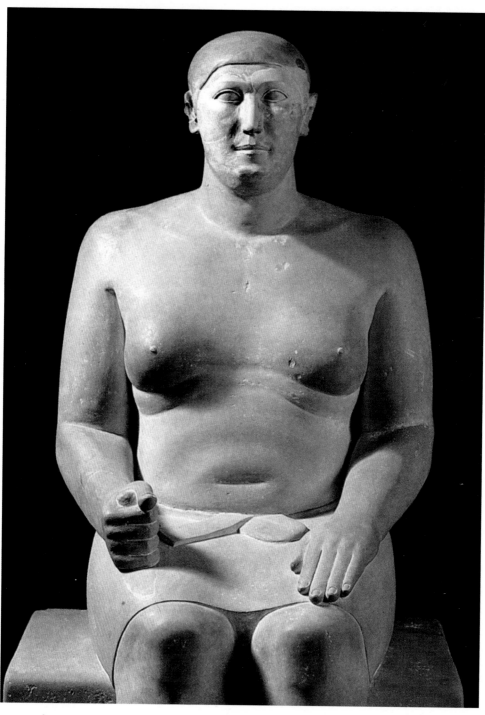

Hemiun the Vizier. Pelizaeus Museum, Hildesheim. (Photograph by D. Forbes)

The tomb of Queen Hetepheres as found by Reisner. After a painting by
Joseph L. Smith. Museum of Fine Arts, Boston. (Photograph by D. Forbes)

Pyramid texts. Pyramid of Unas, Sakkara. (Photograph by S. Ikram)

Hatshepsut. Seated limestone statue. Metropolitan Museum of Art, New York.
(Photograph by D. Forbes)

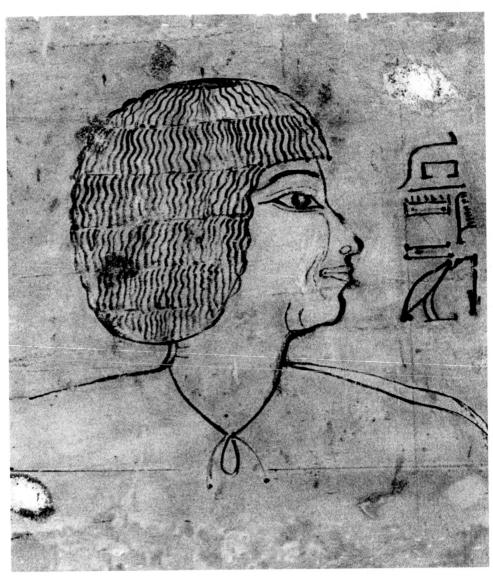

Senenmut. From his tomb at Thebes. (Photograph by D. Forbes)

Deir el Bahri. Temples of Hatshepsut (*foreground*) and Mentuhotep III.
(Photograph by D. Forbes)

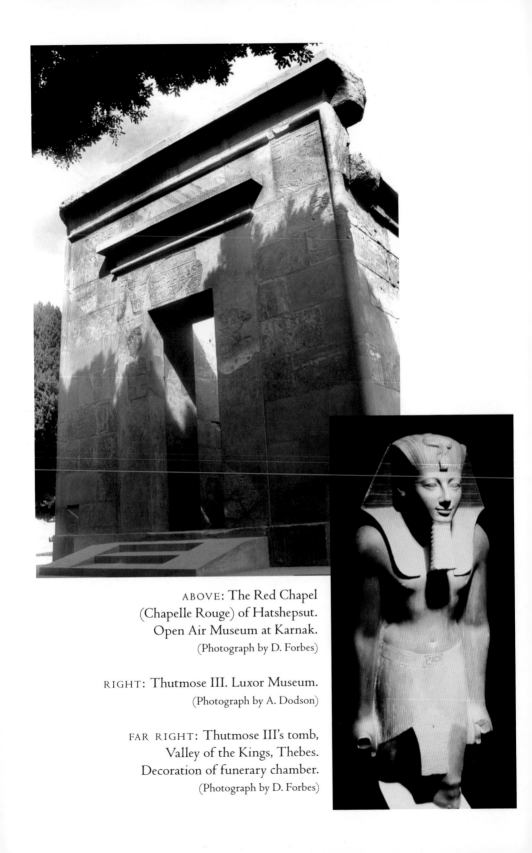

ABOVE: The Red Chapel
(Chapelle Rouge) of Hatshepsut.
Open Air Museum at Karnak.
(Photograph by D. Forbes)

RIGHT: Thutmose III. Luxor Museum.
(Photograph by A. Dodson)

FAR RIGHT: Thutmose III's tomb,
Valley of the Kings, Thebes.
Decoration of funerary chamber.
(Photograph by D. Forbes)

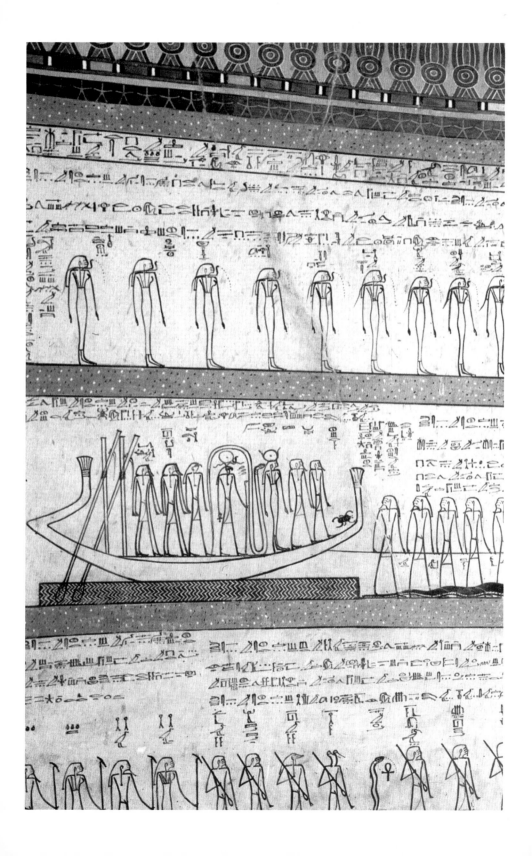

LEFT: Amenhotep III.
Metropolitan Museum of
Art, New York.
(Photograph by D. Forbes)

RIGHT: Red granite head
of Amenhotep III.
Luxor Museum.
(Photograph by D. Forbes)

ABOVE: One of the protective goddesses (Selket) from the Canopic shrine of Tutankamon. Cairo Museum. (Photograph by D. Forbes)

TOP RIGHT: Akhenaton, Colossal Statue. Cairo Museum.
(Photograph by D. Forbes)

BOTTOM RIGHT: Kiya, wife of Akhenaton. From a block found at Hermopolis. Metropolitan Museum of Art, New York. (Photograph by D. Forbes)

Amenhotep, son of Hapu. (Photograph by D. Forbes)

Abu Simbel. Rock-cut temples of Ramses II. Great temple (*above*);
temple of Nefertari (*below*). (Photograph by D. Forbes)

Temple of Ramses III,
Medinet Habu, Thebes.
(Photograph by D. Forbes)

Luxor Temple. Pylon of Ramses II. (Photograph by D. Forbes)

The Pyramids of Meroe. (Photograph by Martin R. Davies)

the entire dramatic scenario of resentment and revenge, female usurper and frustrated king, into disrepute. And it was such a great story!

I won't try to summarize the evidence, since it is extremely complicated. Suffice it to say that investigation of the damage perpetrated on the monuments of Hatshepsut at Karnak Temple seems to indicate that the campaign to destroy her memory did not begin until late in the reign of Thutmose III—twenty years after he became sole ruler, in fact. The relevant monument is, or was, Hatshepsut's Chapelle Rouge or Red Chapel—a handsome little shrine Thutmose dismantled. Many of the separated blocks were found in modern times, inside a later king's pylon. For years they rested on platforms in the Open Air Museum at Karnak until, in 1997, the French Institute decided to rebuild the Chapel. The task was equivalent to working a giant three-dimensional jigsaw puzzle when half the pieces are missing, and the French did a marvelous job. The restored shrine, in the Open Air Museum, is well worth a visit.

The reliefs on those blocks show not only Hatshepsut and her daughter, Nefrure, but Thutmose III. He was acknowledged, if in a secondary role, and it is believed he added to the Red Chapel after Hatshepsut died. Was that why he waited twenty years before dismantling it?

One might also ask why he bothered to do it at all. In fact, Egyptian kings weren't always respectful of their ancestors' monuments. It was easier to "borrow" neatly cut stones from pyramids and pylons than carve new ones out of the quarries. Karnak in particular was an ongoing architectural process that continued for centuries if not millenia. If a later king wanted to expand his building area and somebody else's shrine was in the way, he might take it apart and reuse the stones, without necessarily any hard feelings.

That might account for some of the damage to Hatshepsut's Red Chapel, but not for all. Her image and/or cartouche were removed from it, but the damage is inconsistent, to say the least. Maybe the reliefs weren't attacked until after the shrine had been taken down, and the workers who carried out the job could only reach certain places; but that strikes one as somewhat sloppy reasoning.

Be that as it may, we come back to the question of why Thutmose
didn't go after Hatshepsut as soon as he assumed sole power. Some scholars try to explain the mystery by denying that Thutmose resented his
aunt's occupation of the throne. If I may be pardoned for interjecting a
sexist viewpoint, I can't believe that any normal, chauvinist male—much
less Thutmose III—would have enjoyed being overshadowed by a mere
woman. Either there is something horribly wrong with our interpretation
of the royal succession in Egypt, or Hatshepsut had some means of dealing with Thutmose. But that's only one part of the mystery. What made
him decide, twenty years after her death or abdication, that history required revision?

One recent theory proposes that Thutmose felt no need to act against
his aunt-stepmother until he realized that his end was near and feared his
son's succession to the throne was in jeopardy, threatened by the claims of
another branch of the family. The trouble with this theory is that there
is no evidence of rivals to the throne, legitimate or otherwise. Collateral
branches of the royal family are essentially invisible; they must have existed, given the royal habit of polygamy, but uncles and nephews, cousins
and half-cousins, do not seem to have had any particular status during
this period. Even brothers of the king rate no special title, though the title of "king's sister" is not uncommon. If the king was a minor, someone
would have to act as regent, and this could open up interesting possibili-
ties for pretenders lurking in the wings. However, in almost all the cases
we know about, the boy's mother acted as regent. Furthermore, Thutmose III's heir was no helpless child. By the time his father died he was an
adult and, as we shall see, no weakling. Nor was there any question of his
legitimacy. His father was a king, and his mother a (lesser) royal wife.

So far no one has come up with an explanation that is wholly satisfac-
tory. Thutmose's campaign against Hatshepsut's memory was spasmodic
and inconsistent. He left her images and cartouches untouched in some
places, he concealed part of her magnificent obelisks but left them intact.
But—and it is a large but—the statues of Hatshepsut at her mortuary
temple were pulled down, smashed into bits, and buried. Her images and

cartouches there were erased and, as we have seen, replaced by the names of Thutmose III and his father and his grandfather. We don't know when this took place.

The revisionists also have several ideas about Senenmut's fate. The belief that Hatshepsut turned against him, for one reason or another, is unproven. He may even have survived her. A lot of time has passed, and a lot of tomb robbers, iconoclasts, and vandals have been at work in Egypt; there is no way of telling who was responsible for the random destruction perpetrated on his sarcophagus and in his tombs.

So there they are—the lastest theories and my impertinent criticisms of them. Naturally I have a few opinions of my own. I still believe that Thutmose began abusing Hatshepsut's monuments shortly after she disappeared from the scene, and that it took him a while to get round to the Red Chapel and, perhaps, other places. Personal resentment may or may not have been a factor. Another even more important motive may have been the need to "restore *maat*," the proper order of things, by eliminating the "disorder" of a ruling female. Hatshepsut's name is conspicuously absent from later king lists.

The last word has not been spoken; perhaps it never will be. I wait with interest to see what the next Hatshepsut Problem will be.

Six

THE CONQUEROR

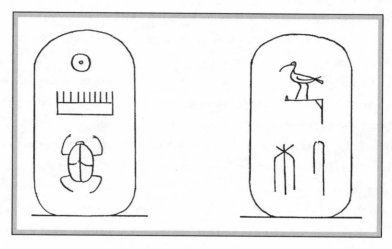

Cartouches of Thutmose III

Thutmose III, everybody agrees, was the greatest warrior Egypt ever produced. He has been compared with Alexander and Napoleon, particularly the latter; for when Thutmose's mummy was found and examined, the anatomist Grafton Elliot Smith reported that he was a little fellow, slightly over five feet tall—pretty short, even for an ancient Egyptian. This led to the usual psychological cliches about little men and their need to prove their manhood. It wasn't until fairly recently that someone actually took another look at the mummy and pointed out that the feet were missing. Remeasurements and recalculations resulted in quite a different figure. Thutmose was of average height for an Egyptian—approximately five feet seven inches.

This is a relatively minor point, I suppose, but I mention it because it is further proof of the advantages of revisionism. To claim that Thutmose's accomplishments were "compensation" for a subconscious sense of inadequacy or frustration is a cheap explanation. He was, as his adult life demonstrates, a man of varied and profound capabilities. Soldier, strategist, statesman, administrator—in each of these roles Thutmose displayed both energy and imagination. To accomplish all he accomplished in one lifetime, he must have been one of those irritating people who sleep only four hours a night and spend their waking hours operating at the highest pitch of efficiency.

It is a pity that physiognomy is not a reliable reflection of character, for while we cannot explain what went on behind Thutmose's face, we know pretty accurately what he looked like. His is not a handsome face, for its regularity is marred by one outstanding feature. Thutmose III excelled his predecessors in nose as in everything else and bore it as proudly as Cyrano bore his.

We happen to have unusually detailed records that relate the military exploits of the Conqueror. The basic source is a long inscription called the Annals of Thutmose III. It was recorded on the walls of the temple of Karnak, and there it may be read today by any visitor who can decipher hieroglyphs. The stone-carved inscription was copied from an original, probably written on leather, by a man named Thaneni. In his tomb, Thaneni says proudly that he followed Thutmose III on his campaigns and "recorded the victories which he won in every land, putting them into writing according to the facts." He was evidently the official army historian or military scribe, and it is to him that we owe the famous tale of the Battle of Megiddo with which the Annals of Karnak begin. But the man who supervised the carving of the copy was a priest, whose chief interest was not in battles but in booty, much of which went to the temple. As the Annals continue, they gradually degenerate into a prosaic list of tributes with only tantalizing hints of battles and brilliant strategies. Fortunately, we have other sources. The most useful is the tomb

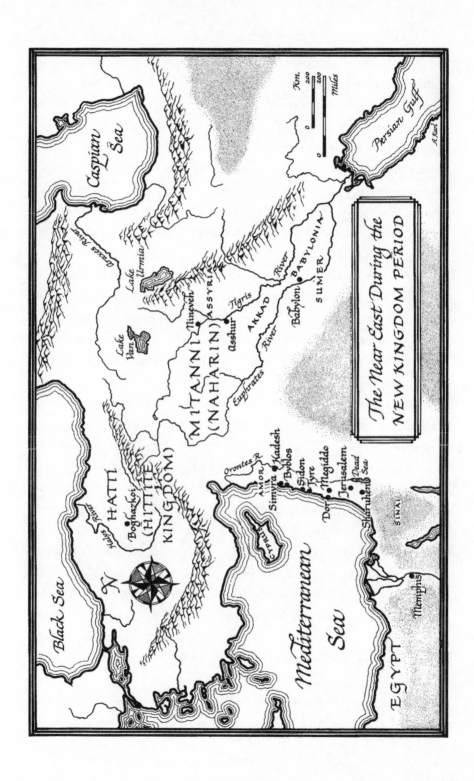

The Near East During the NEW KINGDOM PERIOD

autobiography of a soldier named Amenemhab, who was second only to the royal warrior himself in valor. Other inscriptions that tell of the exploits of Thutmose the Great have been found at Gebel Barkal in Nubia and at Armant.

In the eighth month of his twenty-second year Thutmose left Tharu, the last Egyptian city on the northeast frontier, at the head of his army. His purpose, "to extend the boundaries of Egypt"—a candid avowal of motive, which is not found in the annals of most conquerors. In fact, the expedition marched to counter the threat mentioned in the preceding chapter, a threat posed by the great confederation of north Syrian states and their princes.

Ten days later Thutmose was at Gaza, a distance of 160 miles, not a bad pace for infantry. The date was significant: exactly twenty-two years earlier, Thutmose had been crowned king of Egypt. He arrived at Gaza on the fourth day of the Egyptian month Pakhons, and he left the city on the fifth day. On the sixteenth day he encamped at Yehem, a town on the southern slopes of the Carmel Mountains.

Thutmose's goal was the city of Megiddo, in the plain on the northern side of the mountains. Megiddo had been fortified by the allies, who were under the command of the powerful king of Kadesh, because of its important strategic position as well as its reputation as an invincible fortress; it commanded the best road from Egypt to the Euphrates and was a populous city before and after Thutmose III.

Thutmose called his officers together for a council of war. The problem: how to cross the mountain ridge and reach the plain. There were three possible roads. One came out of the mountains north of Megiddo and one skirted the slopes of the city. The third route was the shortest and most direct. But the direct route had one conspicuous disadvantage, which the officers promptly pointed out.

"How can we go upon this narrow road, when it is reported that the enemy is waiting? Must not horse go behind horse, and soldiers and people likewise? Shall our vanguard be fighting while the rear stands in Aruna, unable to fight?"

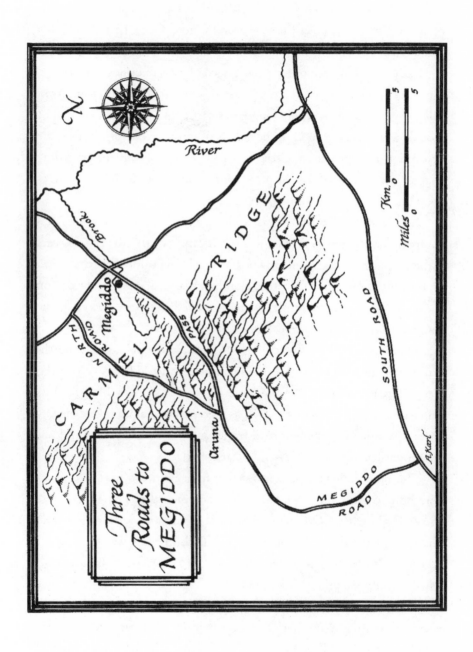

River

Brook

N

RIDGE

CARMEL

Megiddo

NORTH ROAD

PASS

Aruna

SOUTH ROAD

MEGIDDO
ROAD

R. Kurl

Km.   5   0

Miles   5   0

Three
Roads to
MEGIDDO

This makes very good sense militarily. However, as we saw in the story of Kamose, the caution of the royal council is a favorite Egyptian literary device and is intended to contrast with the valor and reckless courage of the king.

"My Majesty will proceed along this road of Aruna," the king swore, with great oaths. "Let him who will among you go upon those roads of which you speak, and let him who will among you come in the following of My Majesty."

Naturally everybody followed His Majesty. Evidently courage was a royal attribute more cherished by the Egyptians than good sense. Thutmose only succeeded in this recklessness because his opponents were equally careless—which, to do him justice, he might have counted upon. He himself led the way through the narrow, treacherous pass, up the mountain ridge to the town of Aruna, where he spent the night. Next morning he pushed forward again and, before long, ran into the enemy. As the council had predicted, the rear of the Egyptian army was still in Aruna; but luckily for the Egyptians, the king, in the van, had reached a widening in the pass. Here the exasperated officers once more pleaded for caution.

"Let our victorious lord listen to us this time, and let our lord await the rear of his army and his people!"

This time Thutmose harkened. He waited till the rest of the army caught up with him. The enemy was not in sufficient force to oppose him, so he was then able to press forward and make camp south of Megiddo, on the bank of the brook called Kina.

Heaven knows what the king of Kadesh and his confederates were doing all this time. They might have won the battle if they had had scouts farther along the Aruna road, or had brought up reinforcements in time to deal with Thutmose when he first came out of the pass. Perhaps they assumed that no soldier of any intelligence would venture upon the Aruna road, so narrow and so susceptible to ambush. Or perhaps they counted on the strong walls of Megiddo, for when Thutmose led the chariot charge against them next morning, they broke with scarcely a fight. "They fled headlong to Megiddo in terror, abandoning their horses and their chariots of gold and silver, and the people hauled them up into the city, pulling them by their clothing."

The Egyptians enjoyed low comic touches of this sort, when the joke was on the enemy; the picture of the mighty prince of Kadesh being pulled up over the walls of Megiddo by his shirttails is rather funny. But what happened after that was not so amusing, and Thaneni, the army scribe, is bitter about it.

"Now if only the army of His Majesty had not given their hearts to plundering the belongings of the enemy, they would have captured Megiddo at this moment!" The sight of the abandoned horses (still uncommon and very valuable) and the jeweled equipment of the allies was too much for the Egyptian soldiers. They loyally carried the loot to the king, but Thutmose was not consoled. He urged the army on to victory: "The capture of Megiddo is the capture of a thousand towns!"

So the troops of Egypt had to pay for their greed with a long siege. They cut down the trees near the city and walled it in. The incompetent rebels had not planned to be besieged. They had left the very grain in the fields, and their empty stomachs must have felt even emptier as they looked over the city walls and saw the Egyptians munching the bread made from their crops. Famine finally took its toll; the "wretched Asiatics" came forth suing for peace.

Somehow or other the pièce de résistance of the confederation, the king of Kadesh, had slipped over both sets of walls one dark night and made his getaway; it is hard to imagine how, but he did. Despite this setback, Thutmose showed amazing clemency toward the inhabitants. Naturally, he took most of their property, but he allowed the allied soldiers transport to their distant homes. "Then My Majesty gave them leave to go to their towns. They all went by donkey, so that I might take their horses."

In his haste to escape, the king of Kadesh had been forced to leave his family behind; either that "fallen one" was not bound by strong ties of familial affection or he relied rather trustingly on Thutmose's clemency. His hopes were justified. Thutmose took them as hostages but did them no harm. It was safer to be besieged and captured by Thutmose III than by most later European conquerors.

After cleaning out the city of Megiddo, Thutmose took the road again, north to Lebanon. He subdued another confederation of three cities here and built a fortress. The season was growing late; the rains were due. Thutmose turned south toward Egypt, but not without a political stroke no less effective than his military exploits. He had appointed new chiefs for the conquered countries, to supplant the "rebellious" princes. The sons of the new rulers were taken to Egypt by the canny king, whose scribe explains: "Now whosoever of these princes died, His Majesty would cause his son to stand in his place." The heirs of the Asiatics served as hostages for the loyalty of their fathers; and when they in turn came to rule their vassal cities they had become Egyptian in custom and language and sympathy, identifying themselves with the cultured Egyptians among whom they had been raised from childhood rather than with their own humble subjects. It was a masterstroke, and this is the first recorded instance of its being practiced, though later conquerors found it equally useful.

The city of Thebes was in celebration when the king returned, and Amon had the best cause to rejoice; he got the lion's share of the plunder. Not only gold and jewels, but also land in conquered Lebanon and in Egypt itself went to the god, with cattle to graze thereon and slaves to tend it.

The following year Thutmose was off again—an easy swing through the conquered territories to check up on the princes he had left in power. The chieftains' collective memory was good; they poured in with tribute and assurances of undying devotion. There were also gifts from the king of Assyria, then a young nation on the threshold of its later power. The Egyptians blandly recorded these gifts, as they would do with other gifts from more powerful monarchs, as "tribute." If a wandering Assyrian reached Egypt and was able to read the Karnak inscriptions—an unlikely event—he would hardly be in a position to contradict them. It's possible that the gifts were reciprocated.

The energetic king had now worked out a schedule to which he would adhere for the rest of his life: half the year in the field, the other half in Thebes, organizing, building, and checking on what had been done in his absence. The army marched from Egypt after the spring harvests, which occurred earlier in that country than elsewhere in the Near East, and arrived in Syria just in time to swoop down on the enemy's ripening grain. When the rainy season approached, Thutmose turned homeward, reaching Thebes some time in October.

Thutmose devoted his third and fourth campaigns to further consolidation of territory already won. The records of the third campaign at Karnak are rather striking, although they do not note any great battles; instead, the walls depict long rows of plants and animals that were brought back, at the king's command, from Syria. This suggests a certain degree of intellectual curiosity on the part of Thutmose; we wonder what other subjects engaged his interest. But few records touch upon this attractive trait; conquest was a more dramatic subject for reliefs than was scholarship.

In Thutmose's early campaigns we may see a leitmotif that emerges more clearly as the years pass. The great adversary at Megiddo, the leader of the allies, was the king of Kadesh. The Egyptians never gave him a name, for reasons which we have explained before, but he was a shrewd and cunning adversary and a constant thorn in Thutmose's side. We recall that the successful siege of Megiddo did not net this wily bird; he had escaped, leaving his family in Thutmose's hands. In the next five years Thutmose must have realized that he would eventually have to face and crush Kadesh and its king, but he was no longer the impetuous youth who had led his army through the dangerous pass of Aruna. His fifth campaign dealt with the Phoenician cities of the coast, hitherto unmolested. This move had its place in a larger strategy; Thutmose could not advance northward toward Kadesh with the potential threat of

Phoenicia behind him. Cunningly, he avoided the southern coast and struck by sea at the wealthy northern kingdoms of Phoenicia. Two great battles, and the coast was won; the other chieftains sent messages of submission.

Thutmose returned home by sea, the first part of his long-range plans completed. The next campaign was to be against Kadesh itself.

Kadesh was a hard nut to crack, even for Thutmose III. It was entirely surrounded by water, with rivers on two sides and a canal on the third; moats and formidable walls made it perhaps the strongest fortress in all of Syria. Thutmose laid siege to the city. Thanks to the materialistic orientation of the scribe who recorded this campaign, we can't even be sure whether he conquered it or not. Amenemhab, Thutmose's trusted officer, was there; but since his memoirs were designed to be carved in his tomb, they naturally concern themselves primarily with the bravery of Amenemhab. We can only conclude that he was not especially brave upon this occasion.

What happened to the adversary, that "fallen one," of Kadesh? The records are infuriatingly silent on this point. Evidently the king of Kadesh repeated his earlier exploit and got away from the beleaguered city. He was certainly a leading advocate of the "he who fights and runs away" school of thought. We have not heard the last of him yet.

Thutmose regarded Kadesh and not its king as the major goal of this campaign, for he went on to the next stage of what had become a truly ambitious plan. Whether he had dreamed of his final goal from boyhood, or whether he dared envision it as his triumphant army proceeded, almost unopposed, through the highlands, we do not know. It was a dream worthy of a conqueror, and it had precedent. Years before, his grandfather Thutmose I, to whom he owed not only filial respect but the admiration of one fine soldier for another, had led his armies to the banks of the Euphrates—that strange inverted water whose current actually flowed from north to south instead of in the normal, decent manner. The inverted water had now begun to haunt the slumbers of Thutmose III. But between him and the Euphrates lay a sizeable obstacle—not a loosely bound confederation of small city states, but the mighty empire of Mitanni, or Naharin.

The kingdom of Mitanni is still one of the unsolved mysteries of Near Eastern archaeology. To be sure, we know it was there, which could not have been said a century ago. But its capital, known as Wassukanni, has never been found, and its language is still imperfectly understood. Most of what we know of this flourishing country, one of the half-dozen great powers of the second millennium B.C., we know from records of other nations. During the fifteenth century before Christ, a group of alien warriors, trainers, and breeders of horses came down from some unknown homeland in farther Asia and subjugated the indigenous peoples of the area near the Upper Euphrates. They spoke an Indo-European language, these cavalrymen, and the gods they worshiped have been connected with the deities of India—Mitra, Indra, Varuna. At its peak the empire of Naharin extended from the Zagros to the Mediterranean, and from Lake Van to Asshur. Its interests naturally extended to the part of northern Syria that lay near its own borders.

These were the people whom Thutmose III meant to face next. The attack on Mitanni was not out-and-out aggression; the king of that nation had backed the confederation of the chieftains of Syria, which was crushed in the battle of Megiddo. However, it is not likely that Thutmose was worrying about justification.

Before undertaking his greatest battle, Thutmose took every precaution for success. He spent a year making sure that his territories in Syria were under control, and a further year in Egypt making ready. The following year he was on his way.

One little touch displayed during this famous campaign shows Thutmose's foresight, as well as his self-confidence. In Byblos, on the Phoenician coast, he had ships built of the famous cedar. Loaded on carts drawn by oxen, "they journeyed in front of My Majesty, in order to cross that great river which lies between this foreign country and Naharin." The river is, of course, the Euphrates, and the poor oxen must have had a time of it, all the way from Phoenicia.

Senzar, Aleppo, Carchemish—one after another the cities of north Syria fell or sent messages of submission. Thutmose's reputation had evidently preceded him. The king of Naharin fled before him, abandoning his country to fire and the sword. Thutmose crossed the river on his cedar boats and laid waste to Naharin, carrying its people away captive to Egypt. Upon reaching the river, he erected a stela beside that of his grandfather Thutmose I.

Thutmose must have been in his glory as he turned back toward Egypt, conquering a town here and there as he marched. By an ironic touch of fate, he came closest to disaster at the time of his highest triumph; his life was saved only by the prompt action of his devoted follower Amenemhab. This was one of the great moments of the general's life, and he remembered it vividly even when, as an old man, he sat recounting his deeds to the patient scribe who would supervise their recording for eternity. One of the cities Thutmose scooped in on his way home was called Niy. After the battle of Niy, word got around that there was a herd of elephants in the vicinity, and the king decided to take time out for relaxation. There were 120 beasts in the herd, which the Egyptians hunted, and one of them—"the largest," according to modest Amenemhab—charged the king. Standing in the water between two rocks, the general placed his body between his king and danger, and cut off the beast's "hand." He was rewarded with gold—and changes of clothing. One would hope so, indeed. An elephant in a river can raise considerable surf, and if Amenemhab really did sever its trunk there must have been other stains than those of water on his linen kilt.

We know only this single narrow escape of the king's, thanks to the "shrivelled soul of the ancient bureaucrat" who recorded the campaigns at Karnak. The epithets are those of Breasted, who goes on to add, bitterly, that the ancient scribe "little dreamed how hungrily future ages would ponder his meagre excerpts." Of course, Thutmose must have had his share of wounds and danger; he never led his regiment from behind. But the myth of the invincible king, armored in his divinity, is never questioned in the official records.

One might suppose that Thutmose could now safely rest upon his laurels. For ten years he had spent half of his time in the field; he had extended the empire farther than had any king who ever ruled Egypt; and the plunder that poured into the capital at Thebes must have dazzled the eyes of the watching populace. He had enlarged the temples and built new ones, sent caravans to Punt and the Sudan, and received gifts from Babylon and Hatti.

But the conquered lands were too new to subjugation to bear it lightly, and Thutmose had to maintain his empire or give it up. He had another twenty years of life before him, and in that time he fought nine more campaigns. One need not suppose that the task was unpleasant; by inclination and by habit Thutmose may have preferred the life of the camp to that of the courtly halls of Thebes, with their rich decorations of gold and faience—and their tedious round of ceremonial duties. He had his staff, well trained and devoted: Thaneni, the scribe who recorded the exploits of His Majesty; Amenemhab, the trusted general who had saved him from the elephant in Niy; Intef the marshal, a prince of Thinis, who had the king's apartments in tent or conquered palace ready for him when he arrived at night; Thutiy, the prince and priest and commander of the army, who conquered Joppa by a trick straight out of the Arabian Nights, if we can believe a folktale of a later date. Thutiy's soldiers entered the city hidden in panniers borne by a train of donkeys—the precursor not only of the Trojan Horse but of Ali Baba. This tale is fiction, but Thutiy is not. His tomb has been found, as well as a beautiful golden dish, bearing his name and titles, which was given to him by Thutmose as a reward for one of his valorous deeds—could it have been the conquest of Joppa?

With such men behind him, Thutmose could venture greatly. And he could do so with his mind at ease about the welfare of the Two Lands, for he had left another trusted servant as vizier, a man named Rekhmire.

Rekhmire's tomb is one of the showplaces of Thebes today. It lies on the hill of the Sheikh Abd el Gurnah, on the west bank of the Nile, where many of the great nobles of the Empire are buried. The walls of the tomb show us, in brilliant detail, how rich and how sophisticated was the life of a nobleman of that imperial age. The tomb also gives an interesting account of the duties of the vizier. And what duties they were! The vizier was in charge of everything. He was a whole cabinet in himself—secretary of state, receiving embassies and reviewing tribute in the king's absence; secretary of the treasury, since the chief treasurer reported to him, and he was responsible for taxation; secretary of the interior and of agriculture, supervising the water supply, the plowing, and the canals; attorney general and chief justice; secretary of war, with both army and navy under his control; secretary of labor, for he regularly inspected the royal craftsmen, from cabinetmakers to sculptors. In his spare time the vizier wore several other hats: he was mayor and chief of police of the residence city and was also in charge of the royal messengers and the king's personal bodyguard. Rekhmire's tomb inscriptions mention all these functions and others; then, just in case something has been overlooked, the writing adds: "Let every office, from first to last, proceed to the hall of the vizier to take counsel with him."

The painted walls of the tomb depict Rekhmire in the process of carrying out many of his onerous duties, which evidently did not take every moment of his time, for there is a spirited scene of a party at the vizier's home, with wine flowing freely and the guests enjoying its effect. Since his accession to the vizierate was the high point of Rekhmire's life, it is natural that his formal investiture in office should be the subject of another scene.

Here we see Thutmose III enthroned. Before him stands the new vizier, attentive to the exhortation that the king delivers. It is a sobering speech, which must have had the same import as a solemn oath of office. "Look to the office of the vizier," Thutmose begins, "and be vigilant over everything that is done in it. Lo, it is the mooring post of the entire land; lo, it is not pleasant at all—no, it is bitter as gall." Foremost among the responsibilities of the vizier is justice. "The abomination of the god is partiality. So this is the instruction: look upon him whom you know like him whom you do not know, upon him who has access to your person like him who is distant from your house."

If Rekhmire took his responsibilities seriously, his position as judge must have been the most sobering of all his duties. He was by proxy the dispenser of that justice which is higher than human. The tomb walls show him to us in this awesome task, seated in the hall of justice; before him are forty leather whips, which were the symbols of the discipline he could wield if he chose. For a long time these forty pictured objects were believed to be leather rolls containing a law code that governed the vizier's decisions; and how Egyptological mouths watered at the prospect of one day finding such rolls! Peculiarly enough, the Egyptians had no such written code of laws. The other peoples of the Near East did; the Code of Hammurabi is the most famous, but there are earlier examples from the same area. Perhaps it was not strange that to the best of our knowledge the Egyptians never developed formal codified law, since the judgment of the god-king and his proxies was, by definition, straight from heaven.

Rekhmire implies that Thutmose kept a close check on the activities of his subordinates; if so, he was satisfied with what he found, for he left Egypt to their administrations half of each year while he carried out his military objectives. Most of the king's remaining nine campaigns were tours of inspection, gentle reminders to the dynasts in Syria that though they might be far from Egypt geographically, they were only days removed from the all-seeing eye and all-powerful arm of the king.

The tenth campaign had to deal with a more serious problem—a resurgence of the king of Naharin and his allies. The battles Thutmose fought on this occasion daunted the proud princes of northern Syria for a good many years. Even on the relatively peaceful inspection tours, Thutmose maintained high standards of efficiency. Harbors were kept permanently supplied and garrisons were trained. "Tribute" continued to pour in, filling the treasuries of king and gods.

Thutmose had outlived Hatshepsut, subdued Mitanni, and conquered an empire; but there was one shadow out of his past which had never been exorcized. Once again, and for the final time, the prince of Kadesh reappears, out of the mists which had shrouded his activities for so long, to stand against the fighting hawk of Egypt. We have not heard of him since the battle of Kadesh, ten years before, when he mysteriously vanished from the beleaguered city. Where he had been, and what he had been up to, we do not know; but now he was ready for his last gamble with fate. He had engaged formidable support—Naharin again, and many of the coastal cities. His chief ally was the city-state of Tunip, to the north of Kadesh. Thutmose had fought in Syria for nineteen years, but if he lost this battle he might lose all that he had won.

The aging king (he must have been in his forties, which was old for that time) was prompt to take up the gage of battle. In the spring of the forty-second year of his reign, Thutmose's fleet could be seen heading for a harbor on the north coast of Syria. Instead of marching up the river to Kadesh, he had decided to cut her off from her northern ally first. Tunip held him for a time, but he took it eventually, and then led his troops up the Orontes to Kadesh. And here Amenemhab, the old soldier who had cut off the elephant's trunk, performed his second great deed.

The battle was fiercely fought by both sides. The stakes were tremendous, and the prince of Kadesh knew it. In his last, desperate attempt to turn the tide in his favor, he thought up a trick that was worthy of him: he sent a mare out of the city and had her driven toward the Egyptian army. The chariotry wavered as the stallions yielded to this exciting distraction. The prize of victory hung in the balance; and Amenemhab moved to weigh the scales. Leaping from his chariot, he ran the mare down and killed her. In a gesture of pure panache, he cut off the animal's tail and presented it to the king. The assault on the city must have followed immediately; in an epic it could not be otherwise, and an epic king would have cried his army on with a great shout of laughter and a flourish of the mare's tail. Amenemhab, carried away by his success, was first over the walls. Behind him poured the hard-bitten veterans of the Syrian wars. Against such men and such a leader even Kadesh the invincible had no chance. The city fell; and with it fell the last hopes of the Syrian cities for independence.

And what of the prince of Kadesh, who did not know when he was defeated? Once again we may invoke Breasted's curse on the withered bureaucrat who recorded this campaign only as a list of booty collected. But we can deduce the fate of Thutmose's archenemy from the silence that followed. Never again, in the ten years that remained to the king, did Syria rebel against her overlord. We cannot imagine such a state of peace and lethargy with the restless spirit of the prince of Kadesh still abroad in the land. The second battle of Kadesh was not a long-drawn-out siege, as the first had been. Thutmose was behind schedule that year, held back by the resistance of Tunip, and he had not time for such niceties. Kadesh was taken by storm, and its prince may not have had the opportunity to repeat his past escapes. Did he die in battle, in the last hopeless fight to save his city when the bronzed troops of Egypt swarmed over the wall; or was he captured by Thutmose and executed, as the greatest rebel of them all? Thutmose's records do not mention the execution of enemies—who were, in the egocentric Egyptian view, guilty of rebellion and treason. It is, of course, unsafe to conclude from this silence that such executions never took place. Still, we may prefer to think of the prince of Kadesh as perishing in battle. We have a certain sympathy for him. Three times he had fought against the most invincible warrior of his age, the man to whom many of his peers had tamely surrendered without so much as a spear being cast. Megiddo, Kadesh, and Kadesh again . . . It would be interesting to find, some fine day, the buried records of the lost capital of Naharin, and see what they have to say about their ally of Kadesh. To his own men he was probably a patriot and a hero; to the Egyptians, just another rebel.

So ended, after twenty years, the active military career of Thutmose III. He was first and foremost a soldier, and that is why we have devoted so much space to the description of his campaigns. His other accomplishments compare favorably with the activities of other kings who did not spend half their lives abroad. Rekhmire mentions the king's omnipotence; some of this can be written off as court flattery, but there is no doubt that Thutmose made good use of his annual six months in Egypt. He toured the country, inspecting canals, buildings, and harvests, and he ordered careful records kept of his campaigns and their results. Of all his building activities the most famous are the great obelisks. They have had a curious history; not one of them stands in Egypt today, but they have literally carried Thutmose's name to the four corners of the earth. The obelisk in Central Park in New York once towered above Thutmose's temple at Heliopolis; its former mate stands on the Thames Embankment in London.

Another of Thutmose's architectural achievements came to light only forty years ago. It is at Deir el Bahri, squeezed in between the larger temple of Hatshepsut and the ruins of the earlier Seventeenth Dynasty temple. An avalanche had buried it completely until the Polish-Egyptian expedition found and excavated it.

I can't resist giving another example of how preconceptions color Egyptological interpretation; surely, some scholars argued, Thutmose would not have tucked his temple so cozily close to Hatshepsut's if he had detested her. On the other hand, one might argue that he felt it necessary to leave his mark at Deir el Bahri too, instead of allowing her structure to dominate it. I suspect he had more sensible reasons, but I don't know what they were.

When he returned from the Second Battle of Kadesh, Thutmose III had another ten or twelve years of life remaining to him. During this time he occupied himself with such minor details as Nubia, which was now pouring fantastic amounts of gold into the Egyptian treasury. He himself visited the south countries in his fiftieth year, and his domains stretched from the Euphrates to the Fourth Cataract—the largest empire Egypt had or would ever have.

Perhaps the most far-reaching consequence of the life of this man was not the empire itself, but the changes that the empire was to produce in Egypt. Almost every aspect of life was affected; and some of the changes were to bear fruit in a far future day, and in a way that even Thutmose the Great could not have anticipated.

Some of the results are fairly obvious. The army was no longer an amateur militia, hastily assembled for specific campaigns. Since Ahmose there had been a hard core of professional fighters, with the Medjay of Nubia as its elite; these men served as the royal bodyguard and city police in time of peace. But an army that has fought yearly for twenty years has lost its amateur standing; the men knew their craft and their officers, and the ones who survived brought home wealth such as their fathers had never seen. The empire, so hard-won, had to be held. This meant garrisons, though not large ones, in foreign cities. The army organization was complex; quartermaster, signal corps, and general accounting had come into being, along with chariotry, infantry, and naval forces. For the first time the professional fighting man, as a group and as an individual, becomes a force in the state.

Another obvious result of empire was the effect of the enormous wealth pouring into Egypt from the north and south. The nouveau riche acquired expensive tastes and demanded foreign products. No wealthy household was complete without an Asiatic slave or two, and sophisticated Egyptians sprinkled their speech with foreign words and even turned to the worship of new gods.

New people and new ideas often have a favorable effect upon the culture they invade; in the optimum cases the new and the old give birth to a civilization higher than either of its parents. But one of the consequences of foreign ideas in Egypt was not so attractive. This was the effect upon Egyptian art. Craftsmen and painters had developed their skills early, and the canons of taste were beautifully harmonious. The avalanche of new techniques that came from the conquered lands and from other empires was not always assimilated easily. The contents of Tutankhamon's tomb show a certain degradation of the pure classic style; many of the objects are exquisitely lovely, all are beautifully executed; but one or two are dreadfully vulgar in taste.

We could go on describing the changes that resulted from the growth of empire, but one point is especially noteworthy—the fantastic wealth and power that began to accrue to the great state god Amon. Among the multitudinous gods of Egypt there were a dozen or so greater than the rest: Re of Heliopolis, the very ancient sun god; Ptah of Memphis, patron of artisans and artists, to whom (among other gods) was ascribed the creation of the world; Osiris and Isis and their son Horus; another Horus, a falcon and a sun god; Thoth, the ibis-headed divine scribe; and others. All of them were older in dignity than the parvenu Amon; none of them, except perhaps Re, had ever enjoyed the preeminence of the god of Thebes. By a convenient process called syncretism, Amon was able to absorb his potential rivals in the pantheon; among other gods he swallowed was Re himself, and he was known as Amon-Re. This does not mean that Re's temples were closed down. His ancient worship continued as before, but Amon could now claim the attributes and the qualities of the honored sun god. As the conquering pharaohs went out to battle under the aegis of Amon-Re, they attributed their victories to his aid, and thought it only fitting that he be rewarded. The whole transaction made a vicious cycle: the more powerful Amon became, the greater the size of his reward; the richer he got, the more his power increased. It would be a mistake to view Egyptian history from this point on as a conflict between the temporal power, residing in the king, and the spiritual might of Amon-Re and his priests. From the Egyptian point of view, no such distinction could exist, and there were many other factors involved. Yet the shadow of Amon-Re, hawk-headed, holding the insignia of power in human hands, began to grow long across the fertile green valley of Egypt. Thutmose III had raised up a number of unexpected monsters to plague the placid immutability of the divine kingship, but this was perhaps the most menacing of all.

Thutmose the king, of course, had no doubts about the future. The tips of his tall obelisks, sheathed with gold, caught the light of the rising sun each morning and sent sparks glittering across the Nile. Slaves in strange, colored garments, speaking a gabble of uncouth tongues, tended the affairs of the land and worked beside the slighter, smooth-faced Egyptians. Even the succession was in order, for Thutmose had a son.

Thutmose's military and administrative exploits so overshadow everything else in his life that we have not mentioned his domestic side.

Actually, not much is known about it. The uxorious Amenhotep III had a queen who was a personality in her own right; Akhenaton cherished an almost Byronic passion for his lovely wife; and that ancient reprobate Ramses II fascinates us solely by the sheer number of women he acquired. But Thutmose III has left an impression of austerity so far as the "weaker" sex is concerned. Perhaps he had had enough of women after Hatshepsut.

Hatshepsut's daughter, Nefrure, may not have lived long enough to marry her half-brother. Thutmose's great royal wife and the mother of his heir was named Meritre Hatshepsut. The coincidence of names led some scholars to believe she was another of Hatshepsut's children, but she was not a king's daughter. Though he may not have found female society particularly congenial, Thutmose was no more monogamous than anybody else. Three members of his harem were found buried in a single tomb, which was published by H. E. Winlock in 1948. These ladies had foreign names, which reminds us of a policy of Alexander the Great; perhaps Thutmose anticipated the Macedonian in seeing the potentialities of foreign conquest through marriage. These three young ladies were never more than junior members of the royal family, however; and in view of this fact, the wealth of their funerary equipment is quite striking. In 1948, Winlock estimated the value of the gold and silver employed as around $6,800. In ancient times its value would have been considerably greater, and the precious metals represented only part of the equipment of the tomb. What then must have been the treasure buried with the body of the king-conqueror himself!

Toward the end of his life, the aging king seems to have placed his son beside him on the throne. About a year later King Menkheperre Thutmose III "mounted to heaven; he joined the sun, the divine limbs mingling with him who begat him."

The epithet "the Great" surely belongs to Thutmose III, if to any king of Egypt, even if we judge him only by the material results of his campaigns. In an age which saw brutality—though not on so grand a scale as Christian Europe was able to work up—he showed clemency; at a time when death was the proper portion of the defeated, he spared the fallen. At the very least he deserves to regain the prestige he has lost to bombastic old Ramses II.

And do not forget to add Thutmose's tomb to your repertory while in Luxor. The central attraction of the Valley of the Kings, on the West Bank, is the tomb of Tutankhamon. During the "season" this part of the Valley is almost too populous, for in the same immediate area are other tombs that are popular with visitors. But if you are wearing sensible shoes you may take a short hike, only a few hundred yards, to a small canyon in the cliffs, apart from the swarming center of things; and here you will have a genuine feeling for the secrecy and loneliness that these Houses of Eternity once conveyed. Today you climb steep wooden stairs to the hole in the cliff where once the swaying funeral cortege carried the embalmed body of Thutmose the Great. In location and in atmosphere it is one of the most impressive tombs in the Valley of the Kings. The paintings are unusual; at first sight they seem sketchier than the conventional Egyptian technique, to such an extent that the human and divine depictions might be called stick figures. Yet they have a sophistication and elegance that some observers, including myself, find highly attractive.

Thutmose's mummy was not found in his tomb. The members of the second oldest profession had gotten to it long before any of our immediate ancestors were born. But his body survived, thanks to the efforts of a group of devoted priests in the last dying days of Egypt's greatness. Today Thutmose's mummy lies in the Cairo Museum with those of his peers. There is nothing particularly majestic about the withered face. Battered by impious tomb robbers, even the once imposing Thutmosid nose has lost its panache. You may draw your own moral.

Seven

THE POWER AND
THE GLORY

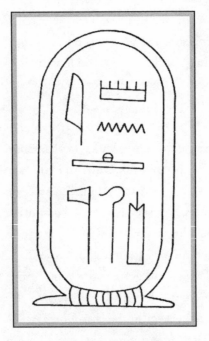

Cartouche of Amenhotep II

AMENHOTEP II

We have exhausted our superlatives on Thutmose III, but that is all right;
we won't be needing them for a while. Not that the Conqueror's son was
not a fair enough fighter himself. If we can believe the stories that have
come down to us—which we probably should not—he surpassed even his
renowned father in feats of arms. Thutmose III had driven an arrow nine

inches out of the back of a copper target two inches thick; Amenhotep II
drove his arrow clean through a target three inches thick. He trained his
horses so ably that they did not sweat, even when galloping. He rowed a
boat (with a thirty-four-foot oar) four miles without stopping, and then
landed it alone; his two-hundred-man crew had collapsed long before. He
could outrun anyone in Egypt, and no man could draw his bow.

All this braggadocio is harmless, though a psychologist might wonder whether Amenhotep II was trying to surpass an impressive father.
But Amenhotep II was not a Nice King. Soon after his father died, he had
to lead a campaign into Syria to suppress a "rebellion" of the local princes
there; these worthies soon acquired the habit of trying out a new king to
see whether he would be as competent or as interested as his ancestors
had been. The account of Amenhotep's first Syrian campaign leaves an
unpleasant taste in the mouth. Probably the actual events did not differ
greatly from what had happened under his father; but there is a difference
in the selection of the details which Amenhotep II wished to commemo-
rate. After capturing seven of the rebel princes, Amenhotep brought them
back to Thebes, hanging head down at the prow of the royal barge. He
then bashed in their heads personally and hung six of the bodies on the
walls of Thebes. The seventh was sent down into Nubia to be draped
over the battlements of the city of Napata as a lesson to the Nubians.

As an act of barbarity, this is pretty tame compared with the daily activities of the Assyrians or the morning prayers of the Aztecs. The technique was still being used in enlightened England, during the enlightened
eighteenth century A.D. The English were more economical with their
corpses; they cut them to pieces in order to spread the effect—a head here, a
torso there—it all added up. A popular artistic motif in Egyptian reliefs was
the bashing of captives by the king; he holds not one but several victims by
their hair, which presumably saved time in the long run. However, one
may reasonably doubt that the king performed this deed in person. Like
so many other rituals, it was either delegated or not done at all; the representation became the deed. So perhaps I am being unfair to Amenhotep II
when I suggest he enjoyed hitting people over the head.

Whatever his methods, they were successful—in large part, perhaps, because of his father's previous prowess. A few campaigns into Syria and Nubia convinced the regions in question that it didn't do to mess with Amenhotep, and the king spent the rest of his life in a normal royal fashion—quarrying obelisks, building at Karnak, excavating his tomb— and, one presumes, shooting arrows through targets. He also amused himself with certain pursuits which might be genteelly summarized as "wine, women, and song." One day when Amenhotep was sitting around in the palace, making a happy hour for himself (as the saying went), he got to feeling nostalgic and decided to dash off a note to an old comrade and drinking companion. This official, who was at one of the forts in Nubia, was so impressed by the letter, written in the king's own hand, that he had it reproduced on stone. It was found by George Reisner at Fort Semna.

I do not propose to translate this text. Authorities differ as to the interpretation of some of the more interesting sections, and the whole document gives an impression of remarkable incoherence. We often have this feeling about mutilated inscriptions, but in this case I am inclined to wonder how much of the incoherence might be due to Amenhotep's condition when he wrote it. What are we to do, for example, with the ladies who are familiarly referred to as a servant girl of Byblos, a little maiden of Alalakh, and an old woman of Arapha? Is Amenhotep insulting his rivals, the princes of these cities, by derisive epithets, or is he reminding the friend of his youth of certain memories they have in common? I suppose this peculiar letter could be interpreted more favorably as a touch of good fellowship from one jolly soldier to another; but I am prejudiced against Amenhotep II. We should, however, say one nice thing about him before we leave the subject. So let us add that there may be a grain of truth in the king's claims about his archery.

His bow was buried with him in the tomb in the Valley of the Kings where his body was found, one of the few royal mummies that survived to our times in their original burial places. Tomb robbers had been at it and had removed everything of value from coffin and body. Then, when

Egypt went into its last illness, and the depredations at the royal tombs passed the bounds of endurance, priests moved the bodies of the kings into secret hiding places, after removing anything of value overlooked by the ancient tomb robbers. One of the places chosen was the tomb of Amenhotep II, and eventually he had fourteen other bodies for company. When this cache was discovered in 1898, Amenhotep's mummy was left in its sarcophagus, and the other royal remains were crated and about to be sent off to Cairo, when orders came to return them to the tomb. There has always been a vociferous minority who feel that the mortal remains of Egypt's kings should be left in honorable burial, not exposed to the gaze of curious sightseers. The procedure ought to be safe, since everyone knows that nothing worth stealing would be left on the mummies. However, the ancient and honorable profession of grave robbing is one Egyptian tradition that has been handed on from father to son, down to the present day; and some of the boys near Luxor evidently failed to read the newspaper accounts which explained that Amenhotep no longer owned anything worth stealing. They broke into the tomb again in 1901 and slit through the mummy wrappings, to find nothing but a mummy. It is surprising that they bothered, since the grapevine among the brothers of the less legal crafts operates more efficiently than archaeological newsletters, and thieves, of all people, ought to "case" a place before they rob it. Perhaps it was just a matter of old habits, which reputedly die hard. They did make off with Amenhotep's bow, however.

As for dignity and honorable burial, Amenhotep II got little of either. After the 1901 break-in his body was left in his open sarcophagus, with a spotlight shining on his unwrapped face. Tourists came in droves. Eventually the king was taken to the Cairo Museum to join nine other royals from his tomb, whose remains had finally been removed in 1900. (In case you're counting, three uncoffined mummies were left in a side chamber of the tomb, since they were assumed to be members of the family of Amenhotep II; a fourth, also uncoffined, was broken to pieces by the frustrated 1901 robbers.)

Amenhotep's wife—one of many, no doubt—was named Tiaa. She is not called King's Daughter, so she was probably a commoner. However, she was the mother of his heir, and that counted for a lot. The son and heir was another Thutmose—the Fourth, by modern reckoning. His is a more elusive personality that fails to convey any positive image, pleasing or the reverse. He made brief excursions into Syria and Nubia in order to put down the usual revolts, and he piously finished and erected the obelisk that his grandfather and namesake, Thutmose III, had begun at Karnak. The largest surviving obelisk, it is now in Rome and commemorates the names of both Thutmoses. The most interesting memorial left by Thutmose IV is the stela that nestles between the paws of the Sphinx at Giza. The stela tells the story of how Thutmose, as a young prince, lay down to rest in the shadow of the great stone beast after a tiring hunting trip. As he slept, the sun god, of whom the Sphinx was believed to be the image, appeared to him in a dream and begged him to clear away the sand that had covered most of the huge statue. As a reward, Re would see to it that the young man inherited the throne. Thutmose got the crown and carried out his part of the bargain. So he says, at any rate.

Some Egyptologists have interpreted this story to mean that Thutmose was not the original heir. Divine intervention was a popular substitute for legitimacy, so the theory may have some foundation. Amenhotep II had several sons, two of them probably older than Thutmose, but they may have died of natural causes before their father. There is no evidence in pharaonic Egypt of a new king executing potential rivals—brothers, nephews, uncles, and cousins—which was a popular and useful custom in the Ottoman Empire, not to mention medieval and Renaissance Europe. That doesn't mean it might not have happened, but without specific examples it is a plot for historical fiction, not legitimate history.

By now, one point should have been made clear—it takes more than a pith helmet and a shovel to make an Egyptologist. Most of the books on archaeology that are written for the "layman"—an opprobrious epithet, for whose use I apologize—tell and retell the accounts of excavations as if that one activity were the sole source of an archaeologist's data. Now and then an attempt is made to give the linguist his due by mentioning the Rosetta stone, and by recounting the life of Jean-François Champollion and the process by which he deciphered the hieroglyphs. Philology and excavation are certainly important subfields of Egyptology, but as I have tried to demonstrate, there is hardly any aspect of knowledge that is not grist for the mill of the archaeologist. One of the unexpected subjects he has had to contend with—in Egypt, at least—is genealogical research. Generally, family trees are interesting only to the twigs of the particular tree. But the genealogies of the ancient Egyptians can give an archaeologist vital information about such matters as inheritance, marital customs, and family life. Royal family trees, of course, are a legitimate subject of historical study. An English historian would have a hard time discussing the Wars of the Roses and the advent of the Tudor dynasty without bringing up the marital—and extramarital—activities of the sons of Edward III. In Egypt, royal genealogies are particularly important because they shed light on a problem that is still in dispute—the problem of the inheritance of the throne.

We are familiar with the relatively modern solutions to this problem, in which the right to rule descended from father to eldest son. Sometimes royal daughters were acceptable in lieu of sons, and sometimes not; but ordinarily it was the offspring of the reigning monarch, whether king or queen, who acquired the mystical sanction of the crown.

This procedure was not universal. In Nubia, to the south of Egypt, the crown went to the brothers of the king before reverting to his eldest son—a practical procedure, which avoided minority rule and the evils which attend upon it. Anthropologists have collected examples of even stranger rules of royal inheritance; there are rumors of societies in which queens were preferred to kings.

Egyptologists once believed that the queen held a peculiarly important position in regard to inheritance. A queen could not rule, but she alone could transmit the right to rule. By dogma, her husband held the throne only by virtue of his marriage to her, and her son had a prior claim—not on the crown, but on the next queen, who would ideally be his sister, the daughter of his mother. The mystical sanctity descended from mother to daughter; her son had no part in it. If the heiress-queen had only daughters, it was all the more incumbent on the next king—who might be her husband's child by a lesser wife—to marry her eldest daughter, the heiress-princess.

This theory of inheritance has now been discarded by the majority of scholars, though you will still find it mentioned in older books. One of the objections to it is the fact that there is no queen's title that distinguishes a royal heiress. If the job was that important, you would think it would have its own proper title. To go one step further—if an heiress-wife was so vital to a reigning monarch, we would expect that she would be honored by the position of chief wife. But not all chief wives were heiress-princesses, or even king's daughters.

The trouble is that the Egyptians did not have family Bibles with pages for births and deaths. Sometimes we have the feeling that kings only mentioned their sons or daughters when they happened to think about them; additional offspring keep turning up, on newly found reliefs and inscriptions. Once in a while a king shows us a collection of sons and daughters; sometimes they are named, sometimes not. But never, or almost never, are we given all the information we would like to have—date of birth, names, parentage.

To further confuse the issue, we should note that Egyptian statements of relationship are often vague. It was recognized early in the game that the words "brother" and "sister" need not indicate ties of blood. They are terms of endearment, equivalent to "sweetheart" or "darling," or even to "husband" or "wife." But it took Egyptologists a few years to arrive at the dismaying conclusion that "father" and "son" are equally misleading. "Father" might be applied by a king to his grandfather, or to an even more remote ancestor; "son" seems to be used for grandson as well, and, at certain periods, as an honorary title. We are still clinging to "mother" and "daughter" as meaning what they seem to mean; but we can never be sure that a newly discovered inscription may not knock the sense out of those words too.

With these cheerful facts in mind, let us take a specific case—the marital situation of Thutmose IV. It presents some interesting problems—not to Thutmose, as far as we know, but to archaeologists. We suspect, to begin with, that Thutmose's mother was not of royal birth. The evidence for the suspicion is negative evidence: the lady is never called "king's daughter."

So until we find a text that states her parentage specifically, we can establish her social status only as a probability. Let us assume that she was a commoner. The next step, for those who followed the "heiress" theory of legitimacy, was to look for a royal princess among the wives of Thutmose IV. If one existed, she would have been his half-sister—the daughter of Thutmose's father, Amenhotep II, by a royal wife who was not Thutmose IV's mother, because she (we think) was a commoner.

One of Thutmose's wives was a princess of Mitanni, who could not have been an Egyptian heiress. Another wife was a woman with an unusual name, which, in view of its uniqueness, may not be a name at all. (And if you find that sentence confusing, the situation it describes is equally so.) A third queen of Thutmose IV was a lady named Mutemwiya, who was the mother of his successor; we assume that she was of nonroyal birth because she, like Thutmose IV's mother, does not have the title "king's daughter."

The ambiguity of the problem may seem complete at this point, but it gets worse. For there may not be three queens involved at all; by the mental dexterity with which all true historians are endowed, we can reduce the three to one. The Mitannian princess could have taken an Egyptian name—Mutemwiya, for example. The lady with the strange name may be the Mitannian princess in disguise, and/or Mutemwiya. The titles of these ladies (however many they may be) add to the confusion. Asiatic princesses are not called "king's daughter." Mutemwiya is not called "king's daughter." The weirdly named queen is called "king's daughter," which makes her identification with either or both of the other two somewhat dubious. In fact, the whole business is extremely dubious, and I see no way out of it. The only point that can reasonably be made is that this is one of several cases that has led most scholars to dismiss the theory of the heiress-princess. It can, of course, be claimed that Thutmose IV had still another queen, unknown to us, who was an heiress-princess, but this is pretty weak logically. You can prove anything if you are allowed to make up the necessary evidence.

The Mitannian princess, whose name is not recorded, was the first such alliance of which we know, but it was not the last. This marriage, together with the relative absence of military activity on the part of Thutmose IV, suggests that he had come to terms with Egypt's rival state to the north and had chosen diplomacy over conquest. His reign was peaceful and quite possibly brief; the mummy identified as his has been described as a frail young man. It was not found in his tomb, which is in the Valley of the Kings; Thutmose IV ended up, like so many of his peers, in one of the caches of royal mummies. His son and successor was destined for greater fame and fortune.

AMENHOTEP THE MAGNIFICENT

The name Amenhotep means "Amon is satisfied." Amon had reason to be satisfied. The old provincial god of Thebes was now Amon-Re, king of the gods, and his priests controlled what was probably the richest ecclesiastical establishment in all of Egypt. To the temple of Amon, with its ever-growing circle of administrative and financial offices, came a goodly proportion of the foreign tribute. The memory of Thutmose III was still fresh in the minds of Egyptian vassal princes in Syria and Palestine; the military campaigns of his son and grandson reinforced Egyptian prestige in those areas and kept Asiatic tribute pouring south into Egypt. From Nubia and from the mines in the eastern desert gold continued to flow into the coffers of the king and the god. And to the king, besides gold and tribute, came letters from the rulers of the great powers of the ancient Near East—not only Mitanni, but Hatti, Babylon, and Cyprus—humbly requesting gold and offering their daughters for the harem of Horus.

As the head of this luxurious and wealthy society, Amenhotep III deserved the epithet "the Magnificent," which has been given him by modern historians. In his youth he showed signs of the athletic ability which had been the boast of his grandfather, Amenhotep II; an inscription claims that he killed over one hundred lions between his first and tenth years of reign. But the third Amenhotep carried out no important military campaigns, not even the customary punitive expedition into Syria at the beginning of his reign.

Among his wives Amenhotep III numbered not one but two Mitannian princesses. They are only names to us—Gilukhepa and Tadukhepa, just for the record—but his chief queen was a more remarkable figure. Her entrance into the royal family was treated in a manner that is unique in ancient Egypt. Amenhotep the Magnificent announced his marriage in a series of commemorative scarabs, the same shape as the well-known beetle amulets, which modern tourists have carried away from Egypt by the thousands, but large enough to contain a short inscription on the flattened base. This inscription read:

> *May he live, Amenhotep III, given life, and the King's Great Wife Tiye, who lives. The name of her father is Yuya, the name of her mother is Thuya; she is the wife of a mighty king whose southern boundary is as far as Karoy, and northern as far as Naharin!*

This announcement can be interpreted in a number of ways, but to me it sounds like a challenge. Tiye was not a king's daughter. The tomb of her parents was found in 1905. It had been entered in ancient times, the coffins opened and some of the grave goods stolen. A lot was left, though, and the exposed mummies were in excellent condition. Tiye's father, Yuya, was a fine-looking man; suggestions that he was non-Egyptian, of Asiatic or Nubian origin, have no actual basis in fact. Yuya's titles are not indicative of high rank. He is called "Master of the Horse," and parts of a model chariot found in the tomb bear out this role. His wife had the usual titles of a court lady, in addition to being designated "Mother of the King's Chief Wife." Yuya's only other title of interest is that of "Father of the God." What god, one might ask? The king? We will defer this question until later, if you don't mind. It's another of those arguments Egyptologists love.

One might also ask why Amenhotep married this daughter of commoners and made her his consort. Queen Tiye was chief wife in the fullest sense, appearing conspicuously upon the monuments of her husband and receiving letters from foreign monarchs which imply that she had a voice in political decisions. There is a small head in the Berlin Museum which is usually assumed to be be a portrait of the lady; although interpretation of physiognomy is always subjective, there is no way that woman could have been a meek, submissive wife. It's a striking face with a full, firmly set mouth framed by hard lines; the chin is outthrust and the eyes hooded. Beautiful, no; but not all the great charmers of history have been beauties.

It is pure romantic fiction to claim Tiye so captivated the youthful king that he defied convention by raising her to such a high position. There are a number of prosaic theories to account for her rise to power. Some are based on the exasperating absence of evidence about family connections and relationships. As I mentioned when discussing Hatshepsut, we know very little about the collateral branches of the royal family. How much power did such cousins have? Did they carry some of the royal prestige—and if so, for how many generations? Maybe Yuya was distantly related to Amenhotep III. Maybe he had enough personal influence with the king and the party in power to push the claim of his daughter. Such suggestions abound, and there is absolutely no proof of any of them. Yuya and Thuya had at least one other child—a son, Anen, who was second prophet of Amon. This is not a neglible title, but it is not on the same level as vizier or high priest. Unlike his parents, who were honored by a tomb in the royal valley, Anen was buried elsewhere. It's all very confusing, but I just don't get the impression that the king's in-laws necessarily had much power at court.

We don't know how old Amenhotep III was when he inherited the throne. The mummy that has been identified as his probably isn't. In the earliest reliefs from his reign he is accompanied by his mother, which has led scholars to suppose that he was a minor when he became king. The marriage scarab is dated to his second year, and if he was hunting lions during his first years of rule, he can't have been a toddler.

One of his first projects, perhaps, was the great colonnaded hall that stands on the east bank of the Nile, not far from the modern Winter Palace hotel. (The original structure was added onto by a later king, Ramses II.) It dominates the view of modern Luxor from the riverbank. At Karnak Amenhotep built a huge new pylon, the third, by today's reckoning.

Though Amenhotep, like most Egyptian kings, had royal residences all over the place, his principal palace was at Thebes, on the West Bank across from modern Luxor. There's not much left of it today, but originally it was a great sprawling structure that covered almost eighty acres and included several subsidiary palaces, presumably for his queen and his heir. Next to it the king excavated a huge harbor connected to the Nile; the resultant earth mounds are still visible, though only an informed eye would recognize them for what they are. The modern name of the site is Malkata. Amenhotep called it "The Mansion of Nebmaatre Is the Dazzling Aten."

Nebmaatre was Amenhotep's throne name. But who, one might ask, was the dazzling Aten?

This is our first encounter with a name—a god—who was to loom large in succeeding years. Originally *aton* was a common noun that referred to the sun itself. Later on the word acquired a "god" determinative and became personified during the reign of Amenhotep's father, Thutmose IV. Just how far his prominence extended under Amenhotep III is open to question. So far as we know, Amenhotep built no temples for him and raised no statues.

Unless, as recent theories propose, he didn't need them because Amenhotep himself was the "Dazzling Aton."

Every Egyptian pharaoh was a god—sort of. He was the Horus while he lived and Osiris after he died. He was called "the good god," and "Son of Re," and like Hatshepsut, Amenhotep III carved a series of reliefs showing his mother being impregnated by none other than Amon-Re. But was Amenhotep III more of a god than other kings?

After he had been on the throne for thirty years Amenhotep III celebrated his first Heb-Sed, or Sed festival (also referred to as "jubilee.") The ritual goes back to the earliest dynasties and was a complex performance involving a number of activities such as making offerings to the gods and receiving offerings, and running races. One can't help wondering whether this originated as an actual test of the ruler's vigor, which was identified with that of the tribe or city. Such procedures are known, not only from Africa, but from other parts of the world; failure could be fatal. It makes a certain amount of sense, really, if one believes in magic. A weak ruler could weaken an entire people and was replaced for the good of the group.

Be that as it may, the Egyptian version was one of rejuvenation. The king was restored, by dogma if not in actuality, to full strength. In theory the first jubilee took place after the king had ruled for thirty years and was repeated at three-year intervals thereafter. There are innumerable exceptions to the rule, however, and it may be that special circumstances required emergency treatment. Amenhotep III celebrated three such jubilees, the last in his thirty-seventh year.

During these years Amenhotep produced an enormous number of portraits of himself—statues all over the place, not to mention reliefs in the temples. Some of the earliest show a baby-faced Amenhotep, with round cheeks, a pouting mouth, and large slanted eyes. This would be in keeping with his age when he assumed the throne, but the change actually begins with his father, Thutmose IV, whose tomb images show him with similar features. Portraits from late in the reign of Amenhotep include several that seem to be more realistic, showing him as paunchy and slumped, with a lined, tired face. A letter from the king of Hatti, saying that he is sending a divine statue to help his brother king back to health, supports the idea that toward the end of his reign Amenhotep was suffering from some form of illness, and some scholars point to the mummy which was identified as his as further proof. It has horribly abscessed teeth. I, and others, doubt that this is the body of Amenhotep, but that doesn't mean he was a healthy man. As we are constantly informed, indulgence and lack of exercise aren't good for people.

Unfortunately the neat progression of artistic depictions, from baby-faced to aged, may not be so neat after all. Not long ago an authority on Egyptian art, W. Raymond Johnson, concluded that many of the statues once believed to date from early in the reign of Amenhotep III were actually produced during that king's later years, after the first Heb-Sed. The change is deliberate, according to Johnson, indicating not only bodily rejuvenation but a change in the status of the king. He became a literal, living god, none other than the Aten himself, and the alteration of his features was accompanied by changes in his ornaments and attire, indicating his divine nature. Like most theories in Egyptology, this one is still being debated.

Like other kings of the Eighteenth and Nineteeth Dynasties, Amenhotep built himself a mortuary temple along the cultivation on the West Bank. Amenhotep's mortuary temple was the largest of the lot. So badly destroyed was it that in modern times nothing remained except a vast plain covered with weeds and prickly camel grass—and two of the most imposing monuments on the West Bank, the so-called Colossi of Memnon. These giant, badly battered statues marked the entrance to the temple. Recent excavations by a German team have uncovered buried remains of the structure itself, including some fine statues.

The man responsible for the erection of these gigantic statues is an interesting character in his own right. His name was Amenhotep, son of Hapu, and like that of another great official, Imhotep, it survived in men's memories for millennia, so that he became a demigod. His only titles were those of a scribe and he is shown in the traditional scribal position, seated, with his writing implements on his lap. But the king Amenhotep must have cherished him, for there are several such statues, carved by the king's order, and the scribe even had his own mortuary temple, a signal token of royal favor. He was eighty years old when he died, and how we wish we knew more about him!

Amenhotep the king broke with tradition by building his tomb in the West Valley of the Kings, not the main East Valley, where his ancestors rested. It was, of course, robbed in antiquity, but it was extensive and beautifully decorated. Some scholars believe that two separate sets of rooms were intended for the burials of the great royal wife Tiye and one of her daughters, Satamon, who also held the title of chief queen, which means that Amenhotep not only married his daughter but had two chief wives simultaneously.

Satamon is another of those elusive princesses. Nothing much is known about her. Maybe she died young. That would explain why she was never married to her brother, the heir, as was customary, but it doesn't explain why she married her father. Amenhotep may have married another of his daughters. Why? Theories abound, but they are only theories. If Satamon was buried in Amenhotep III's tomb she didn't stay there. Her present whereabouts, like those of many royal women of this period, are unknown. Her mother, Queen Tiye, is missing too. We will have more to say about her in the next chapter.

It may seem that we have given rather short shrift to a king who merited the appelation "Magnificent." Yet despite his accomplishments Amenhotep III is less well known (and, to me, less interesting) than his immediate successors. The great royal wife, Tiye, had presented her husband with several daughters and at least two sons. One of the sons, a prince named Thutmose, died before his father, which made his younger brother the heir. Tiye's second son came to the throne bearing one of the traditional names of his house, Amenhotep, which honored the great god of his city. He didn't keep it long. As Akhenaton, the name by which he is known to history, he initiated changes in religion, art, and society that make him the most controversial and intriguing of Egyptian kings; and his successor, under the irreverent journalistic nickname of "King Tut," is better known to the world at large than are any of the great rulers of ancient Egypt.

Eight

THE GREAT HERESY

Cartouche of Akhenaton

The Arabic name is "Biban el Moluk"—the Gates of the Kings. A narrow cleft deep in the western cliffs across the Nile from modern Luxor, it is one of the most desolate spots on earth. Nothing grows there—no tree, nor shrub, nor blade of grass. The sun beats down from an eternally cloudless sky whose brilliant blue is the only color contrast to the monotonous, unrelieved dark gold of rock and sand, hills and valley floor. Yet this wilderness merits its name, so redolent of magnificence. It is literally honeycombed with tombs which, over the millennia, contained some of the richest treasures ever deposited by men to the honor of their dead. From its barren stones Howard Carter and Lord Carnarvon drew the fabulous funerary equipment of Tutankhamon.

Tutankhamon is sometimes on tour, but the most valuable objects don't leave the Cairo Museum—for obvious reasons. Among the hundreds of objects from the tomb, my personal favorite is the canopic shrine with its four protective goddesses, which held the dead king's entrails. The four goddesses are distinguished only by the insignia on their heads; they stand with arms outstretched, embracing and guarding the precious contents of the shrine. They are fragile guardians; the small figures are childishly slender, and the delicate faces lack the awesome stamp of divinity. It has been suggested that the model for the figures was Tutankhamon's young queen. The theory is plausible; the four statues are so much alike that each of the faces might be a copy of the others, and a portrait of the same individual. The faces are charming, and so are the little bodies, which are those of young girls.

Tutankhamon's innermost coffin is three hundred pounds of solid gold. The portrait mask which covered the head of the mummy is also solid gold. There are bracelets and pectorals and rings, earrings, amulets, and collars, all of gold and precious stones. The Egyptians did not work with true gem stones. They did know and use what we call the semiprecious gems—turquoise, amethyst, carnelian, lapis lazuli, onyx, jasper, as well as glass, a comparatively recent invention—and they used them with consummate skill.

Any one of the objects from this single tomb would be the prize of an average museum collection, and there are thousands of such objects. Intrinsically, the contents of the tomb are worth millions of dollars; as examples of the cultural and artistic life of a bygone era, they are literally beyond price. Yet the tomb of Tutankhamon was a disappointment in one sense.

Tutankhamon himself was a minor king who died at eighteen after an uneventful reign of only nine years. Nevertheless, when the discovery of the tomb was first announced, there were hopes that it would contain historical material that would shed light on one of the most intriguing figures the ancient world has ever produced—Tutankhamon's predecessor and father-in-law, the "heretic king," Akhenaton.

If one were to collect the statues of Egyptian kings from earliest to latest times, and arrange them in chronological sequence, one might, at first glance, take them for portraits of the same individual. The artistic canon permitted few deviations, and its rules applied most rigorously to the depiction of the divine king. There are, to be sure, certain stylistic variations from period to period, and it is even possible to distinguish family types. Still, the long row of male figures would be superficially alike: stern, handsome faces and stalwart, muscular bodies, broad of shoulder and slim of hip, with seldom a hint of sagging paunch or double chin. All, that is, except one; and it would stand out from the rest with almost shocking singularity. The long, haggard face, with deep-set eyes and hollow cheeks, the strangely deformed, almost feminine body—this is Akhenaton, whom James Henry Breasted called "the first individual in history" and credited with being the founder of the world's first monotheistic religion. Breasted has been accused of overenthusiasm; some scholars loathe Akhenaton as much as Breasted admired him. Whatever one's bias, it cannot be denied that Akhenaton was a personality, unique and fantastic.

I am planning to spend what may seem to some an inordinate amount of time on this period, for several reasons. First and most important, it interests me. Second, it interests a lot of other people, and volumes have been written on the subject. Third, it shows to what lengths scholars will go to prove a pet theory. One might claim about this period that never has so much been said by so many about so little. In fact we do have more evidence than is often the case, but much of it is fragmented and susceptible, as you will see, to dozens of different interpretations. Here's a brief summary of some of the "facts." Those of you who are familiar with Akhenaton and his lot may regard it as a preliminary test—but remember, there are no right answers.

1. Akhenaton was the son of Amenhotep III and his chief wife, Tiye
2. He ruled for a minimum of seventeen years, either
   a. Alone, *or*
   b. As coregent with his father for one to three years, *or*
   c. As coregent with his father for about twelve years.
3. His chief wife was Nefertiti, who was:
   a. The daughter of a high official named Ay, *or*
   b. Somebody else's daughter.
4. They had six daughters.
5. At the end of his reign Akhenaton was associated with a king named Ankhkheperure, who was:
   a. A young man of unknown antecedents also named Smenkhkare, *or*
   b. Nefertiti
6. He was also associated with a king named Neferneferuaton who was:
   a. The same person as 5a, *or*
   b. Nefertiti
7. They were succeeded by a boy named Tutankhaton, who was:
   a. The son of Akhenaton by:
      (1) A secondary wife named Kiya, *or*
      (2) some other as yet unidentified wife, *or*
      (3) Nefertiti, *or*
   b. The son of Amenhotep III by
      (1) Queen Tiye, *or*
      (2) His daughter Satamon, *or*
      (3) Caught you! Not Nefertiti. Somebody else.

There are a few actual facts in all that mishmash. Akhenaton was the son of Amenhotep III and the latter's chief wife, Tiye. When he became king he took the same nomen as his father—"Amon is satisfied." The early years of his reign appear to have been fairly conventional. Then, at some time before his fifth year, something happened.

The crux of the change was a new god. To honor him, the king changed his name from Amenhotep to Akhenaton, which means "it is well with the Aton." To further particularize the change of allegiance, Akhenaton moved his capital. Thebes was the home of Amon; the Aton should have a city upon soil that had never been dedicated to another god. The court moved, bag and baggage, to a site three hundred miles north of Thebes. Its modern name is Tell el Amarna, and the term "Amarna" is used to characterize Akhenaton's revolutionary ideas in religion, art, and thought. On this site, where the cliffs along the Nile curve back to form a wide bay of land, Akhenaton built a new city called Akhetaton, "The Horizon of Aton." He set up formal boundary markers dedicating the spot to Aton forever, vowing never to change its borders, and declaring that he and his family would be buried in the cliffs behind the city.

This was radical enough, but Akhenaton went still further. He abandoned the worship of the old gods of Egypt—that proliferous pantheon whose complexities must have baffled the ancient Egyptians themselves. In particular, he abominated the greatest of gods, Amon-Re. His agents were sent throughout the land, to temples and tombs and monuments, to cut the hated name from the rock walls even when it appeared in the name of his own father, Amenhotep. The other gods were not spared, and in some cases even the plural word *gods* was scratched out.

Who was this Aton, for whom a king of Egypt committed such monumental offenses against tradition? It is not precisely accurate to call him a "new" god; he had been around for a while. In the previous chapter we gave a brief account of his origins and increasing prominence, but his sudden leap to divine stardom under Akhenaton was without precedent.

The earliest representations of Aton show him as a hawk-headed human figure. This was in keeping with a conventional Egyptian treatment of the gods in art—the animal or bird head on the human body. The hawk was one of the symbols of the sun god, and Aton was originally the sun itself. Akhenaton soon abandoned this tradition too. He showed Aton as a solar disk with rays that end in tiny human hands holding an ankh, the hieroglyphic sign for "life"—the looped cross, or crux ansata—to the nostrils of the members of the royal family. Not all the god's human characteristics were abandoned. He had the titles and cartouches of a king and wore, even as a simple sun disc, the royal uraeus serpent; his jubilee or Heb-Sed was celebrated with that of Akhenaton himself.

Just what was it then that Akhenaton worshiped? The theories vary. By now my own prejudices should be apparent to the intelligent reader. Breasted's *History* was my first introduction to ancient Egypt. It left a permanent impression. Try as I may to become dispassionate and cynical about Akhenaton, I don't always succeed. My own, admittedly subjective, feeling is that it was the spirit of animation and creation implicit in the heat- and light-producing sun that was the object of Akhenaton's adoration. That this spirit implied more than physical well-being is suggested by the king's insistence upon *maat*.

We can translate *maat* as "truth." Abstractions are hard to translate,

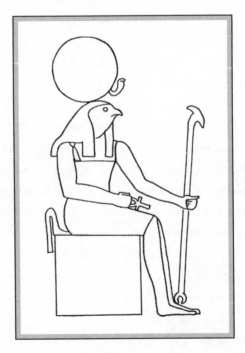

The god Aton in original form

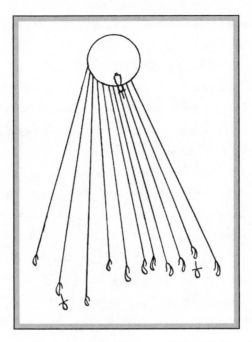

Aton as a sun disk, with rays ending in hands

and the English word *truth* means many things to many people. In Egyptian, *maat* certainly could mean something like our concept of "justice"; the word was personified by a goddess who stood at the side of Osiris at the time of the judging of the soul. The hieroglyph for *maat* is the feather, which was weighed against the heart of the dead man. But *maat* went beyond justice; it has been defined as the universal order, the divine system of correctness—the right way to do things, established at the creation and constantly renewed by religious ritual. Akhenaton's insistence upon his love of *maat* is too striking to be accidental, but there has been much discussion as to just what he meant by it. Some scholars interpreted *maat* as "candor," particularly when it applied to the new art forms of the period, which Akhenaton encouraged.

We have already mentioned the features of this art form in royal portraiture, where its innovations are most noticeable. Akhenaton swept away the old canon of artistic taste; it was, perhaps, inevitable that the original freedom of expression which he may have meant to promote developed into a new canon, with its own set of rules. The strange bodily malformations of the king were copied in the portraits of his wife and children and, to a lesser degree, in those of the courtiers—the elongated skull and slender throat, the narrow, sloping shoulders and heavy hips. There are stages of development in Amarna art, signs of a growing maturity and skill even in the brief years of its efflorescence. The most exaggerated art forms have been described as caricatures, and so they are, if we understand that the deliberate exaggeration of a caricature is not always intended to be insulting or comic. These exaggerated features appear at the beginning of Akhenaton's reign, even before he left Thebes. But when German archaeologists excavated at Tell el Amarna before the First World War, they found the ruins of the studio of a sculptor named Thutmose which contained some portrait heads of fantastic beauty—Amarna art at its latest, and highest, point of achievement. The most famous of these heads, the lovely painted bust of Nefertiti, is world-famous—an idealization of exotic feminine beauty and queenly pride.

It is hard to describe Amarna art objectively. Scholars speak of the increased sense of motion, and of the greater use of curved lines, but none of these criteria explains why the Amarna portraits catch at the imagination as they do. There is certainly a heightened sense of the individual; Khafre is a divinity, and Senusert III is a man of heavy responsibility, but Nefertiti is Nefertiti, and we feel that we would recognize her anywhere and anytime.

The subject matter of sculpture and relief becomes more candid and more natural. Intimate family relations are shown with freedom and charm. The king's devotion to his beautiful wife is a favorite theme. He is shown with his arm around her, kissing her, holding her on his lap. To appreciate how daring this choice of subject really was, one must study the long series of stiff, formal representations of earlier kings and queens.

Akhenaton's six little daughters were, one suspects, badly spoiled by their doting parents. They accompanied the king and queen on drives and excursions, sat on their laps and ate from their tables at banquets. In one scene a small princess is shown slyly tickling the flanks of the horses her father is driving. The picture is one of family affection and peace which strikes the viewer with pleasure in spite of the exaggerated artistic techniques.

Innovations in art, religion, and language—for it is at this time that the dialect known as Late Egyptian is first used in official texts—all these and other changes add up to a genuinely revolutionary spirit. But was the worship of Aton true monotheism, as Breasted believed?

Some scholars prefer to call Atonism "henotheism"—the worship of one god without denying the existence of others. They point out that Akhenaton never relinquished the traditional claim of the Egyptian king to divinity; that his followers worshiped not Aton, but Akhenaton. They say also that Aton's titulary included the names of other gods—all sun-gods, to be sure, but separate gods nonetheless. And to crown their argument, they maintain that Akhenaton's savage attack upon the name of Aton's archenemy, Amon-Re, was in itself a tacit admission of Amon's reality. One does not fight an enemy who does not exist.

Religious dogma is a labyrinth of subtleties, even to the initiate, and it is certainly dangerous to try to impose modern concepts upon an ancient people. But some modern parallels may be illuminating. Akhenaton called himself the son of Aton, and claimed to be the only one who really knew his god; he may have been the first, but he was certainly not the last prophet to make these claims. The Aton titulary does equate the god with Shu and Re and Atum, all solar gods; but this, to Akhenaton, may have had no more effect upon Aton's uniqueness than the concept of the Trinity has upon the monotheism of Christianity. As for the last argument, Akhenaton's attack on the old gods, this too has historic parallels. When Cortez flung the Aztec idols down from before their bloody altars, he was trying to destroy their supremacy in the hearts of their followers, not admitting their reality to him. Proscription of the old gods is a standard practice for prophets of a new faith, monotheistic or not; monotheism is by its very nature intolerant. Polytheistic religions are usually able and willing to identify gods of other regions with their own, or to add a few new ones. The Romans did not throw the Christians to the lions because they were heretics, but because they refused to acknowledge the divinity of the emperor. Hence Akhenaton's persecution of the gods of Egypt can, I believe, be taken as an argument for the monotheistic character of his faith, rather than the reverse.

The terms don't really matter all that much. What matters is that Akhenaton worshipped one god and one god only, in all his manifestations. The particular bitterness of his attack upon Amon may have been influenced by fear of the threat posed by the wealth and power of the Amon priesthood, but the great Aton hymn, which expresses Akhenaton's devotion, does not sound like the work of a politician who cloaks pragmatic deeds in eloquent but empty words. Breasted believed it was composed by the king himself. Whether Akhenaton actually sat down with pen and papyrus in hand (though I love the image of him chewing on the end of his reed pen while he tries to find the right word) is irrelevant. The so-called hymn wouldn't have been inscribed in various courtiers' tombs if it had not been official dogma.

Its striking parallels with the 104th Psalm were first pointed out by Breasted:

Aton Hymn

When thou settest in the western horizon of heaven The world is in darkness like the dead. . . . Every lion cometh forth from his den, The serpents they sting. Darkness reigns. . . . Bright is the earth when thou risest in the horizon. . . . The two lands are in daily festival, Awake and standing upon their feet. . . . Then in all the world they do their work. How manifold are all thy works! They are hidden from before us. Oh thou sole god, whose powers no other possesseth. Thou didst create the earth according to thy desire, being alone: Men, all cattle, large and small; All that are upon the earth.

PSALM 104

Thou makest darkness, and it is night: wherein all the beasts of
the forest do creep forth. The young lions roar after their prey,
and seek their meat from God. . . . The sun ariseth, they gather
themselves together, and lay them down in their dens. Man goeth
forth unto his work and to his labour until the evening. . . . Oh
Lord, how manifold are thy works! in wisdom hast thou made
them all; the earth is full of thy riches.

These similarities do not mean that there is a direct connection between Atonism and Hebrew monotheism, or that Moses learned about
God at the court of Amarna. Rather, the Aton hymn and the psalm represent two examples of a literary tradition that flourished throughout the
Near East over a vast span of time. Certain of the concepts, and even
certain of the phrases, of the Amarna hymn occur in earlier Eighteenth-
Dynasty Egyptian hymns and persist after the heresy of Akhenaton had
disappeared from Egypt. Still, it is interesting to see, in so familiar a
volume as the Bible, echoes of the beliefs of an Egyptian pharaoh of the
second millennium before Christ.

These beliefs, as we know them, were beautiful and kindly—the love
of the creator of all things for his creatures, and their jubilant adoration
of him. All creatures, even the humblest, hail the god's rising:

All cattle rest upon their herbage, all trees and plants flourish;
The birds flutter in their marshes, their wings uplifted in
adoration to thee. All the sheep prance upon their feet, all
winged things fly; they live when thou hast shone upon them.

Aton is the god of Syria and of Nubia also:

Their tongues are diverse in speech, and their forms and their
skins likewise; for thou, Divider, hast divided the peoples.

A spirit of joyousness and of sunlit, open space and an appreciation of the manifold beauties of nature breathe in the liturgy of the Aton faith and are found in other elements of the worship. No longer was the god adored, as was Amon, within a windowless, darkened shrine. The temples of the Aton were illumined by the rays of the god himself, their great altars being set in open courts. According to the tomb reliefs, which often show this scene, the offerings Aton loves to receive are those of fruit and flowers rather than bloody sacrifices.

In its prime, the city of Akhetaton must have been a fitting capital for a pristine new god. The handsome villas of the nobles were surrounded by gardens filled with pools and with flowers, surrounded by high walls for privacy. The workmen's houses were small and monotonously alike, but they compare favorably with some of the twentieth-century fellahins' dwellings. The king himself built several palaces. Like most Egyptian domestic dwellings they have almost disappeared—the tombs were the Houses of Eternity, but a house was only designed for one lifetime. But the palaces were handsome structures, filled with luxurious furniture and ornaments. From the objects found in Tutankhamon's tomb, some of which were doubtless made in Akhetaton, we know that domestic furnishings were designed with an eye to beauty as well as utility.

Akhenaton's palaces had lovely painted floors and walls with scenes of animals, flowering plants, and gracefully flying birds. Here he lived in peace with his exquisite wife and his six little daughters. In the great temple enclosure he worshiped Aton at the appointed hours; and in the cliffs behind the city he prepared his tomb. This tomb, together with those of his chief courtiers, has been excavated. All had been robbed and defaced in antiquity. But from the scenes carved and painted upon the chamber walls, archaeologists have learned much about Akhenaton and his times; perhaps the most valuable inscription is the copy of the great Aton hymn. And from the walls of the royal tomb we learn that the king's life had its tragedies. The first person to occupy the rock-cut sepulcher was not Akhenaton, but his small daughter, the princess Meketaton. The scenes of her funeral covered the walls of one chamber, and the grief of the royal parents is poignantly portrayed.

The loss of his daughter was a shattering blow, but it was only the first of Akhenaton's troubles. It is safe to assume that the displaced priests of the old gods had not taken their demotion lightly. And outside Egypt other clouds were gathering. We know of these foreign problems in some detail, thanks to an archaeological discovery that far surpassed the tomb of Tutankhamon in historical value, though it was composed of no more precious material than common clay.

In 1887, peasants tilling their fields near Tell el Amarna turned up some curious objects—broken squares of dried clay that could hardly be distinguished from the brown earth that hid them. An ordinary cultivator would have thrown them away, but the Egyptian fellah had become sophisticated. He knew that the black soil of Egypt yielded riches other than crops, and that even the most unlikely-looking object might have value. The peasants scraped off the disfiguring earth and found that the bricks were covered with strange scratches, too regular to be accidental.

Eventually the objects found their way to Cairo. They created little stir at first; unprepossessing in appearance and humble in material, they did not attract tourist or scholar. Many of the bricks were broken to begin with, and others were deliberately smashed in order to increase the find in numbers if in nothing else. But finally they came to the attention of specialists, and the queer scratches were recognized as cuneiform writing. Cuneiform, pressed into damp clay tablets by wedge-shaped styluses, was the script of ancient Babylonia; during the fourteenth century B.C. Babylonian was the language of international diplomatic communication, much as French was in the nineteenth century. The ruins of Akhetaton and the antique shops were combed, and some three hundred of the baked clay tablets were found. (Others turned up later.) They are the ancient equivalent of the Foreign Office or State Department archives of our day, covering the reigns of Akhenaton and his father, and including letters from foreign monarchs as well as reports and dispatches from

Egyptian emissaries abroad. They give a vivid picture of the international situation in 1350 B.C.; and the picture is not a bright one for Egypt.

Two of the great powers of this age that are mentioned in the diplomatic correspondence with Egypt were Hatti—the kingdom of the Hittites—and Mitanni, or Naharin. Both kingdoms lay north of the narrow coastal plain of Syria-Palestine, Mitanni on the Upper Euphrates and Hatti in Anatolia. Egyptian-Mitannian relations had changed since Thutmose III crossed the Euphrates with his army. Mitanni was now on friendly terms with the Two Lands, and several Egyptian kings, including Akhenaton, had married daughters of the royal house of that nation. But the Hittites were a horse of a different color.

Like Sumer, Mitanni, and the ancient Indian civilization represented by Harappa and Mohenjo Daro, the Hittite kingdom had vanished from human memory until it was resurrected by archaeologists. The fate of such cultures, once brilliant and flourishing and powerful, may be regarded as an object lesson in the brevity of human vanity. Archaeologists also view them as banners, bearing the word *Excelsior!* If the last one hundred years have brought such discoveries into the light of day, what buried civilizations may yet lie hidden beneath the soil of the several continents?

The existence of the Hittites did not come as a complete surprise to scholars, for there were hints in the Bible and in other sources that such a people had once lived in the Near East; but it was not until after 1906, when the excavation of the Hittite capital at Boghazkoi in Anatolia began, that the full splendor of Hittite culture was really appreciated. The most astounding result of the excavations arose out of the study of the Hittite language; to the surprise of practically everybody, it turned out to be an Indo-European tongue related to Latin and the Germanic languages. To speak of the speech of Boghazkoi as one language is an oversimplification, for there were half a dozen different languages and two scripts—cuneiform and the strange Hittite hieroglyphs. It seems, to put it in simple terms, that Anatolia was, before the second millennium B.C., invaded by a group of warriors who spoke an Indo-European tongue, and who conquered the indigenous, non-Indo-European speakers who lived in the area.

The grammatical awkwardness in the preceding sentence is intentional; "Indo-European" does not apply to peoples, only to the language they spoke, and I want to avoid even the faintest hint of Aryans or other racial wonders. The origins and early history of Hittite civilization are outside the subject of this book; what concerns us is its relationship with Egypt.

By the period we are considering, the Hittites were in good shape. The credit for their flourishing condition, internal and external, seems to belong to one man—Shubilulliuma, the king. The possessor of this mellifluous name must have been a dynamic personality, but we know him only from his deeds, which were admittedly considerable.

Syria-Palestine has long been a focus of strife, no less so in Akhenaton's day than in our own. During the first part of the Eighteenth Dynasty the area consisted of a number of city-states, each with its own local ruler—and all under the control of one of the great powers, Mitanni or Egypt. The Egyptian empire, so called, was always loosely held. Egyptian representatives in the larger centers watched over the pharaoh's interests and kept him informed of events, but there were no large garrisons of Egyptian troops. In spite of the military exploits of Thutmose III and his successors, the small city-states in the area never completely abandoned their dreams of independence. There were frequent "rebellions," as the scandalized Egyptians called them, particularly at the death of a pharaoh, when the internal confusion incumbent upon the accession of a young and inexperienced ruler might have kept Egyptian forces at home. But the great conquerors such as Thutmose I and III had been energetic men, conscious of empire. The rebellions were promptly subdued and were followed by frequent tours of inspection and saber rattling. By the time of Amenhotep III, the Egyptian provinces in Syria had settled down to enjoy the prosperity of the Pax Aegyptiaca. Or so it seemed.

From his perch high in the hills of Asia Minor, Shubilulliuma looked south, and plotted. There is little doubt that the Hittite king's machinations began while Amenhotep III was still alive. Shubilulliuma did not risk direct military attack on Egypt. First he got rid of Mitanni, which left the Mittanian sphere of influence in Syria up for grabs. There was no objection from Egypt, no aid for their former ally. So Shubilulliuma wove his web, casting the strands into the city-states tributary to Egypt even while he was writing flattering letters, couched in the polished terms of diplomatic usage, to his unwitting "brother" of Egypt.

Shubilulliuma soon found the tools he wanted. The most valuable was Abdu-Ashirta, prince of the small state of Amurru on the upper Orontes. One need not be overly cynical to assume that Abdu-Ashirta had his own ideas about who was going to be top dog in Amurru; power politics hasn't changed much. After his death his son Aziru took over the rule of Amurru as a vassal of Egypt; he also inherited the job of cat's-paw for Shubilulliuma. Like his father, Aziru wrote fulsome letters to Akhenaton protesting his loyalty and describing his valiant battles against traitors in other cities.

Aziru's first moves against these "traitors"—the loyal coastal cities of north Syria—were successful and unopposed. Yet even the cities which had not felt the weight of the Amorite prince's hand were under no illusions as to his intentions. The elders of the wealthy city of Tunip sent to pharaoh a plea for help, written with the eloquence of fear and despair:

> Who formerly could have plundered Tunip without being plundered by Thutmose III? When Aziru enters Simyra, Aziru will do to us as he pleases, in the territory of our lord the king; and on account of these things our lord will have to lament. And now Tunip, thy city, weeps, and her tears are flowing, and there is no help for us. For twenty years we have been sending to our lord the king, the king of Egypt; but there has not come to us a word—no, not one!

For twenty years. The trouble had begun under Amenhotep III, but at first Akhenaton took no steps to repair his father's errors. Simyra fell, as the elders of Tunip had feared; the city of Sidon, seeing no help forthcoming from Egypt, made terms with Aziru and assisted him in attacking Tyre. Before long all the coastal cities loyal to Egypt had fallen except Byblos.

By this time the prince of Byblos, an elderly nobleman named Rib-addi, was badly worried. He had been writing to his lord, Akhenaton, for some time concerning the doings of Aziru, and he knew that Byblos would be next. After the fall of Simyra his letters become absolutely im-passioned, and one cannot but marvel at the old gentleman's tenacity, loyalty, and stubborn courage—and his epistolatory exploits. There are more letters from him than from any other correspondent.

However, Aziru seems to have had a friend at the Egyptian court, and this man, in the useful position of chief steward, may have managed to conceal the truth of what was going on in Syria. Aziru himself was no mean persuader; he even convinced the Egyptian army officer stationed in Galilee that Ribaddi was a traitor, and talked him into sending Egyptian mercenaries to attack Byblos. After this unprovoked stab in the back, the city quite understandably rose in revolt against Egypt and ousted Rib-addi, delivering his scepter and his family into the hands of his bitter foe, Aziru. The valiant Ribaddi actually succeeded in regaining Byblos, but his situation was hopeless. Aziru still flourished, as the wicked proverbi-ally do, in spite of being summoned to Egypt to explain himself to a be-latedly suspicious king; the ships of Ribaddi's enemies blockaded Byblos and cut off his supplies; even the old man's wife urged him to forsake the broken reed of Egypt and submit to Aziru. Still he held out, asking for only three hundred men to help him hold the city. To this letter, as to the others, there was no reply. Byblos fell, and Ribaddi became a fugitive.

In the south the situation was equally desperate, although the attack-ers were different—fierce desert raiders called the Habiru.

These people have interested historians because of the etymological similarity between their name and that of the Hebrews. That's probably all it is, an etymological similarity; the Habiru were not a civilized peo-ple, as Egypt and Hatti were civilized, but they were ferocious fighters, and the fortresses of Palestine, weakened by years of neglect under Amen-hotep III, fell to them like wheat under the sickle. And again there was no help from Akhenaton!

"If no troops come in this year," wrote Abdu-Heba, Egyptian deputy in Jerusalem, "the whole territory of my lord the king will perish. If there are no troops in this year, let the king send his officer to fetch me and my brothers, that we may die with my lord the king."

We do not know whether Abdu-Heba gained the safety of Egypt or died in the ruins of his city; but Jerusalem fell, and Megiddo fell, and the southern half of Egypt's Asiatic empire collapsed, as the northern half had done under the hammering of Aziru.

The historian cannot help but ask, at this point: What sort of man was Akhenaton, that he could see his empire crumbling into sand without lifting a finger to save it? If he was the idealist and pacifist that some Egyptologists believed him to have been, how could he watch unmoved the slaughter of his subjects and the betrayal of those faithful to him?

The once-accepted answer, that Akhenaton was a dreamy pacifist more concerned with his god than his country, was always too simplistic. The true facts about the warfare in Syria may never have reached him. The workings of a complex bureaucracy such as Akhenaton's Bureau of Foreign Affairs are in themselves an excellent screen for truth, and there seem to have been traitors in the home office itself. I find it hard to accept the theory of a "let's wait and see" attitude on the part of Akhenaton and his father; after a certain point one or the other ought to have seen enough. Perhaps Akhenaton did. Some of the letters speak of Egyptian troops being sent to certain cities, but there is no actual evidence that Akhenaton himself went to war. Since most of the letters can be dated only by internal evidence, there is still disagreement as to who was doing what to whom, and when.

Here's where we get to the cursed coregency question, as I am sometimes inclined to call it. It's one of the liveliest debates among scholars of this period. Some of them believe that Akhenaton was made coruler with his father somewhere around the latter's year twenty-five. Thus all the revolutionary activities I have described took place while Amenhotep III was still on the throne, honoring the same Amon-Re whom his son was attacking, preparing his conventional tomb in the Valley of the Kings, and continuing the conventional activities of an Egyptian ruler. The evidence for and against this belief are too complicated to go into here, and definitive proof is still lacking. One of the points made by the long coregency school is that in his twelfth year Akhenaton's mother, Queen Tiye, paid a visit of state to Tell el Amarna. Was the death of her husband the occasion for this visit? Did she live thereafter at Amarna? Did she drop a few words of wisdom into the ears of her son, warning him that trouble was brewing? They are reasonable questions, but we don't know the answers.

At about this time or shortly thereafter Nefertiti disappears from the scene. Her name means, appropriately, "the beautiful woman has come." In the early days of their marriage Akhenaton spared no pains to show his love for her. Although she was probably a commoner like her mother-in-law, Tiye, her husband composed a royal titulary for her and gave her the additional name Neferneferuaton, "beautiful are the beauties of Aton." Her titles are phrases of endearment and tenderness: "fair of hands, lady of grace, she at whose voice the king rejoices."

As my little chart indicated, her exact antecendents are uncertain. She was not a king's daughter. One popular theory makes her the daughter of Ay, one of Akhenaton's councilors. Like Yuya before him, he was called "Father of the God"; but this title was held by officials who were not the king's father-in-law, and it has always seemed to me that this is a rather indirect way of describing such a relationship. His wife, another Tiye, has the title of wet nurse to the queen, which makes it unlikely that Nefertiti was Tiye's child. The child of a first wife, raised by the second? Maybe so, though in that case "wet nurse" is surely not to be taken literally. (Figure it out; wives one and two giving birth at approximately the same time, and wife number two passing her own infant on to some other female?) In fact, the position of royal wet nurse was probably honorific, and a high honor it was. Tutankhamon's nurse had a very nice tomb of her own, and so did Hatshepsut's.

Nefertiti shared her husband's beliefs and worshiped Aton at his side. The reliefs of the Aton temple at Thebes show her prominence in the cult. These reliefs come from very early in the reign, and Nefertiti appears without her husband in many of them, worshipping on her own account. What happened, then, to explain Nefertiti's disappearance from the records? Did she die, or did she fall from grace? The so-called evidence is found at Amarna, where, in certain places, Nefertiti's name and titles were cut out and replaced by those of a king named Smenkhkare and his wife Meritaton, who was the eldest of Akhenaton's daughter. Akhenaton showered attentions on his young coregent, giving him the name which had been Nefertiti's—Neferneferuaton.

Or did he? Sometimes I really become irritated with Egyptologists. The narrative I have repeated was a perfectly reasonable, interesting interpretation, accepted by the majority of scholars. In recent years it's been challenged, not by one alternative theory but by several. The most provocative is that there never was a male king named Smenkhkare. Neferneferuaton was always Nefertiti, who became coregent with her husband and, in an infuriating fashion, kept changing her names: Ankhkheperure, Smenkhkare. Her disappearance from the scene was not caused by death or a fall from favor, but by her transformation from queen to king and coruler.

That there was a female king named Ankhkheperure seems indicated by a few examples of the name with a female ending—Ankhetkheperure. An alternative theory (you might have known there would be an alternative theory) agrees that Nefertiti did rule alongside her husband for a while, but that she was succeeded by the male king Smenkhkare. Another one (you might have known there would be another one) claims that Ankhetkheperure was Meritaton, who reigned briefly after the death of her husband.

I may as well give you my opinion, since, at the rate of sounding conceited, it is as good as that of most other people. I am willing to concede the possible existence of a female pharaoh, but I won't give up Mr. Smenkhkare.

In 1907 Theodore Davis, a wealthy American archaeological amateur, came upon a burial in the Valley of the Kings. Within a small unadorned chamber in the rock was a mummiform coffin and a scanty, hastily assembled collection of funerary objects. The coffin was in sad condition; moisture within the chamber had rotted the wooden bier which had supported it, and its fall, as well as the damp, had greatly damaged the mummy, which seems to have been wrapped in grave clothes rather than bandaged in the conventional fashion. Thieves had ripped the gold mask from the face of the coffin, and the name of the dead person had been cut away from the coffin and from the golden bands that wrapped the body.

The battered coffin wasn't the only object in the chamber. A set of canopic jars with beautiful portrait heads, and the pieces of a gilded shrine inscribed with the name and image of Queen Tiye, convinced Davis that he had found the body of the great queen. In his haste to examine it he completed the destruction that had been begun by water and ancient vandalism; the mummy was reduced to bones, and by the time Davis got through there wasn't much left of the shrine either.

Davis's publication, defiantly entitled *The Tomb of Queen Tiyi*, maintains his belief, but from the first Egyptologists doubted the identification. Who but Akhenaton himself, they asked themselves, would be so persecuted even in death that his name would be obliterated and his body hastily hidden in a grave that even a courtier would have considered inadequate? So word spread, among interested Egyptologists, that the mummy of the heretic king had been found.

Sober consideration, and a good deal of careful scholarly work, cast doubt upon both identifications. Physical anthropologists performed their detective work on the bones and pronounced them to be those of a young man, younger than Akhenaton must have been at his death. Smenkhkare, the first of Akhenaton's sons-in-law, fits the age requirements, and for many years this burial was believed to be his.

Recently the whole question of the mummy and the burial arose again, and it may be worthwhile to treat the arguments in some detail, since they illustrate the specialized knowledge and the close attention to minutiae that modern archaeology requires. (They also demonstrates how archaeologists, like other individuals, get stuck on their own theories.)

The inscriptions on the coffin, which are the obvious means of identifying the mummy, are unhappily defaced. They consist of two main
sections: a prayer on the footboard, and a series of titles on bands that
run down and around the coffin. They are the titles of a king, but in all
cases the name has been completely cut away. Certain epithets remain,
and they are epithets associated with Akhenaton: "living in truth, the
beautiful child of the living Aton," and so on. Originally the names in
the missing cartouches must have been his, but they could have stood as
genitives after another name, as for example: "The king's daughter, Meritaton, daughter of Akhenaton, living in truth," etc.

Most authorities agree that the coffin was first made for a woman.
Later it was altered in order to serve for the burial of a man; the original,
presumably female, names have been eliminated. But which man? One
would suppose that definitive evidence could be found in the bones themselves. The detective talents of physical anthropologists, some of whom
have worked with the police forces of various countries, are well known.
It is now possible to tell sex, age, medical history, and other facts from
a skeleton. Archaeology calls upon the talents of many specialists; why,
then, does not a physician or anthropologist examine these bones and
resolve the problem?

Such examinations have been carried out. But the first of them was
performed fifty years ago, when techniques were less advanced, and the
experts, as often happens, did not agree on all points. They did agree on
two basic matters: the bones are those of a man; he was not more than
twenty-eight years of age at the time of his death.

This would seem to eliminate Akhenaton, who had fathered at least
one child before he mounted the throne, and who ruled for seventeen
years. But here we have another example of how preconceptions (dare we
call them prejudices?) corrupt scholarly conclusions. Judging from his
statues, Akhenaton may have suffered from some sort of disease. The archaeologists who wanted these bones to be his asked: Could the king
have been the victim of an ailment that would alter the parts of the bone
structure that determine age?

One of the major criteria used in aging bones (determining the age of their owner, that is) is the evidence of epiphyseal union. The chief center of bone formation in the shaft of a bone is called the diaphysis. The epiphyses are secondary bone masses at the head of the shaft, connected with the diaphysis by intermediate links of cartilage. Bone is a dynamic and active tissue throughout life. It slows down once the individual reaches adulthood, but it's always adapting to demands made on it by the body. However, as a person develops from fetus to adult, changes in his/her stature take place principally by means of growth in the connecting cartilage, which eventually ossifies, thus binding together diaphysis and epiphyses.

The pieces of cartilage connecting diaphysis and epiphyses are clearly visible in a young bone. They fuse completely at various ages until the last, the medial clavicle, completes its union at approximately the age of twenty-eight. Thus an expert can tell, from the degree of fusion, approximately how old the individual was at the time of his death. Epiphyseal union is only one of the criteria used in determining age, but it is an important criterion.

Now for the rub. There is a form of pituitary malfunction known as Froelich's syndrome which can delay the union of the epiphyses. It would be possible for a man suffering from this disease to have, at the age of forty, bones which are in the state normally found in a twenty-three-year-old. What fascinated Egyptologists is the fact that a sufferer from Froelich's syndrome might also have certain of the physical deformities which are seen in the statues of Akhenaton—heavy thighs and thin calves, overdeveloped breasts and abdomen. The pituitary lesion affects the secretion of the sexual glands, producing feminine characteristics in a male.

A neat case, surely. There is only one difficulty. The victim of Froelich's syndrome is necessarily, totally, and unequivocally sterile.

What then do we do with Akhenaton's six daughters?

Some Egyptologists were quite willing to sweep the girls away rather than revise their theory that the miserably buried skeleton was Akhenaton's. We can take it for granted that the children were born of Nefertiti, as the inscriptions specifically state; even the Egyptians could hardly have been mistaken about that. We might deliver ourselves from the manufactured dilemma by blackening Nefertiti's reputation; this would not be chivalrous, but then chivalry cannot stand in the way of scholarship. However, the aspersion is not only unkind, it is ridiculous. Who was Akhenaton trying to fool? Or was Nefertiti trying to fool him? If the king had to hire a substitute to father his daughters, the gentleman overdid it, rather. If I had not been trained to be polite to those who are my elders (admittedly, there aren't many of those left) and betters in the field of Egyptology, I would say that this is one of the sillier theories to come out of a field which, unfortunately, is not devoid of silly theories.

I hope I may be excused for crowing just a little—since I seldom get that opportunity—because the most reliable medical investigations of the remains substantiate the belief I have always held: that they are indeed those of Smenkhkare. In 1963 a thorough anatomical investigation was carried out by R. G. Harrison, of the University of Liverpool. He concluded that the bones were those of a man who was less than twenty-five years old at the time of his death, with twenty years being the probable age. There was no sign of gross abnormality or of a pathological condition remotely related to Froelich's syndrome. Harrison stated that the individual might have had an "ectomorphic constitution"—in other words, that he was slightly built—but that he was definitely a normal male. An even more recent examination, by Joyce Filer of the British Museum, supports Harrison's conclusions.

This should have settled the matter, but the "those bones gotta be Akhenaton's" crowd hasn't given up. Every now and then they find a physical anthropologist who asserts that the skeleton is that of an older man. Then another expert comes along and says no, it isn't. The fact is that the great majority of the best qualified authorities have agreed on the younger age, and their arguments are incontrovertible. I've seen the skull (I get these little treats because I am very, very nice to my Egyptological friends), and although I am the last person in the world to talk authoritatively about bones, even a casual look at the teeth confirms Harrison's conclusions. They are good, healthy teeth, with few signs of wear, and one of the third molars (wisdom teeth) has not yet erupted.

The skeleton can't be Akhenaton. I stick to that. We can't prove yet that the remains are those of Smenkhkare, but the circumstantial evidence certainly points to him. No other royal prince of the Amarna house is known. Blood groupings and the unusual shapes of this skull and that of Tutankhamon suggest a close relationship between the two men—full brothers, or father and son. Smenkhkare seems to have died after a reign so short that there may not have been time to prepare his full funerary regalia, hence the necessity of remaking a coffin and a set of canopic jars intended for someone else. The funerary equipment in Tomb 55 is a motley enough collection; it implies a hasty, perhaps secret, burial. And yet there is a contradiction here; some of Smenkhkare's burial furniture was taken over by Tutankhamon, including the latter's second coffin. If Smenkhkare had all that good stuff (the second coffin isn't solid gold, but it is absolutely beautiful), why wasn't he allowed to use it? It wasn't very nice of Tutankhamon to steal his presumed brother's grave goods. Of course he may not have had anything to say about it, being dead when the final arrangements were made.

This brings us to the interesting question: Who precisely was this boy, the most widely known king of ancient Egypt, whose treasures still draw overflowing crowds to the museums where his traveling exhibits are displayed?

Despite the thousands of words that have been written about him, all we really know for sure was that he was Akhenaton's son-in-law, married to Akhenaton's third daughter, Ankhesenpaaton. Unlike the girls, he is not described as the offspring of Nefertiti. A recently discovered inscription makes it fairly certain that he was a king's son; but which king was his father?

The obvious answer would seem to be Akhenaton. However, Tutankhamon was related in some fashion to Amenhotep III, and a vociferous party of Egyptologists want to make that gentleman Tutankhamon's sire. In order to do this, it is necessary to accept the long coregency theory. At the risk of belaboring the obvious, I will explain.

Tutankhamon was nine years old when he became king, which means he was born before, but not too long before, Akhenaton's year twelve. If Amenhotep had been dead for twelve years by then, he could hardly have fathered a child.

I have, of course, no objection to stating my own opinion; I think Tutankhamon was Akhenaton's son by a lesser wife. It was always a safe assumption that he had some; we know that he took over certain members of his father's harem, including the younger Mitannian princess Tadukhepa. But not until the 1950s did we discover the lady named Kiya. She has now become one of the most popular characters in the Amarna drama, and Egyptologists keep finding her all over the place—in certain reliefs that had been formerly identified as those of princesses, and on the canopic jars and coffin found in KV55. It is hard to know precisely what her position was, for her titles are unique. She was never chief wife; Nefertiti held on to that title throughout, and Kiya's name is not written in a cartouche. Her titulary, if it can be called that, contains no flattering epithets or formal titles. It starts out "greatly beloved wife of" and ends with her name, Kiya; in between is a long string of Akhenaton's names and titles. I leave it to the reader to deduce what, if anything, this implies about the relationship.

Kiya's titles make her the leading candidate for the original owner of the coffin in KV55. Was she the mother of Tutankhamon? If so, Akhenaton must have been his father. Was he also the father of Smenkhkare? Was Kiya the latter's mother? She was for a time high in favor with Akhenaton; the birth of a prince and heir, after all those daughters, might have raised her to prominence over other members of the harem. Some people want to identify her with the Mitannian princess Tadukhepa, pointing out the similarity between the last two syllables of that princess's name and the name Kiya. Something happened to undermine her position, though. In almost every case, her name and image at Akhetaton were replaced by those of one of Akhenaton's daughters. Ah, well; someday an inscription may turn up that will solve the problem. In the meantime, life would be very dull without these arguments about Akhenaton's sex life.

Whatever his parentage, Smenkhkare must have been older than Tutankhamon, since he was the first successor to Akhenaton. He married Princess Meritaton, and either joined his father-in-law on the throne, or succeeded him. His highest known year date is year three. The young man is one of the most ephemeral kings of Egypt, but we do know that he established a temple to Amon in Thebes. It is a small fact, but a significant one, for it meant compromise. Akhenaton had attacked the age-old gods of Egypt for the love of Aton; did he send his son and daughter to the stronghold of Amon to arrange a reconciliation? I think this is a strong indication that Akhenaton had died before that event took place. Fanaticism, or idealism, of the degree that inspired the profound uprooting of the ageless pantheon of Egypt does not often soften with age. Rather the reverse, in fact.

Akhenaton died in his seventeenth year of rule, under circumstances that are unknown. There is no record of his death or burial or mummification. Smenkhkare and his young wife Meritaton disappeared from the stage of history soon thereafter, in the same infuriating silence; and the little king, Tutankhaton, ascended the throne. He was about nine years old. His wife, Ankhesenpaaton, was only a few years older.

For a year or two Tutankhaton remained at the city of Akhetaton. Then he moved the court back to Thebes and Memphis, changed his name to Tutankhamon, and began restoring the temples Akhenaton had desecrated.

The temples and cities of the gods and goddesses had fallen to pieces. The land was in ruin, and the gods turned their backs upon this land. Their hearts were hurt, so that they destroyed what had been made. But His Majesty deliberated plans with his heart, seeking out acts of service to his father Amon. All the property of the temples has been doubled—tripled—quadrupled; their service is charged against the palace and against the treasury of the Lord of the Two Lands.

So reads Tutankhamon's restoration inscription. In other words, pharaoh makes good, fourfold, what pharaoh tried to destroy. The triumph of Amon was complete.

One wonders at the emotions of the two small rulers at this capitulation, particularly at those of Ankhesenpaaton—for she too had taken the name of the god her father had anathematized. Were they in agreement with the surrender to Amon or, being mere children, were they helpless pawns in the hands of older players? There were several of the latter, the two most important being the God's Father Ay and the general Harmhab, both of whom succeeded to the throne after the young king's death.

Tutankhamon had little time to assert his own personality, even if he had wished to do so. He died at eighteen, not, as it turns out, as the result of a blow to the head. The latest examination suggests an accident that caused a serious leg injury resulting in infection. (I've always had doubts concerning the murder theory. If I had wanted to do him in, I wouldn't have hit him on the head; it's a crude, chancy method of murder compared with alternatives like poison or a sword through the gizzard.)

It is safe to say that his death was premature and unexpected. He hadn't had time to finish his own tomb, so he was laid to rest in a tomb that had been designed for a commoner, possibly his immediate successor, Ay. Robbers entered the tomb twice shortly after the burial, but in both cases they were thwarted before they reached the burial chamber, though they carried off a number of small items such as jewelry and left the outer chambers in a state of confusion. The mess was hastily tidied up by inspectors and the passageway was refilled. In the Twentieth Dynasty, Ramses VI excavated his tomb just above and to the left of Tutankhamon's, and the debris and workmen's huts hid the entrance to the boy-king's tomb from sight and from memory until Carter's moment of triumph in 1922. In the tomb were found two other mummies—those of infant girls, born prematurely. So ended the hopes of the Amarna family for a permanent dynasty; but Tutankhamon's young widow made one last desperate bid for power.

This incredible story is known not from Egyptian archaeology, but from the excavation of the Hittite capital in Anatolia. In the royal archives was a cuneiform text of the Hittite king, Mursilis III, telling of a message sent by an Egyptian queen to his father, our old friend Shubilulliuma.

"My husband is dead," she wrote, "and I have no son. People say that you have many sons. If you were to send me one of your sons he might become my husband. I am loath to take a servant of mine and make him my husband."

If Shubilulliuma had acted promptly, he might have changed history. But he was too sly to recognize candor when he met it, and there was reason for his skepticism. "Since of old such a thing has never happened," he exclaimed. So he sent his chamberlain to Egypt to investigate before making a decision. "Perhaps they have a prince; they may try to deceive me and do not really want one of my sons to take over the kingship."

In the columned and painted rooms of the royal palace at Thebes, Queen Ankhesenamon watched her young husband's tomb being made ready and waited for word. No one had consulted her on the succession. She had to act quickly and in secret, for she was no more than a pawn in the current game of politics, to be disposed of as the winner decreed. It is pitifully clear that she could expect no help from any of her father's former friends; Hatti was a last resort.

But the slow days dragged on without an answer from the north, and Ankhesenamon must have found her mask of indifference harder and harder to maintain. Then, at last, came a message. We do not know how it was delivered, nor by whom, but its import is plain from the letter Ankhesenamon wrote in reply. I know of no more eloquent text from ancient times.

Why do you say, "They may try to deceive me"? If I had a son, would I write to a foreign country in a manner which is humiliating to me and to my country? He who was my husband died, and I have no sons. Shall I perhaps take a servant of mine, and make him my husband? I have not written to any other country, I have written only to you. People say that you have many sons. Give me one of your sons, and he shall be my husband and king in the land of Egypt.

Bearing this message the courier set out again on the long journey, beset with many dangers. And this time Shubilulliuma was convinced. It was, in modern parlance, too good a chance to pass up. He sent a son, but too late. According to the Hittite records, the prince and his escort were attacked and murdered on the way "by the men and horses of Egypt." The conspiracy had been discovered.

And what of Queen Ankhesenamon? She was a true granddaughter of the shrewd little commoner Tiye, who had fought for a crown in her own way; but her husband was not "a mighty king whose borders reach from Karoy to the Euphrates." Her husband was dead, and in his place stood the Father of the God Ay, who had just had himself painted on the wall of Tutankhamon's tomb as the boy's successor.

Just who was Ay anyhow? Some scholars believe he was the brother of Queen Tiye and the son of Yuya and Thuya, and thus a member of a provincial family that had, for some reason or other, considerable influence at court. Nothing contradicts this theory, but negative evidence isn't proof; and I've always wondered why, if Ay was a son of Yuya and Thuya, his name does not appear anywhere in their tomb. Thuya is described as mother of the king's great wife, which we knew from the marriage scarab of Amenhotep III, and as mother of a son named Anen, whose modest tomb has been found. This is also negative evidence in a sense, but it strikes me as odd.

Excavators have found a gold ring whose bezel bears the joined cartouches of Ay and Ankhesenamon, side by side, as the name of royal consorts are written. This may indicate a scheme of Ay's to justify his occupation of the throne by marriage to Tutankhamon's widow. If it actually took place, the marriage didn't last long. The queen who stands beside Ay in his reliefs and statues is the same woman who was his wife in his humbler days at Amarna, and Ankhesenamon, like her parents, vanishes from history.

Some scholars deny the clue of the ring and believe that Ay never had any plans to marry his youthful queen. I personally cannot produce any other explanation for the joined cartouches. But for me the "clincher" is the queen's poignant letter to Shubilulliuma: "Shall I marry a servant of mine and make him king?" she asks—not once, but twice. Feminine intuition is as aggravating in historical study as it is in family discussions; yet I venture to suggest that this is precisely the comment a woman would make if she had been offended, as a woman and as a queen, by advances from a man of Ay's age and nonroyal status—especially if he really was her grandfather! It's pure speculation, of course, but the ring, the letter, and the sudden disappearance of Akhesenamon do permit us to suspect that she died before a marriage could take place. She may have been murdered after the discovery of her attempt to deliver Egypt over to the Hittites, but another explanation is possible. Perhaps Ay was actually a "fate worse than death" to the proud daughter of the heretic king.

I really hate to qualify this romantic narrative, but candor compels me to admit that practically every statement I have made is open to debate. Many of the major actors in the drama of Amarna vanish from the scene as mysteriously and as inconclusively as does Ankhesenamon. Her mummy has never been found, nor have the remains of her grandmother Tiye, her mother Nefertiti, or any of her sisters. Every now and then someone claims to have identified one of the numerous anonymous female mummies as Tiye or Nefertiti; then somebody else comes along and proves it isn't. Like other romantics, I believe that there is at least one more royal cache to be found—the burials of the missing royal ladies of the late Eighteenth Dynasty, including those of Nefertiti and her daughters.

Let's suppose that they and Smenkhkare were originally buried at Amarna, like Akhenaton. When the city was abandoned, the mummies and the portable parts of their funerary equipment were moved to new tombs in the protected Valley of the Kings. While this process was under way, Tutankhamon died. He had presumably begun a tomb—every Egyptian king did—but it wasn't ready for occupancy, and his funerary equipment was incomplete. His successor might have decided to swipe some of Smenkhkare's belongings, and bundle the latter into a leftover coffin. Or maybe . . .

Well, that's how it goes with the Amarna debates. We can invent half a dozen scenarios that would make perfectly logical plots for historical novels, but until there is absolute proof the end must be in doubt. At this writing there are rumors of evidence that would identify the occupant of the KV55 coffin beyond dispute. Wait and see. And wait for the latest news from the Valley of the Kings, where the recently discovered cache of funerary materials known as KV63 may indicate the existence of at least one other unknown tomb of Amarna date.

Despite the almost certain identification of the mysterious skeleton as that of Smenkhkare, the theorists have not abandoned their theories about Akhenaton's physical peculiarities, basing them now solely on the abnormalities depicted in the sculptures, which are admittedly odd enough. The latest kick is something called Marfan's syndrome. I still cling stubbornly to the belief that one cannot give a statue a physical examination, and the existence of Akhenaton's daughters, and perhaps his sons, seems clear evidence to me that he was not exactly impotent, whatever his other problems may have been. However, people will undoubtedly go on arguing until, or if, his mummy is found.

Will it ever be found? The possibility seems unlikely. Akhenaton probably died at Amarna and was buried there. His tomb had been prepared for him, and fragments of a sarcophagus found therein belonged to him. It is possible that when Tutankhamon left the city of the Horizon of Aton, he moved the bodies of his royal relatives to Thebes for safekeeping. But if this is what happened, then what became of Akhenaton's own coffin and golden ornaments, which must have surpassed those of Tutankhamon in splendor? He had seventeen or eighteen years in which to prepare them, in comparison with Tutankhamon's nine years of rule, and he was not, as his critics have pointed out, a humble man. The godson of the sole universal god deserved the best that imperial grandeur could supply, and the empire was in better shape at Akhenaton's accession than it was when Tutankhamon took over.

Active persecution of Akhenaton's memory did not begin immediately after Tutankhamon went over to the enemy. The boy-king could still place in his tomb many of the cherished objects he had owned while he was still Tutankhaton, "Living Image of Aton," including the throne, which still bears the name and shape of the solar orb. We are safe in assuming that Akhenaton was laid to rest with all the pomp and reverence due a divine king of a mighty empire. What befell his body afterward is a matter of pure speculation. Perhaps his enemies eventually broke into the tomb and destroyed it. Perhaps it was desecrated by tomb robbers of ancient times, as were the mummies and the treasures of other pharaohs. A third possibility—that when the city of Akhetaton was abandoned, Akhenaton was taken back to Thebes with the other royal dead—isn't as romantically unlikely as it may sound. How it kindles the imagination, to fancy that the mummy of the first great heretic still lies undisturbed somewhere in the Valley of the Kings.

Lest the reader accuse me of going into inordinate detail over this confused era, let me assure him that I have not even touched upon many of the problems which are connected with this reign. More verbiage has been produced on Akhenaton and his times than on almost any other era of Egyptian history, and the work of scholars is remarkable for its heated tone. It is hard to be dispassionate about Akhenaton; you may loathe him or admire him, but you cannot ignore him. He has been described as a sexual degenerate and as a pure spiritual leader; as a destructive fanatic and as a great idealist. Psychiatrists have written about his psychoses and doctors have diagnosed his diseases. And Egyptologists—well, they have theories, and passionate ones, about every aspect of Akhenaton's life except what he ate for breakfast. I know of no better illustration of the subjectivity of some types of historical research than the widely varying approaches to the character and exploits of Akhenaton, and the bias extends to the minor characters. Some people, for instance, persist in viewing that old scoundrel Ay as a dedicated servant of his country, and Ankhesenamon as a traitor to Egypt! I, of course, am completely dispassionate on this subject, as on everything that has to do with Akhenaton.

The city of the Horizon of Aton struggled on for a time after Tutankhamon deserted it, but eventually it died, as cities will when the spirit that animated them is gone. The houses were abandoned and the tombs in the cliffs were emptied or robbed. Some of the latter, designed for high officials, contain reliefs and inscriptions of interest, though many are in poor condition. The royal tomb, at the end of a long wadi, is in even worse condition. After the death of Ay his successor began the demolition of palaces and temples, a process that continued into the following dynasty. The site has been methodically excavated in modern times, most recently by the Egypt Exploration Society of England, whose publications are the definitive work on the city. It yielded its treasures; the painted head of Nefertiti is perhaps the greatest, but there were other pieces of sculpture, some so naturalistic that they were originally taken to be death masks. Fragments of the brightly painted floors of the palaces survived, to find their way into museums and collections. The plans of the villas and the workmen's village have been reconstructed; certain of the massive boundary stelae still exist, sadly ravaged by time and human destructiveness; but there is little left at Tell el Amarna to interest the nonspecialist.

At Thebes, blocks and statues have been found that came from Akhenaton's first temple to his god. They had been torn from their setting and used as filler for the work of later kings in the great Amon temple of Karnak. After a reign of only a few years, Ay passed away and was buried in a tomb in the West Valley, perhaps the one that had been begun for Tutankhamon. But for the miraculous survival of Tutankhamon's burial equipment we would know very little about the wealth and richness of this imperial period. Multiply that minor king's goods a hundredfold and you will get some idea of what the magnificent Amenhotep must have taken to his tomb.

In later times Akhenaton's name and that of his god were cut from the inscriptions and the name of Amon was replaced. Amon-Re resumed his place as king of the gods and took back all the ground he had lost— and more. His devotees had good reason to write, after Akhenaton's death:

> *Woe to him who assails thee!*
> *Thy city endures, but he who assails thee is overthrown;*
> *The sun of him who knew thee not has set, but he who knows thee shines;*
> *The sanctuary of him who assailed thee is overwhelmed in darkness,*
> *but the whole earth is in light.*

The shout of triumph rings hollow, however, after three thousand years. The attempt to obliterate Akhenaton's name failed, thanks to the patient skill of historians, philologists, and archaeologists; he still exists in memory, to stir the imaginations of all who know of him. Even the great god Amon-Re did not live forever. He is as dead today as his old enemy Akhenaton; the sand drifts over his altars, and his sanctuaries are laid open to the stares of the curious.

Nine

THE BROKEN REED

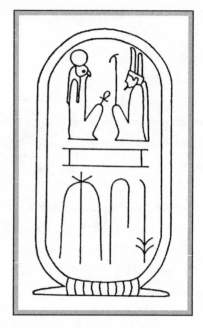

Cartouche of Ramses II

LOOK ON MY WORKS!

There is no apparent reason why Egypt should not have arisen refulgent from the minor brushfires set by the Amarna heresy, as it had been reborn out of the greater conflagrations of the first two Intermediate Periods. To the men and women who lived out their lives under the first kings of the Nineteenth Dynasty, this resurgence was probably taken for granted. Yet to some, the greatness of Egypt is gone.

Greatness is a hard word to define. But whether Egyptian achievements

are defined in terms of the rampantly successful imperialism of Thutmose III or the defiant spiritual challenges of the First Intermediate
Period, the fable-making iconoclasm of Akhenaton or the more than
oriental splendor of his father's court, in almost every sense, Egyptian
culture had passed its high point. Except for short periods of domestic
calm under a strong pharaoh, the internal picture is one of slow but
unmistakable decay. Abroad, the attempts of the Nineteenth Dynasty
kings to regain the lost empire of Egypt fell short of Thutmose III's
achievements, and their descendants were unable to hold even what
they had gained. There is a brief efflorescence of art, incorporating the
best of the Amarna techniques, which produced some beautiful statues
and reliefs, but it did not last. It is a melancholy task to view the decline
of a culture so bright and attractive as that of Egypt, but it would be
futile to try to paint the dying organism in the colors of life. So let us
take up the story where we left it after the tragedy of Amarna was
ended.

Ay, the old councilor who took Tutankhamon's crown and perhaps
his widow as well, did not live to enjoy his dubiously acquired gains for
long. After his death there was no man in Egypt who could put forth
even a faintly legitimate claim to the throne of the Two Lands. Contemporary inscriptions tell us that the internal affairs of Egypt were not
flourishing. Egypt needed a strong hand to put down domestic disorder
and civil strife, and a strong hand was just what she got. Ay's successor
was a military man named Harmhab, who had served under Tutankhamon. It is rather pitiful to see how few genuine converts the creed
of Aton could claim. It was in truth the personal faith of the king and his
family; many of Akhenaton's leading adherents turned their coats with
shameful haste after he died. Or perhaps they had only pretended to
believe.

Tutankhamon had claimed the honor of reestablishing orthodoxy
and repairing the temples ravaged by Akhenaton's decrees, and Ay had
been an eager servant of Amon, but neither of them was as zealous as
Harmhab. He added greatly to the Amon temple at Karnak, using the

blocks of Akhenaton's dismantled Aton temple to hold up his pylons. As a high-ranking official of Tutankhamon he had already had built for himself a very elegant tomb at Sakkara, near the capital of Memphis, but after his accession to the throne he excavated another in the Valley of the Kings. He also took over a number of the monuments that had been erected by Tutankhamon, replacing that ruler's's name with his own. This wasn't an uncommon practice, but Harmhab's motive was, in part at least, political. The Amarna kings were to be eliminated from history. In the great king list of Seti I, Harmhab's second successor, Akhenaton, Smenkhkare, Tutankhamon, and Ay do not appear. Harmhab added their years of reign to his own.

By what right Harmhab claimed the throne of Horus we may never know. Amon, of course, hailed him as his son, and some scholars think he established his legitimacy by marrying a sister of Nefertiti's who had survived the anti-Amarna reaction. It is difficult to see what good this could have done the general. Nefertiti was only a member of the royal house by marriage, and her sister could not by any stretch of the imagination be considered a royal heiress, even if such a concept existed. One wonders what had happened to Akhenaton's daughters. The three oldest may have been dead by the time Harmhab claimed the throne, but what about the younger girls? Were they disregarded, as members of a tainted family, or did they too die before their time, possibly during a plague? It could be that Ay and Harmhab struck a deal in order to avoid a possible, damaging struggle for power; the older man got first crack at the throne, naming Harmhab as his successor.

Though he had led military campaigns in Syria and Nubia under Tutankhamon, Harmhab had little opportunity for warfare after he assumed the throne. The confusion within Egypt occupied him throughout much of his reign, and he seems to have dealt with it ably. A stela at Karnak mentions a number of abuses he had to correct: illegal taxation, extortion, theft, and fraud. He had no surviving son, so when he died he passed the kingdom on to an old buddy, another general named Ramses. With this king the Nineteenth Dynasty properly begins.

Ramses I was an old man when he came to the throne, and he only held it for a year or two. However, his son, Seti I, was a man in the prime of life, with a son of his own; and he proved to be a vigorous, energetic ruler. He must be given credit for a number of more or less laudable deeds: he built largely and with taste, he kept internal affairs under control, and he made the first serious attempt to reconquer the lost Asiatic empire of Egypt. His campaigns were successful but limited; he seems to have realized that it would take more than Egypt had then to offer to regain all the territory Thutmose III had held. He commemorated his victories by a series of very handsome, delicately carved reliefs on the walls of the great temple of Karnak. As they stand today, the outlines of the reliefs set off by brilliant sunlight and sharp shadows, they are among the most beautiful of all Egyptian relief carving. However, to many of us, Seti is chiefly memorable for a somewhat dubious attribute: he possesses (or should one say possessed?) the handsomest mummy ever to come out of an Egyptian tomb.

Egyptian mummies in general are not precisely beautiful, so to call Seti's the best may seem a doubtful compliment. But it is more than the best of a bad lot; it is a positively good-looking mummy, the features being those of a man of truly kingly appearance and noble looks, with the relaxed aspect of a man asleep.

Seti's elegant mummy was not found in his tomb; like so many other royal mummies it had to undergo repeated transfers for the sake of safety. But the tomb was worthy of its occupant. Its total length is about three hundred feet—not including a mysterious tunnel leading down from the floor of the burial chamber. It has not yet been completely explored. The walls of corridors and chambers are adorned with attractive painted reliefs of the king and the gods, many of which still retain their original color. These traces of paint have always given me a queer sense of the insubstantiality of time. Three thousand years have passed since the hands of the artist completed the laying on of orange and white, blue and gold; yet still the colors remain, frail shells of actuality.

Seti was responsible for another tourist attraction, this one at Abydos, which is well worth a visit (if you can get there; Abydos is in Middle

Egypt, and security is very tight). The Abydos temple is a beauty, with reliefs of very fine quality. Being in Abydos, it could only be dedicated to Osiris, which suggests a pleasing irony: the sanctuary to the murdered god built and dedicated by the namesake of his murderer! Seti was named after Set the Enemy, and he paid his tutelary deity cautious honor. Whether he remembered the postulated Set movement of the remote Second Dynasty, or had any desire to imitate it is highly doubtful; it was as much ancient history for him as it is for us. But if he did know about the event, it would have warned him against any attempt to give Set more than his due. At Abydos where, of all places on earth, Set's name would be de trop, the king substituted the hieroglyphic image of Osiris for the figure of Set that formed part of his own name. This was a solution which only a theologian or an Egyptian could regard as sensible.

RAMSES II

I used to wonder, when I listened to the tales of my acquaintances who had been fortunate enough to travel in Egypt, at the animosity they displayed toward Ramses II. I knew nothing particularly favorable about the gentleman then, but I was unaware of any deed of his which might have prompted the snarl of contempt with which his name was mentioned. Now that I have visited Egypt myself I can understand the reaction; I too snarl. One gets so *tired* of Ramses; his face, his figure, and/or his name are plastered over half the wall surfaces still standing in Egypt—at least it seems that way. Egyptian sculpture during his reign was beginning to decline from the high standards of his father, and the statues of Ramses which so weary the eye are often stubby and unattractive. But worst of all is the sheer number of them, which is surpassed only by the number of his cartouches. You can't miss them; they are cut inches deep into walls and columns. One is entitled to suspect that Ramses, who had replaced the names of some of his predecessors with his own, was making sure nobody was going to scratch his off.

He was the son of Seti I and he was the pharaoh who made the name of Ramses practically a synonym for Egyptian kingship. He had some help in this from a later Ramses, the third in number, but the chief responsibility rests with him. Next to that of Tutankhamon, his name is better known to the public than that of any other Egyptian king, and Ramses II's fame was created by the liberal use of a well-known principle of modern advertising—repetition. How well he deserved the reputation he built for himself may be seen by one striking incident of his career, and the expert use he made of it in order to build the desired image.

His father, Seti, had begun the reconquest of Egypt's Asiatic empire. Just how far the older man got we aren't certain, but he had evidently regained control of Palestine and parts of southern Syria. Ramses burned to surpass his father; he wanted to be a warrior. His first campaign was a tentative push into Palestine, in his fourth year. In the following year he was ready for a more ambitious project.

His goal was a famous city indeed. Thutmose III had captured it twice, though not without difficulty. It had been the home of Thutmose's most trying adversary, and it was still an important city; its name was Kadesh. Part of the city's strategic strength lay in its position, near the mouth of the valley between the Lebanons, through which a northbound army would normally pass. Kadesh was a mighty fortress, and it was defended by a mighty army, for Ramses' opponents were none other than the Hittites. Shubilulliuma, who had outfoxed himself only once in the matter of Tutankhamon's widow, was long dead, but his grandson, Muwatallis, still felt that the Hittites had a claim on the city-states of north Syria. Conflict with the Hittites was inevitable to any Egyptian army bent on expansion during these years, just as a collision with Mitanni had been inevitable for Thutmose III. Hatti had replaced Mitanni as the most important power of the area; of the two, the Hittites were probably far more formidable.

At this period the Egyptian army was an impressive institution, professional in character, well trained, and well equipped. In one important particular it had altered since the heyday of Thutmose III: more and

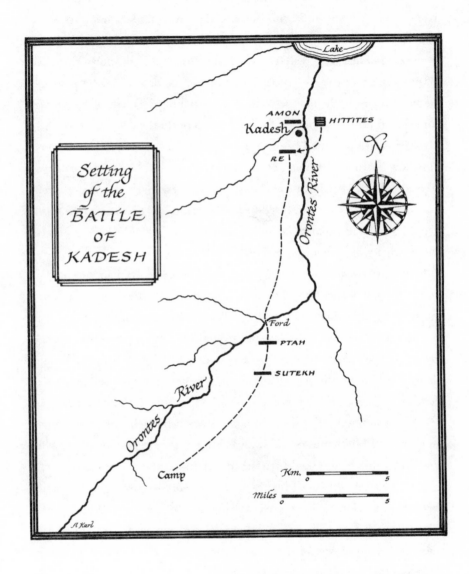

Setting of the BATTLE OF KADESH

Lake

AMON

Kadesh

HITTITES

RE

Orontes River

N

Ford

PTAH

SUTEKH

River

Orontes

Camp

Km. 0 ———— 5

Miles 0 ———— 5

A. Karl

more of the troops were non-Egyptians, mercenaries or conquered enemies forced to serve under the banners of Egypt. Ramses' army was
divided into four sections, each named after one of the great gods of
Egypt—Amon and Re, Ptah of Memphis, and Sutekh, who was a Semitic deity related to—of all people—Set.

A month after the army left Egypt, Ramses found himself standing
on a hill about fifteen miles from Kadesh. No doubt he stood dramatically on the top and shaded his eyes with his hand, straining to see the
dim towers and formidable walls in the distance. The strength of the
army at his back, and his own stunning self-confidence, left him in no
doubt of the eventual outcome. He set out for Kadesh early the next
morning, hoping to get the business settled before dark.

Ramses commanded the division of Amon, which he led down the
steep slopes to the ford of the Orontes—the first spot at which an army
might cross that river. As he was preparing for the crossing, a pair of
wandering Bedouins was scooped up by Egyptian scouts and brought to
the king. They proclaimed themselves Hittite deserters who were anxious
to fight on the right side—the Egyptian side—and they volunteered the
welcome news that the Hittites were not at Kadesh at all. They were in
Aleppo, far to the north. Ramses' reception of this cheering information
was no doubt conditioned by the fact that it was just what he wanted to
hear. He pushed on toward the city, leaving the three divisions of Ptah,
Sutekh, and Re far behind and, in his zeal, even outstripping the division
of Amon. When he set up his camp on the west of the city he was accompanied only by his bodyguard.

Then it happened that two more Asiatics were captured by the Egyptians; and the story they told did not exactly jibe with the first report of
the two Bedouins. The Hittites, as a matter of fact, were not in Aleppo.
They were on the other side of the city of Kadesh, and they had not been
idle while Ramses was trying to outrun his own army.

Even Ramses the Complacent must have lost his breath for a few min-
utes when he heard that news. His reaction was typical; he called his commanders in and told them what fools they were. He then did something

practical, but a little too late, sending messengers speeding south to summon the division of Ptah. The division of Amon had caught up with its complacent leader, and Ramses knew that the division of Re was not far behind. This latter division was actually closer than he knew.

Back at the Hittite camp, matters had been progessing well—from the Hittite point of view. Muwatallis, the Hittite king, was a strategist so superior to Ramses that his talents are obvious even in the Egyptian version of the story, which was not designed to glorify the enemy. Or maybe the strategist was one of his generals. The king would get the credit in any case.

He had, to begin with, completely fooled Ramses with his carefully planted "deserters" and their implausible story. (The nameless Bedouins were patriots of a high caliber; they were risking their necks, in case the Egyptians did not believe their story, and I personally hope they slipped away from their guards in the confusion that was to come.) Then, as Ramses proceeded blithely along the plain on the west side of Kadesh, Muwatallis led his army south on the east side of the city, unseen by the Egyptians; crossed the ford; and smashed into the division of Re before its commanders so much as dreamed that there was a Hittite within fifty miles of the place.

Ramses, stamping and swearing, was not aware of this latest disaster until the fugitives from the broken and demoralized division of Re burst into his camp and on through it, carrying with them the bewildered division of Amon. The pursuing Hittites were not far behind. They surrounded the camp; and there was Ramses, all alone except for the Hittites.

He says he was all alone, and even allowing for poetic license the statement is probably not too inaccurate. A few officers—the remains of the household troops—were not much against 2,500 chariots filled with ferocious Hittite soldiers. According to Ramses, however, he had no support at all. "There was no captain with me, no charioteer, no soldier of the army, no shield-bearer; my infantry and chariotry melted away before them, not one of them stood firm to fight."

So the king addressed himself to Amon:

Have I done anything without thee, do I not walk and halt at thy biddings?
What careth thy heart, O Amon, for these Asiatics, so vile and so ignorant of
maat?

After working himself up to the proper pitch of religious fervor,
Ramses hurled himself upon the enemy. He routed them single-handedly,
driving them into the river. It seems that we must credit Ramses II with
one virtue: he did not lack courage. He was also a magnificent liar, but
then that was expected of him; even if the king had ordered his scribes to
write down a tale of stupidity and defeat, his horrified courtiers would
have carried him quietly away and then made sure the conventional eu-
logy was carved on the walls of his temple. We know that Ramses survived the battle, got back to Egypt, and ruled for many more years. What
saved him was the arrival of unexpected aid.

The divisions of Re and Amon were in headlong flight to the north;
the division of Sutekh was far in the rear, near the ford, and in fact, it
never saw fighting at all. The division of Ptah was his best hope, but with
the scanty resources at his command in the camp he could not expect to
hold out until that division came up. But there were other troops, not
part of the regular army, on the way. We do not know exactly where they
came from, for they are called only "the Nearen from the land of Amurru."
These troops fell upon the Hittites from the rear, and with their help the
king managed to hold the field until the rays of the declining sun caught
the tips of the golden standards of the division of Ptah, toiling along the
dusty road toward the succor of its king.

Nightfall ended the fighting but brought no decision as to victory.
The enemy withdrew to the city, leaving Ramses in possession of the
bloody field; the straggling soldiers of the divisions of Amon and Re
crept shamefacedly back to the king they had deserted. Ramses says the
Hittites then sued for peace, which he magnanimously granted.

At this point we are faced with a major problem in historiography. In
other words, how much of this can we reasonably swallow? We have seen
how varied and how remarkable are the sources from which a student of

history may derive the information he uses to make up a consistent story of what happened in the past. When written records are few the historian uses other materials, which require complicated analyses. But even when an event is well documented, even when we have a written, pseudohistorical account, we must still evaluate the reliability of the source. Many questions must be asked. Is the tale written by an eyewitness or does the author rely on secondhand information? If the former, was he a good observer? If the latter, has he examined his witnesses and tried to test their eyesight and credibility? What is the bias of the author either for or against the people he is writing about? Even if he professes to be moved solely by a desire to record the "truth," is he sufficiently detached from the scene and the players of the drama to write about them dispassionately? Does he have a conscious or unconscious purpose—vilification or glorification of a man or a belief, self-aggrandizement, propaganda? In some cases we must pry into the entire life history of a chronicler or writer of history in order to discover his prejudices and the bearing they may have on his interpretation of the events of the time.

Our task of evaluating the written records of ancient Egypt is relatively easy, since we can start with the assumption that every scribe had an ax or two to grind. The annals of the various kings are not a factual record of events; they are intended to glorify the kings, on earth and in the Hereafter. Hence we can and must take every statement made in such annals with a good-size chunk of salt. We cannot even be sure that Thutmose III was all that good. We think he—and when I say "he" I mean, of course, the scribe who composed the inscriptions under the king's watchful eye—we think Thutmose III was fairly accurate. We can check some of his accounts through other sources, and his story has a certain indefinable, but significant, air of verisimilitude. Ramses II's version of the Battle of Kadesh is transparently, naively eulogistic, and what actually happened was so bad that even the Egyptian scribe could not conceal all the disasters nor all his king's stupidity.

Since we know that the purpose of the narrative was the glorification of the king, we can assume with some confidence that any anti-Ramses or anti-Egyptian remarks are probably correct. Thus, when interpreting the battle inscription, we state that Ramses outstripped the rest of his army; he credulously accepted the story of the two patriotic Bedouins; the division of Re was caught unaware and was annihilated; the majority of the forces encamped with the king were swept away in the rout. We can also state that Ramses survived the battle and got home. Egyptologists generally concede Ramses' personal valor, while condemning him as a poor strategist and a poorer general, but we cannot even be sure about that. Ramses might have spent the battle hours hiding under a baggage cart while some unnamed (and short-lived) hero of Egypt rallied the meager forces in the camp and held them until help arrived. Let no one believe that I am misled by personal animus against a man who has been a mummy for several thousand years. I am perfectly willing to concede that Ramses may have been an Achilles in battle. Achilles was none too bright either. All I am saying is that we will never know for certain.

We do know that the Battle of Kadesh did not have the result which the Egyptians claimed—results that would be hard to believe in any case, just on the basis of the situation that prevailed at the end of the first day of battle. The Egyptian army had been badly demoralized, one-quarter of its strength annihilated at the very beginning of hostilities. The Hittites had certainly suffered severely during the afternoon, but they withdrew to the city in good order and their leader was not killed (the Egyptians would have gloated over his demise if it had occurred, and given Ramses the credit). It is inconceivable that they would have tamely surrendered after such an inconclusive "defeat" as the Egyptian records claim was inflicted.

Fortunately we do not have to rely on logic to prove that the Egyptians lost that fight. By one of those almost miraculous coincidences that do occur, we have at our disposal the Hittite version of the same battle, from the royal archives of the capital of Boghazkoi. According to it, Ramses was defeated and had to retreat, losing much of the territory his father had held.

Of course the same criteria apply to the Hittite records as to the Egyptian; the kings of Hatti were no more averse to flattery than were their royal counterparts to the south. But the Hittites continued to hold Kadesh and certain other cities formerly controlled by Egypt. The final conclusion to the rivalry of Hittites and Egyptians was not a resounding defeat for either side. In year twenty-one of Ramses II a treaty of peace was concluded between the two powers—the first international treaty of which we have record. And to make the wonder more complete, we have both versions, Hittite and Egyptian. The Egyptian copy of the treaty survives from the walls of Karnak and the Ramesseum, and the Hittite copy on two clay tablets from Boghazkoi. The latter was probably an archival version of the original, which was supposed to have been inscribed on plates of silver.

In their essential provisions the two texts are strikingly similar, which indicates that they really were parallel versions of the same agreement. They begin with a reference to former treaties, none of which is definitely known. Then the two monarchs mutually renounce any attempts at future invasion and swear perpetual peace. The treaty establishes a defensive alliance, which holds both in case of external invasion or internal rebellion. It also provides for the mutual extradition of refugees. The Egyptian version reads as follows:

> *If a man flee from the land of Egypt—or two, or three—and they come to the Great Prince of Hatti, the Great Prince of Hatti shall lay hold of them, and he shall cause that they be brought back to Ramses the great ruler of Egypt. But, as for the man who should be brought to the great ruler of Egypt, do not cause that his crime be raised against him; do not cause that his house or his wives or his children be destroyed; do not cause that he be slain, do not cause that injury be done to his eyes, to his ears, to his mouth, or to his legs.*

The same provisions hold in the case of fugitives from Hatti who escape to Egypt. The striking aspect of this section is not the notion of extradition, nor the unmistakable ring of the lawyers' phraseology, but the humanitarianism enjoined upon the two kings. It seems quite inexplicable unless we assume some mutually accepted moral or legal code of—not so much justice as mercy, for the malefactor's crime is to be forgiven him.

The two treaties are almost exact parallels, but not quite exact. The Egyptians felt it incumbent upon them to add a prologue explaining that the treaty was granted by merciful Ramses after the Hittite king came crawling and begging for peace. No comment.

Some years later, the alliance was cemented by a royal marriage, and Ramses' version of this diplomatic stroke is equally—I almost said characteristically—egomaniacal. The Hittites are described as "coming with fearful steps, bearing all their possessions as tribute to the fame of His Majesty. His eldest daughter comes before, in order to satisfy the heart of the Lord of the Two Lands."

Ramses evidently could not recognize an inconsistency if it walked up and bit him. He implies that the poor Hittite princess was thrust into the ravening jaws of the dragon Ramses by her trembling father; but elsewhere he exchanges the role of dragon for that of a chivalrous prince, who rushes out at the head of a well-equipped escort to meet his promised bride with all honor. The tale concludes in the second, fairy-tale strain: "She was beautiful in the eyes of His Majesty, and he loved her more than anything!"

It is a shame to dim the glow of this pretty story, which would make a standard diplomatic marriage into a case of love at first sight; but, of course, the version we have is another of the standard court fictions. The Hittite princess—poor girl—was raised to the rank of chief royal wife, but her throne was uncomfortably crowded. The women's quarters were a standard architectural element of all Egyptian palaces; but it is probable that few kings of Egypt had harem quarters covering as many acres as did Ramses. We do not know exactly how many wives he had. Most of them were not wives, strictly speaking, but occupied a position analogous to that of legal concubine. A higher rank in the harem was held by the king's wives, who were not so numerous as the concubines. We usually translate "king's wife" as "queen," but the woman who really held the place of royal consort was the "king's great wife." Sometimes this lady was a lowly commoner; sometimes she was the king's half-sister or his full sister. Brother-sister marriages were common in the royal house of Egypt, although the practice was rare among humbler folk. The king was a law unto himself, in marriage as in other matters, and we have a few cases of father-daughter marriages; at least the evidence is hard to interpret in any other way.

Ramses II was one of the kings who apparently married some of his own children. It is possible that he had forgotten momentarily that he was related to them; the total sum of his offspring exceeded 150, and no man can be expected to keep that many little faces clearly in mind. Because of paternal pride—or some other reason—Ramses liked to show off his children, and if you visit the temple of Luxor at Thebes you can see a long line of them carved on the wall, all in a row like so many upright sardines.

The Luxor temple, begun by Amenhotep III, was only one of the many monuments dedicated by Ramses to the greater glory of Ramses. He added a forecourt, a huge pylon, and massive statues to the front of the temple. In order to achieve this noble end, he spared none of the works of his ancestors, razing the temples and pyramids of past ages in order to obtain handy precut building blocks. At this time the royal capital was in the Delta region, which has not been so methodically excavated as has Upper Egypt; hence Ramses' most famous temples are in the southern part of Egypt, and they include some of the standard tourist attractions. He was responsible for finishing the great Hypostyle Hall of Karnak, the most spectacular section of that crowded and complex temple. The vast trunklike columns are staggering in their size and number, and no traveler comes away from Egypt without a photograph of a row of them, with a handy guide posed against one to give some idea of relative dimensions. Ramses' mortuary temple, across the river from Karnak, is called the Ramesseum, and it too is on the list of Things to See while in Luxor. The best known of all his monuments is the rock-cut temple of

Abu Simbel in Nubia, with its four colossal statues of the king. A second, smaller temple at the same site was dedicated to Nefertari, one of Ramses' principal and most favored queens.

These temples were the most conspicuous of the Egyptian antiquities threatened by the building of the High Dam at Aswan in the 1960s. The old dam had left the island of Philae under water for part of the year. The new one would cover it entirely and inundate a huge area of lower Nubia, with its temples, ancient sites, and villages. The Egyptian government called on the international community for help, and the response was immediate. For almost twenty years expeditions worked in the area, in a frantic attempt to excavate and record as many sites as possible before the deluge. Some of the smaller temples were moved to safer locations. The biggest problem was what to do with Abu Simbel. It was not a freestanding temple, like the others; its chambers and halls were cut into the solid rock of the cliff.

The problem was certainly one of the most fantastically difficult ever faced by a team of archaeologists and engineers, and some of the solutions proposed were even more fantastic. The simplest suggestion was to build a dam around the temples and install a pumping station to take care of seepage and overflow. But if the pumps had failed, for any reason, the temples would have been flooded in no time. So this scheme had to be abandoned.

The most intriguing suggestion was one proposed by Italian engineers—to cut both temples free of the cliff into which they had been carved, and lift them up above the water level by means of hydraulic jacks. Concrete blocks would be inserted underneath as the temples slowly rose. Impossible as this plan sounds, it was approved by an international committee of experienced engineers, but it too had to be given up because of the prohibitive cost. The estimate was $85 million. It doesn't sound like much compared to the cost of modern wars, but it was a lot of money back then.

The plan that was eventually carried out was to carve the temples up into thirty-ton blocks and move them. They stand today atop the cliffs, two hundred feet above their original location, where they attract as many tourists as they always did. The blocks were stuck back together with one of the new synthetic glues.

Undoubtedly this was a monumental achievement and a magnificent testimonial to international cooperation, but there were a few cynics who wondered whether it was worth the effort. I have already made a number of rude, possibly unfair, remarks about Ramses II, so I will refrain from criticizing his temples, and I would be the first to admit that seeing Abu Simbel, especially at night, is a memorable experience.

Ramses does have one spectacular artistic achievement to his credit— the exquisitely painted tomb of his queen Nefertari. In its present state it is a tribute not only to Ramses but also to the efforts of a modern team of restorers, who spent years repairing the badly damaged walls. In her white pleated robe, her face exquisitely made up, the queen pays homage to various gods who will guide her through the perils of the Afterlife. One can only hope that the astronomical entrance fee and the deteter- mination of the Egyptian government to limit access will prevent future deterioration.

Ramses' own tomb, in the Valley of the Kings, is in poor condition, and most of the decoration is missing. However, a few years ago an American archaeologist, Kent Weeks, made a discovery that electrified not only the world of Egyptology but the world media. The tomb of the sons of Ramses II is the largest ever found in Egypt—well over a hun- dred rooms so far, and still counting. It's even more of a mess than that of Ramses himself, and the work of excavation has been unbelievably difficult.

Ramses probably gave up the ghost with the satisfying feeling that he had done the best he could. Lots of statues, lots of temples. In other mat- ters he was no less diligent. There would be no dangerous uncertainty about a male heir to the throne; Ramses had supplied Egypt almost as abundantly with sons as with statues. He reigned for sixty-seven years and was over ninety when he died—a ripe old age indeed, considering the state of ancient medical knowledge, but then Egypt has a notoriously healthy climate, and clean living tells in the end. A goodly number of crown princes abandoned hope and died while Ramses flourished; it's easy to understand why he was driven to burying them in a group grave. He was succeeded by his thirteenth son, Merneptah, who was himself well past middle age when he gained the long-awaited crown. The poor man deserved a peaceful reign after waiting so long for it, but it was his unhappy fate to meet the greatest challenge Egypt had had to face since the days of the Hyksos.

PEOPLES OF THE SEA

The man who climbed the steps to the throne of Horus was no muscular warrior-king. He had occupied his throne only five years when he received word which must have hastened the loss of his remaining hairs.

For almost two hundred years the military ambitions of Egypt had been directed toward Syria and the east. Since Ahmose pursued the fleeing Hyksos invaders into Palestine, this area had provided the greatest challenges and the most pressing dangers to Egypt. There were always battles in Nubia to the south, and with the Libyans, west of the Delta; but these were lesser enemies than the great confederations of Syrian princes and the eastern empires of Mitanni and Hatti.

Now the status quo was changing, and drastically. A new wind was blowing against the isolated green island of Egypt, a wind cold and sharp with northern ferocity. The immediate threat to Egypt, the news of which reached the elderly king in March of his fifth year, came from the desert regions west of the Delta, which were occupied by various Libyan tribes. Maraye, king of the Libyans, led not only his fighting men but all the peoples of his tribe, women and children, with their cattle and household equipment, in a vast migration. Yet the threat of the Libyans was not new. What was new, and disturbing, was the presence of alien peoples among the military allies of Maraye. They have strange names: the Akawasha and the Luca, the Tursha and the Sheklesh. Perhaps the names will not sound so strange if we give the now commonly accepted equivalent: the Achaeans and the Lycians, the Tyrsenoi and the Sicilians.

The Egyptian records call these tribes "peoples of the sea." We know them from Greece and also from Italy, if the Tyrsenoi are in actuality the ancestors of the Etruscans. How they came to be allies of a Libyan chieftain is a mystery, but it seems that there was ferment and unrest and a great movement of peoples throughout Asia Minor and the Mediterranean. The ancient empire of the Hittites was rocking on its foundations; Merneptah had sent grain to that country in order to relieve a severe famine. With a little ingenuity, we can trace most of the "peoples of the sea" to homelands in Asia Minor. The Tyrsenoi had lived in Lydia before they emigrated, and the Achaeans may have inhabited the Mycenaean colony at Miletus just south of Lydia.

If the famine and the general brouhaha that can be read in the Hittite records of this period affected the whole area of Asia Minor, the "peoples of the sea" may have been forced to migrate by hunger, or by pressure from other tribes to their rear. Whatever their motive, they and the Libyans posed a formidable threat to Egypt, and Merneptah, in his extremity, sought advice from the gods.

They were reassuring. Ptah himself appeared to the king in a dream and offered him a sword. Merneptah, on this symbolic advice, sent out the army. We cannot condemn him for not taking part himself, for he was probably too old and possibly too fat for such exercise. But victory, in the orthodox view, was a gift of the gods who employed men and weapons as their tools, so Merneptah's "pull" with divinity very properly received credit for the Egyptian success. Over six thousand of the enemy were slain, and nine thousand were taken prisoner.

Merneptah commemorated his victory in writing, upon a wall at Karnak. He also caused a stela to be carved—on the back of a stela of Amenhotep III, but he was not about to apologize for a minor usurpation of that sort after the outstanding example his father had given him. The inscription on this stela is one of the best known texts in Egyptology, and for a rather unusual reason. It gives the standard shouts of praises for the warrior-king, ending with a long list of conquered towns and tribes. The style of this hymn of victory is reminiscent of modern football reporting, which seems to have an unwritten rule against the use of the word *defeated*. Southern Cal smashes or flattens, or walks over, or edges an opponent; Merneptah plundered, and laid waste, and destroyed. Among the variegated verb forms we find the following phrase: "Israel is desolated, and has no seed."

Naturally, this stela is called the "Israel stela," and the reader can understand why it is so widely known. This is the one and only mention of the Israelites in all the Egyptian inscriptions we possess. And, of course, it provides a terminal point to the vexed question of the Exodus, which we glanced at earlier and then put off for future consideration.

The wicked pharaoh of the Exodus has long been sought by biblical scholars, and formerly Merneptah was a leading contender for the job. Proponents of the theory were confounded when Merneptah's mummy was found, resting in peace though in poverty, in 1898; they had expected that his body would long since have dissolved in the waters of the Red Sea. The mummy is irrelevant to the problem, really; the thing that eliminates Merneptah as the pharaoh of the Exodus is this very stela, which demonstrates that Israel was a recognized entity by the time of Ramses II's son. It is interesting to note, however, that the determinative of the word is not the sign for city or country, but for people—a tribe, rather than a state.

Who then was the pharaoh of the Exodus? Or was there a pharaoh of the Exodus? Was there, in fact, an Exodus at all?

A popular compromise answer holds that there was no single, massive exodus as described in the Old Testament. Asiatic peoples were continually wandering in and out of Egypt, as visitors or traders or conquered slaves, according to the vicissitudes of the Egyptian empire in Asia. A group of the people whose descendants formed part of the kingdom of Israel may have entered Egypt with the Hyksos; another group may have been led in chains behind the victorious chariot of Thutmose III; one group was active in the deserts of Palestine during the reign of Akhenaton, if the Habiru who devastated the southern half of Egypt's empire at that time have any connection with the Hebrews. Or none of the above may be true. The biblical narrative specifically mentions the treasure cities of Pithom and Ramses, which implies that some of the Hebrews dragged stones under Merneptah's father. However, there is the possibility that the names of the cities were added by a later compiler of the original tale, for the name of Ramses early came to loom large in the minds of men who thought of Egypt. As you can see, the problem is not simple, and the solutions to it are strongly influenced by the prejudices of the theorists. The archaeological evidence is equally conflicted. I don't intend to go into details, since the subject is really outside the mainstream of our symposium.

Gallant (or lucky) old Merneptah, who was not the pharaoh of the Exodus, had a few years left to him after the battle with the Libyans and the Sea Peoples, and he spent them emulating his father; he tore down as many monuments as he could get at and built himself some memorials. Since he did not reign as long as Ramses II, he was unable to wreak so much havoc, though he did manage to dismantle the superb mortuary temple of Amenhotep III. When he died, a time of anarchy ensued, as Egyptologists like to say. It ensues, henceforth, with depressing frequency.

During this particular ensual, Seti II, Merneptah's son, succeeded him. But he wasn't the only king of Egypt at that time. A fellow named Amenmesse also occupied the throne. Did he control only Upper Egypt, with Seti II ruling in the north? Or did he snatch the throne away from Seti for three years, or five, or six? His mother was apparently a queen, but his father is unknown. Merneptah, Seti II? Take your pick. Seti II eventually ended up having sole control, and proceeded to replace Amenmesse's name with his own wherever possible. Seti in turn was succeeded by a youth named Siptah, who was probably his son, but maybe Amenmesse's. Siptah's mother has an unusual name—Sitailja, or Shoteraja— certainly non-Egyptian, possibly Canaanite. He was only about eighteen when he died, after a reign of six years. His mummy has a severe deformity of the left foot, probably the result of polio.

Obviously a twelve-year-old king required a regent. Since his mother was almost certainly a concubine or lesser wife, the logical candidate, in accordance with tradition, was the chief wife of Seti II, Tausert.

Here's where the sense of déjà vu all over again begins. In addition to the female regent we have a mysterious character named Bay, who held the title of chancellor. His name suggests that he was Syrian, possibly related to Siptah's mother; his exalted position (for he was granted the high privilege of a tomb in the Royal Valley) has prompted the same sort of rumors that gathered around Hatshepsut and Senenmut. After Siptah's death Tausert proclaimed herself king, as Hatshepsut had done before her, assuming kingly titles. We have no depictions of her in male attire and form, but that could be because only a few monuments of hers have survived.

Not very exciting, is it? Yet there is material for a thrilling historical novel here, and hints of dark events, murder, betrayal, and conspiracy. Bay's influence did not endure; a recently discovered inscription calls him the great enemy, and proclaims that the king has had him killed. One would love to know why Siptah (or someone else in power) took this step. Chancellor Bay would make a splendid eminence grise, like Cardinals Mazarin and Richelieu three thousand years later and, like them, the lover of the queen regent. Or was he a hated rival of the lady, who finally became powerful enough to order his execution? It's pure fiction. The players in this drama are two-dimensional; we don't know much about them, except for the fact that they all, including Tausert, had rather nice tombs in the Valley of the Kings. There is another tomb in the valley connected with Tausert and her husband, Seti II; the so-called Gold Tomb, though small in size and obviously not of royal dimensions, contained a cache of jewelry that was one of the most impressive found up to that time.

Among the loot was a pair of very small silver gloves, with a number of rings inside the fingers. Nothing organic had survived. It may well be that the theory suggested by one scholar is correct: that the burial was that of a small prince or princess, and that when the modern excavator cleaned out the silver gloves he threw away the rotted flesh and bone of a royal child.

Tausert's successor was Setnakhte, a man of unknown antecedents, who took over her elegant tomb in the Valley of the Kings and was buried there after a reign of only a few years. Like Hatshepsut's, Tausert's mummy is missing, unless one of the unidentified females in the royal cache is hers.

Setnakhte is considered the founder of a new dynasty—the Twentieth—but his chief claim to fame is that he fathered Ramses III.

The name had already become one to reckon with, and Ramses III's aping of his predecessor was certainly deliberate; it is too exact and too consistent to be otherwise. Ramses III built grandly and without undue modesty. His most famous monument is his mortuary temple, which today bulks large upon the West Bank of the Nile across from Luxor, not far from the mortuary temple of his idol, Ramses II. Medinet Habu is the name given to the temple of the third Ramses; it has been studied with more intense concentration than has any other Egyptian temple. The Oriental Institute has been copying texts and excavating in and around the temple for more than thirty years. The results fill several immense volumes, each about half as tall as I am, and they may truthfully be said to be as precise and accurate as any product of modern archaeological methods can be. If you visit Medinet Habu—which you certainly will do if you go to Luxor, since it is part of the standard tour—you will be struck by the yards and yards of inscriptions. I have a personal interest in these texts because I spent one semester translating some of them, and I contemplated the inscribed walls with loathing. The laudatory texts are as turgid and repetitive and pompous as the architecture. Once again— compare it with Deir el Bahri.

Medinet Habu was more than a temple. The king had a palace here, one of a number that he maintained, with the usual offices and servants' quarters. Ramses entertained his harem in the gatehouse, and the reliefs that survive here are chastely indicative of the purpose of the structure. In defense of the adverb, let me add that the Egyptians saw nothing shocking about nudity; climate and common sense alike decreed relatively few garments in informal situations.

The Medinet Habu reliefs and inscriptions tell of more serious matters than dalliance with the girls of the harem. When Merneptah crushed the Sea Peoples and the Libyans, he may have believed that he had settled one problem for good and all. But he had only encountered the first wave of the great migrations, or Völkerwanderungen, which marked the first millennium before the Christian Era, and revamped the political map of much of the Middle East. The Sea Peoples and the Libyans were on the march once more; the old tribes who had harassed Merneptah had acquired fresh allies. Some of the new names may be identified; the Danu are possibly the Danaoi of the *Iliad*, and the Peleset are surely the Philistines, who settled along the coast of Palestine and irritated the Israelites in succeeding years. These people were not so much an army as a swarm of army ants, a vast column of warriors, oxen, children, wagons, and baggage carts which swept like a scourge through the eastern lands. They dealt the Hittites their death blow and came down on Egypt by sea and by land.

Ramses III defeated them in ferocious fighting on land and water. In three separate engagements he took care of the Libyans and the Sea Peoples, which makes his military accomplishments much more impressive than those of Ramses II. But there was one important difference. Ramses II was fighting at Kadesh, in what might be called a war of aggression hundreds of miles from Egypt. The men who fought under Ramses III had their backs to the wall, and they fought with the knowledge that defeat meant slavery or annihilation. The Egyptian empire was dead. Later there would be attempts to resurrect it, just as there would be imitations of other elements of past glory. But the ka of Thutmose III, safely settled in the Land of the Westerners, was not reembodied in Egypt.

The end of the Twentieth Dynasty is a sad spectacle. Almost every document that survives from this time, beginning with the last years of Ramses III, tells the same tale of corruption and abuse, a deadly rot that invaded every cell of the body politic. The death of Ramses III is an example; it does not seem appropriate to call it a "good" example. He was probably murdered by members of his own household in a case involving the blackest treachery, witchcraft, and subornation. The conspirators were headed by a queen named Ti, who wanted to see her son upon the throne of Egypt. The true heir, Ramses IV to be, did not succeed in saving his father's life—was it, one wonders cynically, his primary aim?— but he defended his own rights with a vigor which he displayed in no other activity during his brief reign. The queen, her son the pretender, and certain harem officials were seized and condemned to trial.

During the hearings the ghastly tale of black magic emerged. One of the criminals began to make humans of wax, inscribed, so that they might be taken in by the inspector of the harem. To what purpose? one wonders. Were the waxen images used as they have been used in European witchcraft? Such a doll could be identified with a particular individual by means of fingernail clippings, hair, or the like kneaded into the wax; torments worked upon the image inflicted corresponding injuries upon the victim's body. The use of these "humans of wax" or clay is very, very old, but it is impossible to be sure that this is how they were used by the Egyptians. There is a suggestion that one of the figures may have been that of Ramses III, animated by means of a magical roll and thus a puppet in the hands of the conspirators. Though we do not fully understand the means, the deadly purpose of the magic is clear enough. To make matters worse, some of the judges fell under the influence of two of the accused criminals, consorting and carousing with them while the trial was under way. All the criminals died. The lesser were executed, but those of higher rank were accorded the privilege of supervised suicide.

We are told of only one other attempt at assassination, that of Amenemhat III back in the Twelfth Dynasty, but one can't help suspecting that this sort of thing happened every now and then. If successful, the usurper would piously proclaim himself the chosen of Amon and bury his victim with suitable ceremony. If unsuccessful, why talk about anything so distasteful, so threatening to *maat*? The only reason why we know so much about this one is due to an accident of survival—a record of the court proceedings—or perhaps it's only part of the proceedings. There is no mention of witnesses, no questioning of the accused by the judges, only a methodical list of the condemned and their punishments.

Up to this time the priesthoods had done well for themselves. A document called the Papyrus Harris, written at the end of the reign of Ramses III, lists the extent of the temple property. We are not sure whether the fantastic figures indicated only the gifts of Ramses to the gods, or the total amounts, including his donations; but in either case the holdings of the ecclesiastical foundations must have been enormous. Estimates range from 2 percent of the people of Egypt and 15 percent of the land, to 20 percent of the people and almost one-third of the total acreage. The figures would not be so formidable if the wealth had been equally divided; Egypt had so many gods and so many temples that the grand total would have been safely fragmented. But the great gods of Egypt held the lion's share of the wealth, and the greatest of them all, Amon-Re of Thebes, was mightiest in temporal terms as well. One scholar has estimated that Amon alone owned one-fifteenth of the population and one-eleventh of the land.

The last kings of the Twentieth Dynasty are a dreary roll of Ramses—eight more of them. The events of their reigns are equally dreary. Asia, as a field of conquest, was closed to Egypt, and Ramses VI was the last king to work the mines in Sinai. At home, the stain of decay spread and deepened. The necropolis workers of Thebes, the men who built and maintained the tombs on the West Bank, went on strike on numerous occasions, demanding the pay that was overdue them. Each time the responsible officials met them with soothing words and promises that were never, or inadequately, fulfilled.

The priests were no less venal than their counterparts in the civil bureaucracy. Indeed, the distinction between civil and religious functions was far from sharp, and a man might hold offices in the temple and in the court simultaneously. But if he had to choose between the two, the service of the gods was preferable. As far back as the Eighteenth Dynasty the convenient omniscience of historians allowed us to utter dire predictions of the danger of the trend that Papyrus Harris illustrates so vividly. We were able to view the generosity of Thutmose III and his successors to their patron god as a portent because we knew what was going to happen. It has been suggested that there was an element of political expediency in Akhenaton's religious experiment, if not in Akhenaton himself. However, this interpretation necessitates the assumption that someone possessed a remarkable degree of insight into a situation that had not, at that time, taken on the shape it was to assume later, and which was probably never defined in such clear-cut terms. The conception of church and state as separate, rival entities was antithetical to the Egyptian worldview.

Whatever the causes of the heresy, the results did not weaken Amon but gave him renewed strength. With the progressive debility of the state, and the succession of feeble pharaohs clinging to the name of Ramses as to a talisman, the power of Amon continued to wax.

The last Ramses, number eleven, marks the end of the Twentieth Dynasty. Egypt was in bad shape by then, impoverished and torn by what was essentially civil war. It ended with the country again divided, Ramses XI being allowed to retain the titles of king and control of the north, while the high priest of Amon controlled the south.

By this time even Amon-Re must have been feeling the pinch. Presumably the temples still owned a great portion of the country, but no longer did tribute from abroad enrich the gods. However, there was one source of wealth available to the man who ruled at Thebes—the tombs in the Valley of the Kings.

Tomb robberies, which had never been completely suppressed, increased as the necropolis workers increasingly suffered from nonpayment of wages and official corruption. They knew where the loot was buried, and they may have figured it was of more use to them than to the silent dead. At first the authorities tried to carry out regular inspections and repair the damage they found. It was extensive; in some cases even the bodies had been dismembered and left scattered on the floors of the burial chambers. Eventually the priests decided they were fighting a losing battle. The only sure way of protecting what was left of the royal dead was to collect them and tuck them away in secret hiding places.

An honorable, pious enterprise, to be sure. Or was it?

Well, partly. The ruined bodies were rewrapped and relabeled, but it now seems clear that anything of value left on or with the mummy was recycled by the emissaries of the high priests. Two of them, scribes of the tomb named Djehutymose and his son, Butehamon, have achieved belated and somewhat dubious fame among Egyptologists. Their names appear all over the cliffs of the West Bank, noting the presence of the tombs they had located—and emptied. A series of letters between the High Priest Piankh and these two men makes their activities clear. The process went on for years, and by the time it was finished the tombs in the Valley of the Kings had been cleared of their former occupants and what had remained of their possessions—all except one. The location of Tutankhamon's tomb had been forgotten by the end of the Twentieth Dynasty. The mere fact that its contents survived is proof of that.

The gold in the other tombs, even the gilding on the coffins, went into the coffers of the high priests. Stripped of their valuables and in some cases mislabeled, the pathetic remains of the royal mummies found final resting places where they lay undisturbed for three thousand years.

Even before this time the office of high priest of Amon had become hereditary, like the kingship. The High Priest Amenhotep had been preceded in the office by his brother and his father, and he had shown signs of increasing presumption by having himself carved on a temple wall the same size as the pharaoh whom he faced. This would have been inconceivable in earlier times. He had to appeal to Ramses XI, however, when the viceroy of Nubia, Panehsy by name, marched north with an army and actually besieged the high priest at Medinet Habu, the mortuary temple of Ramses III, which had formidable walls. The royal army, led by a general named Piankh, eventually met and overcame Panehsy's army, which retreated to Nubia. Not too surprisingly, General Piankh seems to have settled down at Thebes, where he eventually took the additional office of high priest of Amon.

His successor in both high offices was a figure of some stature. Here the presumed conflict between church and state is seen in its true light; Herihor was church and state in one person. As a soldier and viceroy of Nubia he commanded a large and effective army. The high priesthood was probably a prize of his prowess rather than the source of it. When he added the title of high priest to those of his military rank, he had more prestige than any man in Egypt except the pharaoh, and more real power than any man, including the pharaoh. It was only a matter of time before he would adjust the fiction to suit the fact and climb into the throne from behind.

The reliefs on the walls of the Khonsu temple at Karnak tell the tale with an ironic clarity that needs no words. In the outer courts the high priest usurps the functions of the king and makes offerings in his own person; inside the temple, the latest part to be built, he assumes the crown and the cartouche. So pass the Ramessids—unwept and unhonored, perhaps, but not unsung, thanks to the strenuous efforts of the second and third bearers of that now diminished name.

Ten

THE LONG DYING

Cartouche of Psamtik

ADVENTURES OF A MAN OF NO CONSEQUENCE

In the spring of a year some thirty centuries ago an Egyptian official set out from Thebes on a long and tedious business trip. His destination was Byblos, his mission the acquisition of cedar wood for the divine boat of Amon-Re. The name of Amon's messenger was Wenamon, and his adventures are told in one of the most famous papyri of ancient Egypt. The story may be the ancestor of all historical novels, a felicitous blending of fact and fiction.

True or not, it is a wonderful tale, a tragicomedy of adventure and mis-adventure; and it incidentally tells us a great deal about the state of affairs in and around Egypt in the twelfth century before Christ.

The nominal king of Egypt was the last of the Ramses, number eleven, but as we have seen he exercised very little power. Wenamon's overlord was the high priest of Amon, Herihor, who was master of Upper Egypt. When Wenamon left Thebes he soon entered the territory of an-other man who was to claim royal status—Nesubanebded, known to Manetho as Smendes, of Tanis in the Delta. His approval was necessary before Wenamon could continue his journey. This was easily done, for Smendes and Herihor had an "understanding"; but this divided authority is one of the symptoms of the breakdown which the story illustrates.

Wenamon took passage on a ship leaving for Palestine—another bad sign, for an emissary sent on such a mission by the god in better days would have had his own fleet. By the time the boat reached Dor in Pales-tine, Wenamon's store of money—not too great at best—had been stolen by a member of the crew. Raging, Wenamon made his way into the pres-ence of the prince of Dor and demanded justice or restitution, preferably the latter. The prince met his unreasonable demand with remarkable for-bearance; indeed, he appears much more urbane than the Egyptian. We can almost see his eyebrows lifting as he inquires coolly, "Are you serious, or are you inventing? Indeed, I know nothing of this tale which you have told me." The prince pointed out that the thief was not one of his own subjects; if this had been the case he would have replaced the money—an offer that diminishes the amount to a bagatelle unbefitting an Egyptian envoy of Amon. But since the thief belonged to Wenamon's own ship, the prince felt that he had no obligation. He did offer to institute a search. When this proved fruitless, poor Wenamon went on his way, his heart despairing and his eyes wide open.

Shortly after he reached Byblos, Wenamon had made good part of his loss. Although he is understandably vague about details, we are led to understand that he had "liberated" thirty deben of silver from certain subjects of the prince of Dor, blandly informing the victims that he was taking their money in compensation for that which was stolen by their fellow countrymen. This specious argument, if it can be called an argument, was accepted by the victims with surprising meekness, which leads the reader to wonder whether Wenamon waited around the scene of the crime long enough to discuss the problem.

So Wenamon sat down by the shore in the harbor of Byblos and congratulated himself. His rejoicing was premature. For reasons which Wenamon does not mention, the prince of that city had taken a dislike to him. "I spent twenty-nine days in his harbor, and he sent to me daily, saying 'Get yourself out of my harbor!'" Wenamon remarks morosely.

After twenty-nine days of this, Wenamon took the hint. He was looking for a ship back to Egypt when a strange incident occurred. We would call it luck, or coincidence—or, if we wish to be cynical, maybe Wenamon had enough money left for a bribe. During a ceremony in the temple, one of the prince's attendants was "seized by the god" and cried out, "Bring up the god, bring up the messenger who is carrying him; it is Amon who sent him!"

It happened that Wenamon, in lieu of cash, had brought along a portable statue of his god, which was called "Amon of the Ways." The frenzied youth's reference was too exact to be ignored. The prince of Byblos sent for Wenamon.

"I found him sitting in his upper room with his back to a window, so that the waves of the great Syrian sea broke behind his head," says Wenamon poetically. The two men got down to business, and with every word Wenamon was deeper in trouble. The prince spared the humiliated Egyptian no embarrassment. He admitted that Amon was supreme, that Egypt had once been the hub of the world, and that his own land owed much to the skill and learning it had acquired from Egypt. But this was in the past. Where was Wenamon's ship? the prince asked sarcastically—for surely a man on so important a mission would have been given an official vessel for his journey? Where were his credentials? Most important of all—where was his money? Byblos was not subject to the ruler of Egypt. Even in the past, when a king of that land ordered a shipment of the fine cedar wood, he had paid for it, and paid well. The prince brought out his account books to prove it.

Wenamon "was silent in that great moment." There really wasn't much he could say. But he hit on the one argument he did have, and hit it hard—the power and might of Amon and the spiritual benefits he could bestow, benefits beside which mere gold and silver were trivial. His speech was masterful, fully worthy of the man who could talk his way out of a robbery, and it had its effect. The prince of Byblos let him send back to Tanis for goods with which to trade. Smendes and his queen Tentamon came through, and the prince began to load the cedar.

Wenamon's troubles were not over. Just as he was finally about to set sail for Egypt with the hard-won cedar, he saw ships speeding into port. The ships belonged to the prince of Dor, who was in hot pursuit of the money Wenamon had liberated. Wenamon knew, as soon as he identified the ships, that he was in for it. Stiff upper lips and Anglo-Saxon phlegm were unknown to the ancients; when they suffered, they wanted everybody to know about it. Wenamon suffered all over the beach of Byblos, in a tone of voice that was clearly audible up at the palace.

One can only marvel at Wenamon's oratorical talents. His character or personal habits apparently induced instant hatred in the people who met him, but when he started talking he had the situation under control. The prince of Byblos was as responsive as a hypnotized rabbit to the Egyptian's rhetoric. Although Wenamon's loud laments—before the boats had even landed!—were an open confession of guilt, the prince stood by him. He sent the woebegone Egyptian a message telling him not to worry, and reinforced the advice with gifts of food and drink and the temporary loan of an Egyptian singing girl. The following day he got Wenamon on a ship and out of Byblos—with, no doubt, a hearty sigh of relief. The Egyptian ended up in Cyprus, and the inhabitants met him with curses and threats; this seems to have been the instant reaction of most of the people Wenamon encountered. He forced his way through the enraged throng and appealed to the queen of Cyprus for protection. The papyrus unhappily breaks off at this point, but no doubt the eloquence of Wenamon once again saved his life. He got back to Egypt to tell his tale.

The most important historical fact about this picaresque story is what it tells us of Egyptian prestige in the areas that had once been controlled by swaggering Egyptian troops. The breakdown at home was reflected by the contempt in which the once powerful nation was held abroad.

We may as well stop for a minute and get the terminology straight. Egyptologists like to break history up into periods. The Nineteenth and Twentieth Dynasties are sometimes referred to as the Ramesside Period. The Twenty-first through Twenty-sixth (Saite) Dynasties now constitute the Third Intermediate Period. (I can't quarrel with the logic of that term, since for almost the entire time Egypt consisted of separate states and kingdoms, just as it had during the first two intermediate periods. I just think there are getting to be too many "periods.") That leaves us with the Late Period, from the Twenty-seventh Dynasty, depending on which authority you happen to be reading, through the Persians, down to Alexander the Great. Oh, I almost forgot about the "Renaissance." It didn't last long, only for about ten years at the end of the Twentieth Dynasty; it overlapped the last years of Ramses XI and was—let me be fair about this—named by Egyptians, not Egyptologists.

The capital of the northern kingdom was at the city of Tanis. The kings of the Nineteenth Dynasty had moved their political center northward, from Memphis to Tanis in the Delta, but had always returned to Thebes in death, to be buried in the holy cemetery on the west bank of the Nile. The Twenty-first Dynasty gave up Thebes entirely. The royal tombs of this period were found by the French archaeologist Pierre Montet, who worked at Tanis during the 1920s and 1930s. He had the good fortune to run into one of the gilded caches which now and then reward the efforts of archaeologists. The tomb of Smendes's successor, Psusennes I, somehow managed to escape the notice of the industrious tomb robbers. The king himself still rested in it, richly adorned, and in side chambers of the tomb were the mummies of two members of his court, one of whom wore a distinctive and rather handsome gold mask. Montet found seven tombs and half a dozen kings, plus a few favored commoners. The Tanis burials are not as impressive as the unique collection of Tutankhamon, but if the latter had not been known (and if, in 1939, the world had not been preoccupied with grimmer news), the discovery would have made a sensation: the vases and bowls of precious metals, the elegant jewelry, the solid silver hawk-headed coffin and the other treasures of the tombs. The evidences of decline are there, however, not only in the quantity but in some cases the quality of the objects. Some of the best had been recycled. Psusennes's very sarcophagus was stolen from Merneptah of the Nineteenth Dynasty.

THE QUICK AND THE DEAD

The official transfer of the royal residence to the north stripped Thebes of much of its glory. Long before this time the city of Amon had, for all practical purposes, become a twin entity. On the east bank of the river were the great temples of Karnak and Luxor, the harbor and its attendant buildings, and the residential area inhabited by civil servants, temple officials, and the usual motley lot of anonymous commoners. Across the Nile, under the western cliffs, lay the greater city, which belonged to the dead. For generations the tombs of kings and commoners had honeycombed the hills; a row of great mortuary temples lay along the edge of the narrow cultivated land. The dead were not the only inhabitants of western Thebes, for they required an army of workmen, priests, soldiers, and artists to maintain their Houses of Eternity.

The royal necropoli on the west bank of the Nile had never been completely safe, but with the decline of the throne after the Nineteenth Dynasty, the grisly depredations of the tomb robbers multiplied and often went unpunished. We have a document, one of the most fascinating papyri ever discovered, which gives the details of a series of tomb robberies under Ramses IX, around 1120 B.C. The picture is one of depressing, widespread corruption. The accused are humble workers whose poverty might excuse their crimes, but the most casual reading between the lines makes it clear that more important people were criminally involved. The only bright and shining figure of virtue is that of the accuser, Paser, mayor of eastern Thebes, the city of the living. Paser's counterpart in western Thebes was named Paweraa. He was not only mayor of the western city but chief of the necropolis police, and one of his primary responsibilities would be the safeguarding of the tombs, royal and otherwise. This was the man whom Paser accused—of negligence at the very least.

If we wanted to be cynical we might speculate about Paser's motives; like his counterpart across the river, he was a politician, and when politicians fall out the worldly-wise may reasonably look behind the noble speeches. But it is kinder to view Paser as the one little candle in a naughty world. He certainly sounds righteous. Having received information to the effect that tomb robbers had been flourishing in Thebes of the Dead, under Paweraa's control, he promptly filed charges with the vizier. His informant had been specific; Paser mentioned by name ten kings, four queens, and many nobles whose Houses of Eternity had been recently defiled.

The vizier appointed a commission to investigate (what a discouragingly modern sound that has) and put the mayor of western Thebes in charge. This was a perfectly logical appointment, considering Paweraa's position, although a Solomon of a vizier might have realized that it was tantamount to appointing the fox to check on the henhouses. The commission accordingly tramped out across the steaming sands—this was in August, when most people simply collapse between the hours of twelve and four—and checked all the questioned tombs. They reported their results. Only one of the kings' and two of the queens' tombs mentioned by Paser had been robbed; with respect to the nobles' tombs, the mayor of eastern Thebes racked up an astonishing 100 percent accuracy.

On the face of it, this report would seem to confirm the charges. Robbery was certainly progressing at a rapid rate; the exact proportion of tombs violated was really beside the point. But the mayor of western

Thebes interpreted the findings of the commission differently. Or to put it another way, the technique of political "spin" is of ancient origin. On the following night, he allowed—the verb may be rather weak—his people, the workers of western Thebes, to demonstrate in celebration of his "vindication." The mob made its way to the house of Paser, the accuser, and stood around jeering at him. Paser was vexed. He lowered himself so far as to come to the door and exchange insults with the crowd. During the flow of repartee, the infuriated Paser bellowed that he was not ready to give up; he had heard about other tombs that had been robbed.

His rival across the river promptly reported the latest doings to the vizier, taking a tone of injured innocence. A new commission of inquiry met next day in the temple of Amon, with Paser on the bench along with certain high nobles and the vizier himself. This gentleman, the highest appointed official in the land, then proceeded to render impotent the commission he had set up. He opened the hearings with a statement which implied that he had already checked the suspected tombs and found nothing wrong! This took the wind out of Paser's sails. Imagine him, squirming on the bench and growing paler and paler as the suspects he had dragged in took their cues from the vizier and denied everything.

That was the end of Paser; reformer or not, he was trying to swim against the tide. He sank. We never hear of him again, whereas his opponent, Paweraa, was still mayor and chief of police seventeen years later. The tomb robberies continued and increased under the latter's administration. Every now and then a petty carpenter or a humble coppersmith was tried and executed, as a sop to the proprieties, but it is so obvious from the papyrus itself who the guilty parties really were, that we wonder how anyone reading the report could have missed the truth. The answer may lie in the fact that the highest official who dealt with the matter was the vizier; and I have my doubts about him.

Recorded confessions of tomb robbers make it clear that part of the normal business expense in the trade was the bribery of officials. The situation went from bad to worse; by the time of the Twenty-first Dynasty, the priest-kings of Thebes were ready for drastic measures. Most of the royal mummies were still intact. How long they would remain so was a question. If they were left in their tombs, whose location was almost a matter of public record, some disappointed thief might destroy the sacred remains, as was in fact done by one set of robbers whose trial records we possess. So the successors of Herihor, who were in power at Thebes, made a plan. A royal commission met and took council on the problem of the dead, and the solution it proposed was the one we mentioned in the last chapter. One by one the despoiled bodies of the ancient kings were gathered together, repaired, and rewrapped (and, incidentally, stripped of any remaining valuables), and hidden away, most of them in a small rock-cut chamber tomb not far from Hatshepsut's temple of Deir el Bahri. The coffins were shoved in, one on top of the other, until the small tomb was nearly filled. Then the weary officials retired, the entrance was concealed—and silence descended until a modern Egyptian named Ahmed went looking for a lost goat.

TOMB ROBBERS AND ROYAL MUMMIES

The Egyptians of the nineteeth century A.D. were among the most accomplished tomb robbers the world has ever seen. One cannot help but have a certain sympathy for their point of view. The tombs were on their land and had belonged, if not to their direct ancestors, to their predecessors. Ancient artifacts had no value to the dead (devout Moslems go to their graves without so much as a coffin), but they were fetching high prices from tourists and museums. Furthermore, the busy citizens of Gurneh and Giza could reasonably claim that their activities were no more destructive than those of many of the archaeologists of the time.

Among the busiest and most successful of these entrepreneurs were the members of a family of Gurneh, on the West Bank at Luxor. The Abd er Rassuls had a well-nigh uncanny instinct for locating hidden tombs. They are the only tomb robbers mentioned in *Who Was Who in Egyptology*. One of the brothers, Mohammed, was in the service of Mustafa Agha, a consular agent at Thebes. Ahmed and Hussein, the other brothers, "dealt in antiquities." Their most spectacular discovery occurred in the early 1870s—the precise date is unknown—when Ahmed Abd er Rassul was strolling around the western cliffs for purposes unknown. He said he was looking for a lost goat. One may legitimately wonder whether he was looking for something else. He could not have anticipated the magnitude of his actual discovery, in a cleft in the rock going down to a small tomb. Packed helter-skelter within were dozens of coffins and many other pieces of funerary equipment.

Ahmed couldn't read the inscriptions that identified the occupants of the coffins, but he knew enough to recognize the shape of the cartouches, which were only used by royalty. No doubt overwhelmed by the richness of the find, he let his brothers in on the secret, and they began marketing some of the smaller objects such as ushabtis and funerary papyri.

The world of archaeology is a small one, and collectors and scholars keep in touch with one another. Within a few years after the Abd er Rassul brothers struck it rich, objects began to turn up in museums and private collections all over the world. They were important objects, and yet no new tomb discovery had been officially reported. The matter came to the attention of Gaston Maspero, the French director of the Egyptian Antiquities Service. Maspero kept an alert eye on the antiquities market, and gradually a pattern began to emerge. The probable source of the new objects was narrowed down to the Luxor area; although they came from the burials of different persons, the fact that they had been put on the market more or less simultaneously indicated that they had been found together. What was sought, then, was not a single royal tomb, but a cache where many mummies were concealed. Maspero asked the police to look out for a man from Luxor who was spending too much money.

The Abd er Rassul family soon came under suspicion, but nothing could make them divulge their secret, although the methods of interrogation were brutal; Ahmed was permanently crippled by being beaten on the soles of his feet. However, it was the eldest brother, Mohammed, who finally cracked. Mohammed thought his brothers were getting the lion's share of the loot, nor could he give them the complete trust which brothers ought to feel for one another. In pure self-protection, fearing they were about to betray him, he betrayed them first.

Maspero was not in Egypt when Mohammed's revelation broke, but his assistant, Emile Brugsch, went at once to Thebes. He was led to the cache, which was entered by a deep shaft descending from a small opening at the base of a sheer rock wall. Brugsch was stupefied by what he found—the coffins of the mightiest pharaohs of Egypt piled one atop the other like kindling wood. According to his later account, he read some of the cartouches as he moved slowly along the dark, cluttered passages, squeezing past mummy cases and stepping carefully over a litter of smaller objects. The liberator, Ahmose I, Amenhotep I, founder of the Eighteenth Dynasty, the warrior Thutmose III—thirty-five mummies in all, including the family of the later priest-king Pinudjem, whose coffins filled the final chamber.

Dazzled and disbelieving, Brugsch had to make a hard decision. He knew that he had to get the coffins into safekeeping as soon as possible; it was not unheard of for fellahin to attack archaeologists, and the richness of the find was a strong incentive to violence. He was probably right, but the result was that no records were kept, no plans or sketches made. Wrapping and securing the objects, maneuvering the heavy coffins through the narrow passages and up the shaft, took fewer than six days. They were then carried across the river and loaded onto the government steamer. It is said that as the slow vessel moved downstream the villagers gathered on the shore, wailing and keening in a form of mourning millennia old. It was a touching sight, but one wonders whether they were mourning the loss of their ancient kings, or the removal of a reliable source of local employment.

The Deir el Bahri cache was perhaps the most dramatic discovery ever made in Egypt: the actual physical remains of men who ruled one of the world's mightiest empires thousands of years ago, men whose names and reputations were as old as legend. Scholars found it a trifle disconcerting to acknowledge that the momentous discovery was made by a pack of crooks, but these lucky intuitive moments do occur, even to the uneducated. They were willing to forgive and forget. In a burst of generosity, the Antiquities Department hired the stool pigeon, Mohammed. It was a good demonstration of the practical value of high moral gestures. In 1891, some ten years after the Deir el Bahri find, Mohammed came to Eugene Grébaut, Maspero's successor, and ended what must have been a long and painful mental struggle—his new loyalty to the Antiquities Department against his instincts and family ties. The uneducated but inspired Abd er Rassul boys had found another tomb and had made good use of it while Mohammed was wrestling with his principles (the fight had lasted quite a long time). It was the third of the big multiple reburials, that of the high priests of Amon-Re. The second, in the tomb of Amenhotep II, had been found in 1898 by Loret, a professional Egyptologist, who thus retrieved some of his colleagues' battered reputation for luck. With Amenhotep II's mummy were, among others, those of Thutmose IV, Amenhotep III, and Seti II.

The royal remains found by Loret were eventually brought to Cairo and united with those of their peers in the Cairo Museum, where, after many journeys, they lie today. Tutankhamon's sadly decayed mummy, marred by the very unguents and ointment that were meant to increase its hopes of survival, and dismembered by the modern archaeologists who discovered it, still rests within its gilded and guarded outermost coffin in the Valley of the Kings. The skeleton of his brother, Smenkhkare, is also in Cairo.

One might assume that after the bodies of the kings were found in modern times they could expect a final end to their wanderings, in whatever dignity the museum could afford. But such was not the case. The royal mummies had one more journey to make—a short trip but one that, unfortunately, had touches of macabre comedy.

In the early 1930s, when the National Party came to power in Egypt, the prime minister, Nahas, erected a costly mausoleum to shelter the body of Saad Zaghlul, the founder of the party. Later the Nationalist government fell and was replaced by a hostile coalition that wanted to lessen the propaganda impact of Zaghlul and his mausoleum. In order to diffuse public interest, the new prime minister ordered the royal mummies to be placed in the tomb alongside the Nationalist idol. Then the Nationalists got in again and decided that too much admiration was being lavished on the mummies, and not enough upon their hero. They sent a curt message to the museum, ordering the authorities to come and get their old kings. Somewhat nonplussed, the museum authorities hired a couple of ambulances, and in the dead of night entered the mausoleum. The last funeral cortege—to date—of the royal dead of ancient Egypt wound through the streets of the sleeping city into a court of the museum, and the bodies were reverently placed in an unused room.

For some time thereafter it was necessary to secure permission to see them from the appropriate Egyptian ministry, and only scholars and distinguished visitors were accorded the privilege. Now the only criterion to which tourists are subjected is the payment of a sizeable fee. Not all the mummies are on display, only those that have been stabilized and put in climate-controlled glass cases. Among them is Ramses II, the greatest traveler of the lot; a few years ago he was taken to Paris to be treated for insect infestation by experts there.

Perhaps the exorbitant admission charge does deter the great majority of the irreverent. There is so much to see in the Cairo Museum that only mummy buffs and archaeologists are apt to pay an additional sum for the privilege of gazing on the ghastly remnants of the long dead. Certainly these tattered specimens deserve the courtesy of silence, at the least, and their present setting, quiet and dimly lit, is conducive to respect. We had a couple of mummies at the Oriental Institute when I was a student there—two little old ladies (they were certainly old) who were known to the students as Mert and Mabel. I found them just as interesting as anybody else did, but I used to cringe at those nicknames. I am not sure that I would recommend a visit to the royal mummies at Cairo as an enjoyable experience. Sekenenre is there, the holes of the battle ax piercing his skull and his mouth agape in the last horrid scream of anguish; Ramses II, the great warrior and womanizer, still has some nasty, rusty white hairs on his withered skull; even Seti I, who must have been a particularly stately and handsome man, is very dry. One comes away with a great thirst, and with a dim reluctance to eat or drink anything for a little time. The sunlight seems too bright, and the noises of the city streets strike strangely on the ear.

MUMMY MUSICAL CHAIRS

The two caches of royal mummies did not contain such spectacular artifacts as did the tomb of Tutankhamon. In terms of historical value, however, they ought to have been more important; for, as we have mentioned, anthropologists can learn a great deal from human remains. One group of mummies from the Deir el Bahri cache dates to the Twenty-first Dynasty, family members and associates of the priest-kings Pinudjem. Another group from that cache includes kings, queens, and officials from the late Seventeenth through the Twentieth Dynasties. Add to this latter collection the royal mummies found in the second cache, in the tomb of Amenhotep II, and we have almost all the great kings of Egypt's glory— Thutmoses, Amenhoteps, Rameses, Seti I. An examination of these mummies, surely, could answer some of the questions still remaining about length of reign and family relationships.

Once the mummies were in the museum, Maspero called in Sir Grafton Elliot Smith, one of the foremost anatomists of his time, to unwrap and examine them. The process went on for several years; not until 1886 were the majority of the remains unwrapped.

Maspero knew that the mummies weren't in their original coffins or bandaging. Hieratic inscriptions, written on coffins and shrouds by the priests who had restored the bodies, were the only way of identifying them. Maspero had no reason to doubt these identifications; but even at the time Smith expressed doubts about certain of them. Not until 1967, when X-ray examinations of the royal mummies were made, did serious questions arise. To take a single example, the individual identified as that of Thutmose I was probably no more than twenty years old at his death. The historical evidence indicates that Thutmose had to have been a lot older.

By the time the later investigators, Edward Wente and James Harris, got through, they had proposed not one but three schemes of reidentification, based on the assumption that the priests who restored the bodies in ancient times hadn't been paying attention. It's a somewhat entertaining and very complicated subject; the reader who wishes to pursue it will find an excellent summary in an addendum to Dennis Forbes's *Tombs. Treasures. Mummies.* (See Additional Reading.)

THE THIRD INTERMEDIATE PERIOD

As we have seen in the story of Wenamon, the Twenty-first Dynasty started out with Egypt effectively divided. The generals and high priests of Amon following Piankh and Herihor controlled the southern half and the Smendes and his successor ruled the Delta. The northern throne then passed to Psusennes, son of Pinudjem I of Thebes. Nominally the country was then under a single king, although the line of military high priests continued to hold political control in the south. The two houses were closely connected by birth and by marriage, and relations between them were cordial. The dynasty ended around 950 B.C. and was succeeded by the first ruling family of non-Egyptian stock, if we do not count the Hyksos.

The founder of the Libyan or Twenty-second Dynasty had the barbarous (from the Egyptian viewpoint) name of Sheshonk. We have a neat family tree that carries his genealogy back to the Twentieth Dynasty, when his ancestors settled in Egypt. They were Libyans, who called themselves "chiefs of the Meshwesh." The Meshwesh were one of the Libyan tribes whom Merneptah and Ramses III had defeated, but the particular Meshwesh who became kings of Egypt were thoroughly Egyptianized and had lived in Egypt for generations.

Sheshonk I, as he is known, was one of the more effective leaders Egypt had seen for some time. By sending his son to Thebes as high priest of Amon and army commander, he was able to take control of the southern part of Egypt, and he made the first military incursion into the Levant in over one hundred years. As Shishak, Sheshonk is well known to biblical scholars, for it was he who sacked Jerusalem in the fifth year of King Rehoboam (I Kings 14:25–26). The only source for this is the Old Testament; "Shishak" did not consider Jerusalem worth mentioning on the great entrance portal he built at Karnak, though he gave a long list of other conquered towns in Palestine. We may therefore conclude that he campaigned there, but precisely where and with what results are unknown, since neither account can be taken literally. *Indiana Jones and the Lost Ark* is wonderful fun, but there is no mention in either the Egyptian or the Hebrew account of the Ark of the Covenant being taken to Egypt and no reason to suppose that if it had been taken, which it probably wasn't, it would have been reverently tucked away in a secret tomb at Tanis.

Tanis was one of the major cities of this dynasty, but Bubastis in the Delta, home of the cat goddess Bastet, was equally important. The Twenty-second Dynasty is therefore sometimes called the Bubastite. The other kings are either Osorkons or Takelots; there were several of each, and it's impossible to tell them apart without a scorecard, unless you are an Egyptologist specializing in this confused period.

By the end of the Twenty-second Dynasty the kingdom was dissolving, back into the small states from which it had arisen. At one point there were four or five people claiming the titles of king. The Twenty-third Dynasty was probably contemporaneous with the Twenty-second, and the Twenty-Fourth consisted of a single king, whose Greek name was Bocchoris. He was the son of a local prince named Tefnakhte, and why he rates a separate dynasty, only heaven and Manetho know; centered in the Delta city of Sais, he certainly never ruled all of Egypt. The only continuity, of an unusual sort, was at Thebes, where a series of women held the office of God's Wife.

We have seen this title before; it was used by queens during the Eighteenth Dynasty, presumably to refer to their unique relationship with the god Amon. The title appears sporadically during succeeding dynasties, always being held by the king's wife. We can't be precisely certain when the situation changed, since identifying holders of the title during the Twenty-second Dynasty is difficult. By the beginning of the Twenty-third Dynasty, however, the God's Wife of Amon had become an independent power, functioning alongside the male rulers of Thebes. These women were not kings' wives. All were kings' daughters; the office was not passed on from mother to daughter but by way of adoption. It is safe to assume, as most scholars have done, that the ladies had no mortal husbands but remained faithful to Amon in body as well as in spirit. Two of their other titles, those of Adorer of the God and Hand of the God, are known from earlier times, but presumably had different implications at this period.

In practical terms, the procedure had a number of advantages. Each new king, whatever his antecedents, sent a (presumably virgin) daughter to Thebes, to be adopted by the current God's Wife—thus gaining a certain degree of legitimacy and a loyal adherent, who might help to counter the prestige of the high priest. How much political power the God's Wives actually wielded is questionable, but the office continued unbroken, through changes of dynasty, invasion, and usurpation, until Egypt fell to a conqueror who worshipped other gods than Amon-Re of Thebes.

In the meantime the nation was ripe for invasion, which was just what it got. The Assyrians were coming down, and they were not the only ones. The Egyptians were not as adept in the "mysteries" as the Rosicrucians believed them to have been, and their varied contributions to civilization did not include the Ouija board. But if they had contacted the shade of Thutmose III he would probably have warned his remote successors to watch out for the Asiatics. Thutmose was too long dead; he would have probably been astounded at the direction from which the inevitable conquest finally came.

HORSEMEN FROM THE HOLY MOUNTAIN

Out of the level stretches of sand rise the pyramids, row on row. The gray smoke of incense ascends to heaven, and the voices of white-clad priests chant the old sacred hymns to the god. "O Amon-Re, Lord of the Holy Mountain..."

Wait a minute. Amon-Re—and pyramids? An anachronism has reared its ugly head. Pyramids were replaced by rock-cut tombs at about the time Amon began his spectacular rise to supremacy.

No, no anachronism. The pyramids and the great temples to Amon were contemporaneous, but not in Egypt. We must go back now in time, and south in space, to witness the flourishing of a strange hybrid that was to have a significant impact on the dying culture of ancient Egypt. Men of a distant clime and an alien race (I use the word poetically) once again carry weapons into the land of Horus; but they come as saviors, not as conquerors, and represent themselves as the true heirs of the son of Osiris against the degenerates who call themselves pharaohs.

We talked about Nubia when we were discussing the Middle Kingdom, but we have had to neglect the region since for want of space. Other developments of the New Kingdom deserved more attention, for Nubia was not a problem during that period. At the beginning of the Eighteenth Dynasty the kings of Egypt regained the Middle Kingdom heritage in the south without difficulty, reoccupying the old forts and building new ones. They also built towns and temples; there was no longer any need for the strong defenses Senusert III had erected. The New Kingdom frontier in the south was eventually set at the Fourth Cataract. Trade flourished; Egyptian traders, priests, and craftsmen kept the river crowded. Even during the struggles of the post-Amarna period Nubia remained peaceful, and it may have been the uninterrupted flow of riches from this region that allowed the later kings to maintain their imperial courts and raise their expensive temples, even though their sources of income to the east gradually diminished. These kings built in Nubia as well as in

Egypt, and some of the temples are quite splendid. All this activity had its effect on the Nubians. As early as the Second Intermediate Period there are signs that the native peoples of the area were getting interested in Egyptian wares and opening their minds to Egyptian ideas.

Politically, the land of Nubia must have been an increasingly important factor in internal Egyptian affairs. The office of the "king's son of Cush," who was viceroy of all the southern lands, was established during the Eighteenth Dynasty. During the Twentieth Dynasty, Nubian strong-men had a hand in the harem conspiracy that ended the rambunctious career of Ramses III, and also in the establishment of Herihor, viceroy of Nubia and high priest of Amon, in control at Thebes.

The collapse of Egyptian unity and prestige in the years that followed—remember poor Wenamon and his journey to Byblos—is reflected in Nubia by a failure of inscriptional and other material. We do not know exactly what was going on down there.

When the curtain does rise, it is upon a scene which we have never observed before in our study of Nubia. The locus is neither town nor Egyptian fort, but a handsome city, with a royal palace and a great temple to Amon at the base of a high, flat-topped hill. The hill is now known as Gebel Barkal, and the ruins of the city of Napata are to be found near the Fourth Cataract, at the far end of the fertile Dongola Reach. To the north is the royal cemetery; the tumbledown pyramids once housed the bodies of the kings of Napata.

The kingdom of which this city was the capital is that which the Greeks later called Ethiopia. We usually apply this term to Abyssinia, but the Greeks evidently used "Ethiopians" to designated any dark-skinned people in remoter Africa. We will avoid confusion by referring to this Nubian nation by its Egyptian name—Cush.

So much for the scenery and the program notes. Now let the play begin.

There is a Prologue, whose details are vague; it concerns a king of Cush called Kashta, whose mission it was to carry regeneration into Egypt. We have no inscription of his, so we do not know when, or even if, he invaded Egypt; but we think he got as far as Thebes, since his daughter was adopted by the God's Wife as her successor. The real protagonist of act one is Kashta's son, once known as Piankhi. You will find him referred to, in more recent works, as Piye.

See him as he occupies the seat of Pharaoh—he claims those titles and wears the full regalia of an Egyptian king. The great god Amon extends his protecting hand over Piye, his son; and Piye worships the god devoutly and purely. The petty bickering of the local nobles far to the north keeps them occupied and allows them no time for transgression upon the realms held by Cush.

Then, in the first month of the twenty-first year of Piye, comes ominous news. One has arisen among the dynasts of the Delta, a man named Tefnakhte, of Sais. He has seized the whole west, coming southward with a numerous army, while the Two Lands are united behind him, and the princes of walled towns are as dogs at his heels. Herakleopolis is besieged, and Namlot, prince of Hermopolis, has submitted himself to Tefnakhte as his lord, forswearing his allegiance to Piye.

Piye received this news with a shout of laughter.

His loyal courtiers wondered if the old gentleman had lost his wits. But Piye was only expressing his nonchalance. The stela describing his reaction and future actions—one of the most remarkable historical documents ever found in Egypt—is a little vague on the subject of precisely how much of Egypt was subject to Cush before Tefnakhte took up arms. That didn't matter, since Amon was about to bestow the whole country on his devoted Piye. Piye was so confident of the result that initially he did not even take the field himself. The troops he sent to Egypt received noteworthy instructions: they were to conquer, of course, but equally important was their conduct when they came to the sacred city of Thebes, the home of Amon-Re. "Bathe in the river, dress in fine linen, unstring the bow, loosen the arrow; do not boast to the lord of might, for there is no strength without Amon."

After paying its respect to the god at Thebes, the army proceeded to Herakleopolis and lifted the siege. Among the besiegers were Namlot,

the prince of Hermopolis who had cast his lot with his fellow countrymen against the Nubian Piye, and Osorkon III, the last king of the feeble
Twenty-third Dynasty; though he has the title of king he is obviously
only one prince among a lot of princes.

Piye's army drove the Egyptians away; Tefnakhte headed for Sais, his
hometown, while Namlot escaped to Hermopolis, and shut himself in.
The Cushites settled down around the latter city and sent word home to
Piye.

Piye was not pleased at the news of victory. He had expected to hear
of annihilation, and he must have known that he would have no peace
to worship Amon while Tefnakhte and Namlot were still on the loose.
He contemptuously ignored "Pharaoh" Osorkon, and with good reason.
When Piye, deciding to take matters into his own hands, came north in
person, Osorkon hurried to make his submission. Piye had stopped at
Thebes on his way, of course, to take part in the great feast of Amon, and
when he went out to battle, he was well fortified with the grace of the
god. The big battle was at Hermopolis, where Namlot was still holding
out, but in great discomfort: "Days passed, and Hermopolis was foul to
the nose, without breathable air." According to Piye's story, the citizens
of the dying city came forth to plead for terms. Piye was stern until the
ladies made their appearance. Namlot's wife and daughter sought out the
womenfolk of Piye (what they were doing on a military campaign is never
explained), and on their bellies begged the Cushite queens to intercede
with their lord, which they did. Evidently chivalry was not dead; perhaps
Piye was also moved to clemency by the rich gifts that Namlot sent him.

Piye's behavior on entering the city in triumph is so pious and austere
as to be priggish. First of all he visited the temple—Thoth, the patron of
scribes, was in charge at Hermopolis—and only then did he turn his attention to the loot. Among the booty was the harem of Namlot, whose
members hopefully "saluted his majesty in the manner of women." Piye
would have nothing to do with them. (This touch of chastity is all very
well, but it does not jibe with the fact that Piye could not even fight a war
without dragging his own women along.)

Namlot's horses aroused Piye's passions, as Namlot's women had failed to do. When he visited the stables he found that the horses, naturally enough, had suffered from the siege. "It is more grievous in my heart," said Piye reproachfully to the humble Namlot, "that my horses have suffered hunger than any evil deed that thou hast done." This is a truly royal "my"; but Piye was being a little unreasonable. The horses were lucky to be there at all, if the city had reached the state of woeful hunger implied by the narrative. Perhaps Namlot tended them with anxious care, knowing of the Cushite king's major weak spot. Piye's love of horses is attested by other evidence, notably the fact that he began the custom of burying his favorite steeds honorably near the royal tomb. Whenever a penitent rebel wanted to get in Piye's good graces, he offered him a horse.

Piye then went on to Memphis and took it by storm. His first act was to protect and cleanse the temples. During his stay in the city, all the local dynasts came trooping in to offer allegiance and the contents of their treasuries. Piye would have taken the latter anyhow, but it makes a nice gesture, especially when the humble princes proposed to hand over their best horses. Despite Namlot's neglect of "his" horses Piye dealt mercifully with him and the other rebels he encountered on his northward march. This was a mistake, but an attractive one. Piye was hopelessly old-fashioned in his piety, and perhaps he trusted in the oaths of others because he did not readily break his own word. There is no point in worrying about the moral rights involved in the conquest of Egypt. Piye was in one sense a foreigner and an invader; but the native Egyptians he fought had been squabbling unpleasantly among themselves for four generations, and would squabble again as soon as he left the country. There has been a lot of debate about Piye's "race," or ethnic connections; some Egyptologists want to make him a Libyan, others claim he was a descendant of Egyptian emigrants to Nubia. But there is no reason not to take Piye for what he seemed to be, a Nubian—whatever that means. Judging from the most significant factor, that of cultural and religious affinity, Piye was an Egyptian of the Egyptians and considered himself the heir of Egypt's long, rich past.

Piye had one more little "rebellion" to deal with as he headed south. His success brought a bunch of other would-be rulers to beg for mercy, including the archenemy Tefnakhte, who was allowed to surrender, with solemn vows not to do it again. So Piye sailed happily home to Napata, leaving Tefnakhte, no doubt, rubbing his hands together and chortling like Iago.

When he stopped at Thebes, Piye requested that the current God's Wife take his daughter under her wing, which she did all the more readily because she herself was the daughter of Piye's father, who had installed her in the office as the successor to the daughter of the last king of the preceding dynasty.

As soon as Piye left, Tefnakhte was up to his old tricks. We do not know what Piye was doing while his enemy was breaking his solemn vows; he lived long enough to set up a handsome stela, written in good Egyptian, in the temple of Amon at Gebel Barkal, the Holy Mountain. It is from this stela that we get the story of Piye's conquest. Certain it is, however, that Tefnakhte was successful enough to set up his son as pharaoh. This son, known to the Greeks as Bocchoris, is the aforementioned sole king of Manetho's Twenty-fourth Dynasty. The Nubians, beginning with Piye, are the Twenty-fifth, a slight confusion chronologically, but that is the least of the confusion that attends upon the last years of Egypt.

Bocchoris did not last long; Manetho says he was burned alive by Shabaka, the successor of Piye. The burning may be apocryphal, but Shabaka did put a premature end to Bocchoris and his dynasty. The Cushite conquered all of Egypt, transferred his capital to Thebes, and ruled as the "king of Egypt and Cush." He was as pious as Piye; almost every temple in Egypt was enlarged or restored by him, and he was remembered by Greek historians as a righteous king.

At this point we acquire some new sources of information. The most important comes from the kingdom of Assyria, which was fighting its way to world supremacy in a series of bloody battles in western Asia. From this time on we can also see Egypt and Assyria through the eyes of the Israelites. The books of Kings tell of the terror of Assyria and the broken reed of Egypt, upon which the small kings of Judah and Israel tried to lean in their struggle for independence against the fierce warriors of Sargon and Sennacherib. The Egyptians are typically silent on the subject of Assyria.

This is the time of Hosea, when Sargon II carried Israel away captive, and Egypt sent no help. The name given to the Egyptian pharaoh in the biblical account cannot be identified with any of the men ruling in Egypt during this period; it may have been that of a viceroy or general. A few years later, perhaps under Shabaka, came the rebellion of Hezekiah and the first meeting of the two powers—Assyria, young, arrogant, in the early morning of its strength, and Egypt, the tottering wreckage of the colossus that had for thirty centuries towered above the east. The event is described in Kings II, which is more to be commended for its literary style than for historical accuracy; the chronicler may have confused this Assyrian campaign with another one twenty-five years later. For what it's worth, he says that Sennacherib of Assyria led his armies against the "rebels" in Jerusalem. When the soldiers of Egypt came to defend their ally, the Assyrian king jeered at them, using the familiar analogy of the broken reed. But plague—or the visitation of God—decimated the Assyrian ranks, and the army had to retreat. The crucial meeting between Egypt and Assyria was yet to come.

Shabaka was succeeded by his brother, or perhaps his son, named Shabatka; and he in turn was succeeded by his cousin (?) Taharka, the last of the strong Cushite kings. Taharka built largely in Egypt and at Napata, and left a number of stelae at various places in Nubia, which is one reason why we know more about him than about some of his predecessors. One of the Greek historians accused him of murdering his predecessor, but this may be just a nasty rumor. His pyramid at Napata is the biggest of the lot, but it is pretty pathetic compared with even the Middle Kingdom royal tombs of Egypt. Despite their poor construction, the pyramids of Napata still stand upon the plain near Gebel Barkal. They are in ruinous condition and look peculiar because of their slope, which is much steeper than the standard fifty-two-degree angle of Egyptian pyramids. All of them were robbed in antiquity; in modern times they were excavated by Reisner, whose precise methods allowed him to reconstruct the genealogy of many generations of Cushite kings.

Before Taharka concerned himself with his pyramid, he had other problems to face. Thebes was too far south for his tastes; he resided most of the time at Memphis, where, one supposes, he could keep an eye on the activities of the threatening Assyrians. Sennacherib, the scourge of Jerusalem, was dead, but his son, Esarhaddon, was an even more formidable warrior. He had to deal with a number of rebellions among the vassal cities of Phoenicia, in some of which we may see Taharka's fine Nubian hand. His attempts to distract the Assyrian only delayed the inevitable. In 671, Esarhaddon marched south, driving Taharka's army before him, until at last he stood before the walls of the most ancient city of Memphis, Menes's capital. There is a ring of truth in the Assyrian king's grim record of the campaign; Egyptian records, needless to say, are conspicuously silent on the matter. Esarhaddon gives Taharka his due; the battles he fought were bloody ones, and he claims to have inflicted no less than five wounds upon the person of the Cushite king. Taharka's valor was in vain. Assyria took Memphis and leveled its legendary walls. Among the captives were Taharka's brother and the women of his household.

In succeeding years the fortunes of life and death turned the struggle between Egypt and Assyria into a deadly seesaw; Esarhaddon's departure enabled Taharka to recover Memphis for a time, but after the death of the Assyrian king, his son Asshurbanipal returned to quell the stubborn Egyptians. Once again Taharka fled from Memphis to Thebes and then to Napata. This time he stayed there.

Up to this point the Assyrians had committed one important error, which later conquerors did not repeat. They conquered and departed, taking heavy loads of booty with them and extorting great oaths of fealty from the Egyptian vassals they established in office. And as soon as they left, the rumble of rebellion began again. Even in the final throes of

degeneration and defeat, the Egyptians were hard to conquer. Like wheat
before the storm they bent and were not broken.

When Asshurbanipal left Egypt, after chasing Taharka home to
Cush, he left a power vacuum. The various petty princes of the country
started their aping of imperial dignity. Taharka died soon afterward; his
nephew, Tanutamon, stepped into his place. Again a Cushite king came
north, besieged Memphis, and ruled Egypt. But Taharka's sandals were
too big for Tanutamon, and even Taharka had not been able to stop the
Assyrians. Asshurbanipal returned, and Tanutamon followed his uncle's
example, retreating first to Thebes and then, when that city was threatened, to Napata. In the far regions of the south the Cushite kings were
safe, for no Assyrian wanted to pursue them through the difficult regions
of the cataracts. But Thebes, abandoned by its soi-disant king, met the
full fury of Assyrian wrath. The sack of Thebes was an effective object
lesson to rebels; for over fifty years its fall haunted the memories of men
and found an echo in the words of the prophet Nahum when he threatened Nineveh with a similar fate.

Asshurbanipal also left a description of the destruction of Amon's
holy city. "Heavy booty, beyond counting, I took away from Thebes.
Against Egypt and Cush I let my weapons rage and showed my might."
The conquest ended the glory of Thebes, and the pretensions of the
Cushite dynasty.

If we want to think in terms of national psychoses, we might say that
the Cushite kings had developed a trauma about Egypt. Up and down,
back and forth; every time they had sallied forth to Memphis, the Assyrians had appeared and sent them packing. Enough was enough. They
were safe and prosperous in their own kingdom, and there, from this
time on, they stayed. The subsequent history of the kingdom of Cush,
which turned its eyes away from Egypt and to the south, is fascinating,
and I wish we had time to talk about it in detail. The capital was finally
shifted even farther south, to Meroë, and here a version of Egyptian culture lingered for centuries, mixed with various native elements. The last
pyramids in Africa were built in Cush, odd little redbrick imitations of

the towering monuments of Giza and Dahshur. A new language developed, called Meroitic; temples and palaces were built and maintained. Cush looked to Egypt as the font and origin of its culture, but never again did it contemplate the Two Lands as a field for conquest. The splendor of Egypt, which had dazzled the vision of Piye and Taharka, had blinded Tanutamon.

BACK TO THE DRAWING BOARD

Sooner or later, most historians succumb to the urge to discover causes in history. We have had occasion to ponder causality once before when we talked about the genesis of civilization and hauled out the homely analogy of the wagon on the slope. I could belabor this figure of speech further. It lends itself, with an aptitude I had admittedly not foreseen, to the process of decline as well as to the process of growth. But I will assume that the reader is imaginative enough to invent his own images: wagons grinding to a halt, level and monotonous plains, etc. Let us, instead, go on to consider some of the factors which have been suggested as causes for the decline of Egyptian civilization: the rise of the priesthood, which not only controlled a paralyzing amount of the national wealth, but exercised a stagnating influence upon experimentation and new ideas; the power of the army and the military leader; the appearance of iron, which is not found in Egypt, as a material for weapons and tools; the pressure exerted by the great folk migrations; the corruption of the native Egyptian genius or ethos by poorly assimilated influences from without; the increasingly formalized social structure, with the rich getting richer and the poor getting poorer; the substitution of form for content and resignation for struggle in the intellectual and spiritual realms.

There you are; a nice representative sampling. None of the above is original with me, as far as I know. Perhaps I ought to invent a couple of my own: (I) that fatal something in the psychology of the Egyptian people, the desire for regimentation and blind obedience; (2) the will of God.

I doubt if I can persuade the reader to take my second cause seriously; even devout historians assume that the Deity works through certain ascertainable rules. The first of my suggestions may not sound so immediately implausible. Its absurdity should become apparent when I explain that I copied the sentence from a context that has nothing to do with ancient Egypt—a commentary on the events leading up to World War II. I changed only the names of the people referred to. An appeal to "the fatal something" in a nation's psychology is not an explanation of anything, only an admission of the inability of the commentator to produce an explanation.

The fact that acceptable theories of causation fluctuate is a disturbing phenomenon if we would like to believe that real reasons really exist. A number of theories have come in and gone out in the past century, in addition to the will of God. *Causality* is a dangerous word for a historian to play with; if he presses it too far he finds himself, sooner or later, locked in a death-grapple with a philosopher. Historians—and who can blame them?—try to avoid such encounters. Their causes are not philosophical profundities, as a rule, but prosaic, matter-of-fact explanations that are comprehensible to any well-read person. But historical causes are inevitably affected by the intellectual climate of the times. We no longer accept supernatural explanations—God and the devil are equally out of style—because our present worldview does not include a belief in the direct intervention of such forces in man's affairs. Economic explanations are still respectable, despite the unfortunate use which has been made of poor Karl Marx, but most historians would not regard them as valid exclusive causes.

One very popular class of causes these days is the psychological, applied to nations or to individuals. It does not require much insight to identify the Egyptian who is most popular with the psychologists. Freud found Akhenaton perfectly fascinating, even though his childhood memories are irretrievably lost. One so-called psychologist has gone Freud one better: he not only supplied the missing details of Akhenaton's childhood and pronounced him to be suffering from an Oedipus complex, but proposed the novel theory that Akhenaton was, in fact, Oedipus.

I am doing historians who employ psychological techniques a slight injustice by mentioning the Oedipus-Akhenaton theory, for it cannot be taken seriously, either as psychology or as history. It is representative of one of the lunatic schools, which flourish around the fringes of many fields of scholarly discipline, and it differs from the outpourings of the Pyramidiots only in the air of verisimilitude it creates. Its basic crime against true scholarship, the same error that mars the books of the pyramid mystics and more recent volumes on the age of the Sphinx and the identification of Akhenaton with various biblical characters, is that the author is not working with an open mind. He is not using facts to construct a theory, but is selecting facts to support a preconceived and unshakable belief. Whatever the techniques a historian chooses to work with, he must use them without prejudice and be prepared to revise, or dismiss, his theory when he runs up against a fact his tools cannot handle.

An excellent example of the whimsy of historical fashion is given by the rise and fall of the Great Man theory. Simply stated, this is the biographical approach to history. The plot of the past is produced by the players; Great Men (and a few Women), by virtue of their personalities or their positions, not only influence the shape of events but bring them into being. After a period of relative respectability, this attitude was to some extent replaced by its converse, which has been called the Cultural Process. Men do not make events; events make men. Hitler did not "cause" World War II; the circumstances in Germany and the rest of Europe would have produced that fatal event even if Hitler had never been born, and some other leader would have been coughed up by the body politic to assume the role that the character of the times demanded. Akhenaton did not initiate a religious revolution; Egypt was ripe for an attempt at reform, and the general sentiment of the time would have forced such a move with or without Akhenaton.

You may feel that the Cultural Process is a rather extreme way of looking at history. I think it is; and I am happy to tell you that the Great Man is coming back into fashion. Some sort of middle ground is probably necessary; any man is the product of his culture in the broad-est sense, but to deny the particularity of Hitler or Akhenaton is ratio-nally impossible.

It seems, then, that we are still a long way from final causes. Not only do we find that categories of explanations change their status with alarm-ing frequency, but we always have with us certain more elementary problems. We can isolate discrete cultural or political phenomena—the advent of iron, the wealth of the priesthoods—but what is a cause and what is an effect? The effect on one cause may be the cause of another effect; or it may be neither or both, but simply a—thing. Sometimes you can't tell one from the other without a scorecard, and the scorecard has not yet been written. The situation is trying enough for the modest scholar who is only attempting to explain an isolated phenomenon in a single culture. When a historian tries to extend explanations into the world at large and compose a universal theory of history, he is really in trouble.

This has been a very superficial, limited probing of some of the types of problems we encounter when we talk about causes in history. We have not even settled the important question of whether there are causes. Yet we will probably go right on looking for them, and talking about them. The intellectual climate of our own era asks for explanations. We would like, if we could, to reduce all phenomena to systems of logical sequence. In part this is the effect of the prestige of the physical sciences, and this effect is not always for the good. History may be "scientific" in its ap-proach, and the social studies may be "social sciences" in the sense that they apply dispassionate, critical, and rigorously logical analyses to the subjects of their discourse. But the disciplines that deal with man and his peculiar affairs cannot expect to use the methods, or anticipate the re-sults, of the physical sciences. The human experiment will not reproduce itself under laboratory conditions; we can never control our specimens to such a degree that we can isolate a pertinent stimulus or determine a spe-cific conclusion. My personal antipathy toward the use of the term "sci-entific" in the humanistic disciplines is that the very application of the word sometimes suggests to the user that such isolation and such determination are possible. Sometimes I wish they were.

We have a more personal need, in our time, to dissect the past in search of its pathology, for according to some historians our own culture is showing disturbing signs of disease. However you define the developmental stages of civilization, and upon whatever step you put us here, in this twenty-first century of the Christian Era, it seems unlikely that we are at the beginning of a process. This leaves us with the dismal possibility that we may be nearing the end. If so, it behooves us to discover, insofar as we are able, where we are, and why. If there are universal causes, and if we are able to see them plainly, we may learn how to avoid their more disastrous consequences.

That is one of the reasons why we look for reasons. Whether we have any grounds for supposing that we will find them is another question. At the moment, it appears that our only recourse, if we are about to fall, is to go down gracefully.

THE FINAL HUMILIATION

Let us leave this depressing subject and proceed to view, with comfortable detachment, the decline and fall of somebody else. The Assyrians had ended the power of Cush, but they had not yet done with Egypt. Assyrian strength was extended to its uttermost; the vast, dissatisfied empire required constant sorties in force to keep the vassal areas under control. Asshurbanipal could not spare enough troops for a military occupation of Egypt. He had to rely on the loyalty of the vassals he selected. And Egyptian oaths of fealty were written on water. Whether one commends the Egyptians for their stubborn hatred of foreign domination, or damns them as oath breakers, one must confess that they did not lie down until they were dead. Asshurbanipal left a man called Necho, of Sais, in charge of Egypt when he went home. Necho, of course, rebelled the first chance he got, and Necho's son Psamtik I was the founder of what Manetho calls the Twenty-sixth, or Saite, Dynasty. Psamtik must have had some of the old spark. He succeeded in persuading his bickering fellow nobles to unite against the Assyrians and got control of Thebes by ordering the God's Wife at that place to adopt his daughter. Of course Psamtik didn't put it so crudely; the famous stela describing the adoption of the princess by her predecessor stresses the fact that Psamtik did not arbitrarily remove this lady, who was of the family of Taharka. (In fact, Psamtik's daughter didn't actually assume the title until after the death of the older lady. All very civil and, if I may say so, ladylike.) By uniting Egypt he ended the Third Intermediate Period, so, just for the record, we are now in the Late Period.

The success of Psamtik gave his subjects an illusion of rebirth, and modern scholars sometimes refer to the Twenty-sixth Dynasty as a renaissance. A surge of real vitality produces new cultural features, which resemble the products of other renaissances only in the strength and creativity of the impulse that gave them birth. But when the impetus and the vigor are lacking, a backward-looking society may strive to emulate the past by imitating its external symbols. That is what happened in the Saitic revival of the Twenty-sixth Dynasty.

Copying is the most striking manifestation of the revival of painting—a copying so anxious and so exact that the men of this time reproduce, line for line, the decoration of the tombs of the Old and Middle Kingdoms. To be fair, not all art was slavishly imitative; beginning in the preceding dynasty, perhaps under the influence of the energetic Cushite rulers, we see a new style in sculpture. It is found, at its best, in certain heads of kings and nobles. They are hard—hard in surface and in style, formalized, and yet giving an impression of realism. These two seemingly contradictory impressions, naturalism and formalism, are found in the same work of art, and the result is remarkable. Some of the most interesting sculptures belonged to a certain Mentuemhat, who was not a king but a priest and major of Thebes.

The altered mood of the wisdom literature is equally indicative of the change in national attitudes, though it began earlier than the Twenty-sixth

Dynasty; dating such texts is difficult, since they were copied and recopied, but it is likely that the first dates from the late Ramesside period and the second from even later. There is a wistful charm in some of the late wisdom texts; in some ways the sentiments they express are more sympathetic to us than the rather cold-blooded practicality of earlier advice to the young. Take this section, from the "Instructions" of a father to his son:

> *Double the food which thou givest thy mother, carry her as she carried thee. She had a heavy load in thee, but she did not leave it to me. After thou were born she was still burdened with thee; her breast was in thy mouth for three years, and though thy filth was disgusting, her heart was not disgusted. When thou takest a wife, remember how thy mother gave birth to thee, and her raising thee as well; do not let thy wife blame thee, nor cause that she raise her hands to the god.*

There is plenty of sentiment in this passage, although the tone and the candid selection of details raise it above mere sentimentality. Now compare the words of Ptahhotep of the Fourth Dynasty on a similar subject:

> *If thou art a man of standing, thou shouldst found a household and love thy wife at home, as is fitting. Fill her belly, and clothe her back; ointment is the prescription for her body. Make her heart glad, for she is a profitable field for her lord.*

Tastes may differ as to the relative wisdom of these excerpts, but there is no doubt about the change in attitude. The dominating theme of the later texts is submission and patience; the key word, terrifyingly reiterated, is "silence." An Old Kingdom Egyptian would have laughed incredulously at such guides to success; what, sit silent like a fool while some glib talker shoves his way ahead? The self-assertion of the earlier dynasties is not unattractive; it is breezy, bouncy, a little naive, and wholly sympathetic. In its greatest form, it dared to question the immortal gods as to the meaning of life. The spirit of ancient Egypt was indeed dead when men could boast of being silent.

The theme of silence is found in another late "instruction," the Wisdom of Amenemopet, which has an unusual interest beyond the fact that it gives the attitudes of a particular age.

The reader may recall that we mentioned the parallels between Akhenaton's famous sun hymn and one of the Psalms, and then rejected a romantic story by claiming that the resemblance did not prove a direct connection between Egypt and Israel at that period. With the Amenemopet text, the dramatic conclusion is hard to avoid, for its parallels with the biblical book of Proverbs are so close that only the dependence of one upon the other can satisfactorily explain the resemblance. It has been suggested that the Egyptians borrowed their text from the Hebrews, but most scholars incline toward the opposite interpretation. There is nothing "un-Egyptian" about the contents of Amenemopet; the text is perfectly consistent with the feeling of the age, as expressed in a variety of other cultural phenomena. If we compare Amenemopet with the biblical text, especially with Proverbs 22:17 through 24:22, we find the same precepts repeated, often in almost the same words. But the final proof of relationship is a really beautiful bit of research, which enabled an Egyptologist to correct the Hebrew text.

The Egyptologist was Adolf Erman, the teacher of an entire generation of philologists, British and American as well as German. In looking over the passage, Erman noted Proverbs 22:20–21, which, in the King James version, read as follows:

Have I not written unto thee excellent things in counsel and knowledge,
That I might make thee know the certainty of the words of truth; that thou
mightest answer the words of truth to them that send unto thee?

The words "excellent things" were marked with a question. The Hebrew had *shilshon*, "formerly," which is obviously an error; the original editors had suggested *shalishim*, "officers," which is hardly an improvement. Now Hebrew, as it was originally written, resembled Egyptian—and other Semitic languages—in that it wrote only the consonants. Much later a system was developed that indicated vowels by means of "points," small marks written above or below the line. The reader will note that the Hebrew words that have been suggested for the disputed reading differ only in the pointing, their consonants being the same.

Erman, of course, was familiar with the Amenemopet text, and he had found a passage which in many ways seemed to resemble the two verses of Proverbs. But the Egyptian text reads: "See thou these thirty chapters; they entertain, they instruct. They are the foremost of all books; they make the ignorant man to know."

As Erman studied the text he was struck by the recollection that the Hebrew word for "thirty" is *sheloshim*—a word that involves only a small change in pointing and makes better sense of the Hebrew than do any of the suggested renderings. The Egyptian text contains precisely thirty chapters; the Hebrew passage is not so divided, but it does contain thirty different precepts. Erman's discovery not only settled the question of borrowing between the two sources, but made the direction of the borrowing pretty sure, for the use of the word "thirty" is more logical in the Egyptian. The applicability of the numeral to the Hebrew text is not so obvious, and it is easy to understand why later copyists misread the word or tried to substitute a—to them—more logical alternative.

After the transitory reflection of greatness which appeared during the Twenty-sixth Dynasty, the aging giant on the Nile stumbled ever faster down the ignominious path to annihilation. It is a depressing subject for Egyptophiles, and very confusing; for those reasons, most general works, including this one, tend to pass rapidly over the details. Assyria fell, but Babylon took its place as a conquering power; the last pharaohs of Egypt fought their hopeless battles with the aid of mercenaries, Greeks who had settled in large numbers in the Delta. Toward the end of the dynasty the decline of Babylon left Egypt temporarily at peace, but Babylon had fallen to the conqueror Cyrus, the Achaemenid. Cyrus left a far-flung empire to his son Cambyses; it included most of the known world—except Egypt. Cambyses remedied this lack. In 525 B.C., at the Battle of Pelusium, he broke the back of Egyptian independence. The country became a province of the vast Persian empire, and Manetho's Twenty-seventh Dynasty consists of Persian kings. The Twenty-eighth through Thirtieth Dynasties were "native" again, feeble princes who took advantage of Persia's preoccupation with other areas to attain an illusory independence. In 343 B.C., the Persians found time to remember Egypt. As a result we have a Thirty-first Dynasty, another Persian one, which was later combined with Manetho's Thirtieth—to make them symmetrical, I suppose. The last king of pharaonic Egypt was Nectanebo, and that is probably all you need to know about him.

Meanwhile, in the barbaric backwaters of Macedonia, a new Great Man was coming of age. Alexander is one of those overpowering personalities who leave a mark not only on history but on the imagination. He added Egypt to his growing empire in 332 B.C. There's a legend that he took the long desert road west to Siwa Oasis, to consult the oracle of Amon located there—and that Amon, predictably, named him son and pharaoh. After Alexander's premature death in 323 B.C., his empire, the greatest known until then, was eventually divided. Egypt fell to Ptolemy, one of his generals, whose descendants held sway for over two centuries. Being polytheists anyhow, the Greek pharaohs had no problem honoring the Egyptian gods. The temples were maintained, and new ones built. Many of the most famous religious edifices popular with tourists date in whole or in part from this and the following Roman period—Philae, Denderah, Edfu. It isn't difficult to distinguish Ptolemaic art and architecture; art forms became a strange (and in the views of many, awkward) amalgam of Greek and Egyptian techniques. Ptolemaic hieroglyphs are hard to read, even for a student of classical Egyptian.

However, political and cultural institutions were maintained. The Ptolemies were divine pharaohs, their names written in cartouches, their images prominent on temple walls, paying homage to the ancient gods. The city of Alexandria became a magnificent capital and a center of learning; its library was world famous and its prestige was enhanced by the tomb of Alexander himself. The conqueror had died in Babylon; his embalmed body was being taken back to Macedonia for burial when it was "hijacked," as one scholar has put it, by General Ptolemy. Much of ancient Alexandria lies underwater today, and Alexander's tomb has never been found. It is unlikely that people will stop looking for it, though.

The Ptolemies continued the ancient royal custom of brother-sister marriage. They were not a loving family. The last two Ptolemies, numbers thirteen and fourteen, were brothers; they and their sister Cleopatra the Seventh were constantly at one another's throats. She is the Cleopatra we all know, the lover of Mark Antony, who tried in vain to hold off the mighty power of Rome. Under Octavian, better known as Augustus, Egypt became a province of the Roman empire, and one of the first to adopt Christianity. The Greeks and the Romans had respected the old gods and adopted some of them; the cult of Isis spread through the empire. But monotheism is by its very nature intolerant; the Coptic Christian church of Egypt began the destruction of the pagan monuments and inscriptions. The language passed from the knowledge of men, and the hieroglyphs became a source of wild speculation and mystical theorizing. The wisdom of Egypt would become a legend, but its learning was lost beneath the weight of twenty centuries of dust and ignorance. Yet still today the forested pillars of Karnak trumpet the name of Ramses to men and women from lands that the conqueror never knew existed, and until the last stone falls from the sides of the Great Pyramid of Giza, men will marvel at the might and the presumption of its builder.

A goodly number of books on archaeological subjects end with resounding sentences like that last one. There is a perfectly good reason for the popularity of the theme. The physical survival of the great Egyptian monuments is a noteworthy phenomenon in itself, when one considers that most of the other civilizations of comparable antiquity are visible to us only as mud-brick-foundation outlines, or as verbal reconstructions. Structures such as the pyramids, the Karnak temple, and the temples of Philae, Abu Simbel, and Abydos would be astonishing even if they were not so old; in size and magnificence they compare favorably with the ruins of almost any other past culture that is known to us.

Still, I have a prejudice against an emphasis of this type; or perhaps it would be more accurate to say that I have a predilection in favor of another sort of emphasis. The tombs, the temples, the golden coffins of Tutankhamon, are exciting and dramatic, yet they have not so much fascination for me as have other, less tangible, contacts with an antique and alien world. My interest in archaeology was stimulated initially by the lure of buried treasure; but eventually I found myself allured by the ideas of the past even more than by its artifacts. And this development led to another, very personal and perhaps subjective, discovery. People who read and write about history, particularly about ancient history, are wont to marvel at the "unexpectedly modern" sound of an ancient institution or expression. I do it myself, and I enjoy the small thrill of recognition which results from such an encounter. Yet in a broader sense the works of the past to which our emotions respond are not "ancient" or "modern," not "Egyptian" or "American," but simply—human. The specific expression of a given motivation may be one which our society no longer uses or accepts; but it may be completely valid for the culture in which it operates, and as we come to understand other elements of that culture we will see, behind the unfamiliar facade of exotic custom, human urges that should be as recognizable as our own features in a mirror.

This is not to disparage, nor to disregard, the uniqueness of history. The richness and variety of the attempted solutions to man's numerous problems are marvelous and appalling, and a lifetime is not long enough to begin to comprehend their manifold complexities. This unending diversity is one of the attractions of historical study, and the glamour of exotic custom is another. Egyptian mortuary practices, to take a single example, have understandably intrigued students for generations: the process of mummification, the elaborate tomb, the magical rite, the rich equipment of the dead. As we read the descriptions of the fantastic tombs, we marvel at the ingenuity of their builders, who provided for every conceivable mishap that might befall the naked soul wandering through darkness toward immortality. How richly grotesque—how bizarre—was the spiritual world which these long-dead aliens envisaged!

And then we come upon a single sentence, or an isolated phrase, and the mask of ceremonial vanishes to expose the familiar poignancy of man's quest for immortality, with all its uncertainty and its aching desire. "No one has returned from there to tell us how they fare."

The lament for a dead child, the demand for justice, the lover's yearning for his beloved—before our recognition of the universality of human emotion, time and distance shrink, the barriers of language, color, and nationality go down; we look into the mind of a man three millennia dead and call him "brother."

Additional Reading

GENERAL

Arkell, A. J. *History of the Sudan*. Athlone Press, 1961.

Breasted, J. H. *History of Egypt*. Charles Scribner's Sons, 1948.

Dodson, A. *Monarchs of the Nile*. Rubicon, 1995.

Forbes, D. *Tombs. Treasures. Mummies*. KMT Communications Inc., 1998.

Gardiner, Sir A. H. *Egypt of the Pharaohs*, 3rd rev. ed. Oxford University Press, 2006.

James, T. G. H. *A Short History of Ancient Egypt*. Cassell, 1995.

O'Connor, D. *Ancient Nubia: Egypt's Rival in Africa*. University of Pennsylvania, 1993.

Shaw, I., ed. *The Oxford History of Ancient Egypt*. Oxford University Press, 2000.

Wilson, J. A. *The Burden of Ancient Egypt.* University of Chicago Press. Also in University of Chicago paperbacks under the title *The Culture of Ancient Egypt,* 1956.

————. *Signs and Wonders upon Pharaoh.* University of Chicago Press, 1964.

TEXTS

Lichtheim, M. *Ancient Egyptian Literature,* vol. I, *The Old and Middle Kingdoms.* vol. II, *The New Kingdom,* vol. III, *The Late Period.* University of California, 1973, 1976, 1980.

Simpson, W. K., ed. *The Literature of Ancient Egypt,* 3rd ed. Yale University Press, 2003.

ANCIENT EGYPTIANS

Aldred, C. *Akhenaten, Pharaoh of Egypt.* Thames and Hudson, 1968.

Arnold, D. *The Royal Women of Amarna: Images of Beauty from Ancient Egypt.* Catalog with articles by J. P. Allen and L. Green. Metropolitan Museum of Art, 1996.

Clayton, P. *Chronicle of the Pharaohs: The Reign-by-Reign Record of the Rulers and Dynasties of Ancient Egypt.* Thames and Hudson, 1994.

Dodson, A., and D. Hilton. *The Complete Royal Families of Ancient Egypt.* Thames and Hudson, 2004.

Forbes, D. *Imperial Lives: Illustrated Biographies of Significant New Kingdom Egyptians,* vol. I, *The Eighteenth Dynasty Through Thutmose IV.* KMT Communications, 2005. (Volumes II and III in preparation.)

Freed, R., Y. J. Markowitz, and S. H. D'Auria, eds. *Pharaohs of the Sun: Akhenaten, Nefertiti, Tutankhamen.* Boston: Museum of Fine Arts, 1999.

Kitchen, K. *Pharaoh Triumphant: The Life and Times of Ramses II, Pharaoh of Egypt.* Benben-SSEA, 1992.

Montserrat, D. *Akhenaten: History, Fantasy and Ancient Egypt.* Routledge, 2000.

Redford, D. *Akhenaten: The Heretic King.* Princeton University Press, 1984.

Tyldesley, J. *Chronicles of the Queens of Egypt.* Thames and Hudson, 2006.

————. *Hatchepsut: the Female Pharaoh.* Viking, 1996.

ARCHAEOLOGISTS AND THEIR WORK

Breasted, C. *Pioneer to the Past: The Story of James Henry Breasted, Archaeologist. Told by his son.* Charles Scribner's Sons, 1943.

Chubb, M. *Nefertiti Lived Here.* Thomas J. Crowell, 1954.

Drower, M. S. *Flinders Petrie: A Life in Archaeology.* Victor Gollancz, 1985.

James, T. G. H. *Howard Carter: The Path to Tutankhamon.* Kegan Paul Int., 1992.

Reeves, N., and J. H. Taylor. *Howard Carter before Tutankhamun.* British Museum Press, 1992.

Sources of Quotes

Quotations from Egyptian and other ancient texts have been made more accessible to nonscholars by omitting symbols such as brackets and parentheses, and by a certain freedom of rendering, when the meaning of the literal translation is not immediately apparent to a modern reader. I believe I can claim, however, that I have not altered the basic sense of the texts. Those who want to check up on me can refer to the following sources.

The indispensable three-volume work of Miriam Lichtheim (see Additional Reading) has translations of many of the texts I have cited, including the Annals of Thutmose III and the Kadesh battle text of Ramses II. The new, revised edition of *The Literature of Ancient Egypt*, edited by W. K. Simpson, includes much of the same material.

Unfortunately, there is no equivalent up-to-date source for historical texts. James H. Breasted's *Ancient Records of Egypt*, in five volumes, has never been supplanted, and although individual texts have been studied and revised it remains a basic reference work. It was reprinted by the University of Illinois in 2001. A selection of Egyptian literary and historical texts can be found in the translations by John A. Wilson, in *Ancient Near Eastern Texts Relating to the Old Testament*, edited by James B. Pritchard (Princeton, 3rd ed., 1969). This invaluable source also contains translations of Hittite texts by Albrecht Goetze, including the Hittite version of the treaty with Ramses II and Ankhesenamon's letters to Shubilulliuma. Certain of the Amarna letters are translated by W. F. Albright. A recent, complete translation of the Amarna letters is that of William L. Moran, *The Amarna Letters*, Johns Hopkins University Press, 1992.

The great Aton hymn is taken directly from Breasted, *The Dawn of Conscience*, Charles Scribner's Sons, 1933, hence the poetic language. Apparently he felt it was appropriate for a hymn, and it does make the parallels with the King James version of the Psalm more obvious. A more recent translation is that of William Murnane, *Texts from the Amarna Period in Egypt*, Scholars Press, 1995, pp. 113 ff. Murnane's excellent volume contains up-to-date translations of the restoration stela of Tutankhamon and other documents of the period, including Harmhab's Karnak stela. The triumphant hymn to Amon is also from Breasted, *The Dawn of Conscience*.

There are a number of editions of Manetho. The one I use is the Loeb Classical Library version.

The stories of Sekenenre and the crocodiles and the Kamose stela can be found in Simpson's useful volume (see Additional Reading). More recent translations of some texts have appeared in articles in such journals as the *Journal of Egyptian Archaeology* and the *Journal of the American Research Center in Egypt*, as well as in journals in languages other than English. I leave it to advanced and/or obsessed students to track them down.

Index

Page references in *italics* refer to illustrations.

Aakheperure, 148
Aamu, 127
Abd er Rassul, 277–79, 280
Abdu-Ashirta, 220
Abdu-Heba, 221–22
Abu Roash, 72
Abu Simbel, temple of, 91, 254–55,
   305–6
Abusir, 79
Abydos, 20, 22, 32, 37–39, 40, 41–44,
   58, 102, 106, 137, 243–44, 305–6
Abyssinia, 287
Agha, Mustafa, 277–78
A-group, 85
Aha, xxii, 33, 35–36, 37, 40
Ahhotep, 138–39
Ahkhetaton, 216
Ahmed, 277
Ahmes, 139
Ahmose, King, xxii, *126*, 133–34,
   135–36, 137, 139, 186, 279
Ahmose, Queen, 148–49
Ahmose, son of Ebana, 134–35, 136,
   139, 140
Ahmose-Nefertari, 138
Ahmose Pen-Nekhbet, 134, 139, 147
Akawasha, 257
Akhenaton, xxii, 188, 204, *205*,
   207–14, 216–18, 220, 221–23,
   224, 225, 226–31, 236–39, 241,
   242, 259–60, 266, 296–97, 298,
   302
Akhetaton, 209, 217, 230, 231, 237
Akhtoy, 100
Aleppo, 247

Alexander the Great, xxiii, 188, 273,
   304, 305
Alexandria, 304–5
Amarna letters, 314
Amarna Period, 224, 229, 230, 232,
   235–36, 240, 242
Amelineau, Emile, 37–38
Amenemhab, 171, 177, 179, 180, 183
Amenemhat I, xxii, 107–10
Amenemhat II, 108–9, 116
Amenemhat III, 111, 116, 118–19,
   120–21, 122, 264–65
Amenemhat IV, 122
Amenemopet, wisdom of, 302, 303
Amenhotep I, xxii, 139, 279
Amenhotep II, 154, 190–93, 194, 197,
   199, 280, 282
Amenhotep III, 188, 198, 199–204,
   208, 209, 219, 220, 221, 222,
   229–30, 234, 239, 254, 258, 260,
   267, 280
Amenhotep IV. *see* Akhenaton
Amenhotep (son of Hapu), 203–4
Amenmesse, 260
Amon, 102, 140, 148, 149, 150, 152,
   155, 159–60, 161, 175, 186, 187,
   198, 200, 209, 214, 216, 231, 232,
   238, 239, 241, 242, 247, 248–49,
   264, 266, 267, 268, 271, 272, 276,
   283, 284, 285, 287, 288, 289, 291,
   304
Amon-Re, 102, 144–45, 148, 187,
   198, 202, 209, 213, 222, 239, 265,
   266, 269, 280, 286
Amratian culture, 15

Amurru, 220, 249
Anatolia, 218
Ancient Records of Egypt (Breasted), 27–28
Anedjib, 40
Anen, 200, 234
ankh, 210
Ankhesenamon, 232–35, 238
Ankhesenpaaton, 229, 231, 232
Ankhkheperure, 208, 224
Apopi (Apophis), 130, 131, 133
Archaic Period, xvii, xxii
archeologists, 121–22
  see also specific archeologists
architecture, monumental, 18, 19–20,
  74, 123, 304
Arkell, A. J., 90–91, 114
Armant, 171
army, 185–86, 221, 245, 247, 249, 251
art, 17, 72–73, 83–84, 212, 241, 300,
  304
  see also sculpture
Aruna, 171, 173
Asia, Asiatics, 108, 110, 111, 127–28,
  129, 130, 174, 175, 178, 186, 197,
  198, 243, 245, 247, 258, 259
  see also specific Asiatic peoples
Asshurbanipal, 293, 294, 299
Assiut, 105, 114
Assyria, Assyrians, 175–76, 191, 285,
  291–92, 293, 294, 299, 300, 303
Assyria, king of, 175
Aswan, 14, 21, 64, 85
Aswan Dam, 14, 91, 255
Atbara, 140
Aten, 201, 203
Aton, 209–10, *211*, 213, 214–16, 223,
  226, 231, 237, 241, 242
Atum, 213
Augustus, 305
Avaris, 128, 132–33, 135
Ay, xxii, 223, 232, 234–35, 238, 241,
  242
Aziru, 220, 221, 222

ba, 80, *82*
Babylon, Babylonia, 6, 180, 198, 217,
  303, 305
Badarian culture, 15
Baka, 72

Bastet, 284
Bay, 261
beer, 67, 106
Belly of the Rocks, 113
Bent Pyramid, 56, 57–58
Berlin Museum, 200
Biban el Moluk, 205
  see also Valley of the Kings
Bietak, Manfred, 128
Bocchoris, 284, 291
Boghazkoi, 218, 251, 252
bones, determining age of, 227
Book of the Coming Forth by Day, The, 80
Book of the Dead, The, 80
Breasted, James Henry, xiii, 27–28,
  148, 179, 183–84, 207, 210, 213,
  214
British Museum, 5, 73–74, 137, 228
British School of Archaeology, 117
Brugsch, Emile, 279
Brunton, Guy, 117
Bubastis, 284
Butehamon, 267
Byblos, 178, 192, 220–21, 269, 270,
  271–72

Cairo, 12, 62
Cairo Museum, 69, 74, 103, 105,
  117–18, 162, 189, 193, 206,
  280–81
calendar, 30–31
Cambyses, 304
canopic jars, 83, 225, 229, 230
carbon 14, 24–27
Carnavon, Lord, 206
Carter, Howard, 152–53, 206, 232
cartouche(s), 35, *46, 95,* 116, *126,
  142,* 165, 166–67, *168, 190, 205,*
  234, 235, *240,* 244, *269,* 278, 279,
  304
Caton-Thompson, Gertrude, 10, 15
cemeteries, 22, 71, 72, 108
cenotaph, 39–40
C-group, 85
Champollion, Jean-François, 195
chariots, 136, 174, 183, 186
Cheops. *see* Khufu
Chephren. *see* Khafre
chronology, Egyptian, 23–32

City of the Dead, 71
civilization, Egyptian
  origin of, 14–21, 123
  decline of, 186, 295, 303–4
Cleopatra, xxiii, 305
coffins, 3, 70–71, 80, 125, 224–26,
  267, 277, 278, 279, 282
Coffin Texts, 80, 125
Colossi of Memnon, 203
conspiracies, 264
Coptic Christian Church, 305
coregencies, 108, 222–23, 230
C peoples, 112, 115
crowns of the king of Egypt, 23,
  33–40, 85, 151
culture(s), 10, 16–21
cuneiform, 217, 218, 233
Cush, 114, 115, 132, 133, 135,
  287–95
Cyprus, 198, 272
Cyrus, 303–4

Dahshur, xxii, 56, 57, 58, 65, 72, 108,
  116, 122
Danaoi, 263
Dante, 40
Danu, 263
Darfur, 90
Davis, Theodore, 224–25
death, 88–89, 97–99, 101, 125
Deffufa, 113–15
Deir el Bahri, 103, 148, 150, 151–52,
  153, 154, 155, 156, 158, 185, 279,
  282
Deir el Medina, 138
democratic principles, 125
de Morgan, Jacques, 116, 117
Den, xxii, 40
Denderah, 304
Diffusion, cultural, 18–19, 20
Diodorus, 82
Djadjaemankh, 76–77
Djau, 91
Djedefhor, 77
Djedefre, 72
Djedi, 77, 78
Djehutymose, 267
Djer, xxii, 38, 40
Djeser-djeseru, 152, 154, 158

Djet, 40
Djoser, xxii, 25, 47–50, 49, 76, 79
documentation, 249–50
Dongola Reach, 113
Door of the South, 85, 87
Dor, prince of, 270–71, 272
Double Crown, 23, 33–40, 85, 139,
  151
Drovetti, Bernardino, 31–32
dwarf, 88
Dynastic Race, 42
dynasties, origin of, 28–29
Dynasty O, xxii, 15, 22, 32

Edfu, 304
Edwin Smith Papyrus, 51, 52
Egypt, map of ancient, 11
Egypt Exploration Society of England,
  238
Eighteenth Dynasty, 29, 31, 32,
  56, 74, 137, 138, 139, 148,
  215, 219, 235, 265–66, 285,
  286–87
Eighth Dynasty, 29, 100
Elephantine, 85, 87, 88, 89
Eleventh Dynasty, 29, 105–6
El Kab, 134, 139
Eloquent Peasant, The Tale of the, 124–25
embalming. see mummies,
  mummification
Emery, Walter, 49–50
Empire, Egyptian, 29, 39, 137, 219,
  222
  see also New Kingdom
Eneenkhet, 88
Erman, Adolf, 27, 302, 303
Esarhaddon, 293
Ethiopia, 287
Etruscans, 258
Euphrates River, 140, 171, 177,
  178–79
Exodus, 259
extradition, 252

face, of kingship, 123
Fakhry, Ahmed, 58
Fayum, the, 100, 108, 118–19, 124
Fayum A culture, 15
Fields of Yaru, 80

Fifteenth Dynasty, 29, 130

Fifth Dynasty, xxii, 29, 39, 75, 77–78, 83–84, 100

Filer, Joyce, 228

First Dynasty, xxii, 16, 17, 23, 29, 30, 32, 33, 35–36, 37–40, 44, 47–48, 85, 90

First Intermediate Period, xvii, xxii, 29, 97, 98–99, 241

flints, 2, 4, 15, 17, 105

Forbes, Dennis, 283

forts, 112, 115, 192, 286

Fourteenth Dynasty, 29, 130

Fourth Dynasty, xxii, 25, 29, 54, 64, 72, 74–75, 78, 83–84, 93–94, 98, 119, 123, 301

Fourth Pyramid, 92–93

French Institute, Cairo, 137–38, 165

Freud, Sigmund, 296

Froelich's syndrome, 227, 228

Gardiner, Sir Alan, 110

Garstang, John, 36

Gaza, 171

Gebel Barkal, 171, 287, 291, 292–93

Gerzean culture, 15

Gilukhepa, 199

Giza, xxii, 59–64, 68, 69, 71, 72, 92, 108, 119, 194, 277, 305

God's Wife, 300

God's Wife (title), 284–85, 288, 291

gold, 38, 53, 67, 69, 85, 88, 99, 112, 116, 149, 150, 151, 174, 175, 179, 180, 185, 187, 188, 198, 206, 225, 236, 267, 274

Gold Tomb, 261

Goneim, M. Zakaria, 53

graffiti, 56, 156–57

Great Man theory, 297

Great Pyramid of Giza, 59–63, 119, 305

Grébaut, Eugene, 280

Greece, 152, 258

Greeks, 63, 73, 82, 92, 116, 118, 119–20, 152, 284, 287, 291, 303, 304, 305

see also specific Greeks

Gunn, Battiscombe, 55

Gurneh, 277

Habiru, 221, 260

Hapdjefa, 114, 115

Hapu, 203

Hapuseneb, 146, 147, 159, 160

Harkhuf, 87–88, 89–90

Harmhab, xxii, 232, 241–42

harpers' songs, 97–98

Harris, James, 283

Harris, Papyrus, 265–66

Harrison, R. G., 228, 229

Harvard University, Giza expedition of, 68

Hatshepsut, xxii, 103–4, 141–67, 188, 223

Hatti, 180, 198, 202, 218, 232, 233, 245, 252–53

see also Hittites

Hawara, 108, 120–21, 122

heart, weighing of, 99

Hebrews, 99, 128–29, 259–60, 302–3

Heb-Sed, 202, 203, 210

Heliopolis, 185, 187

Hememieh, 15

Hemiun, 64–68, 71

henotheism, 213

Herakleopolis, 100, 101, 102, 103, 106, 288

hereditary succession to throne, 195–98

Herihor, xxii, 268, 270, 277, 287

Hermopolis, 288, 289

Herodotus, 63, 82, 92, 119–20

Hetepheres, Queen, 64, 65, 67, 68–71, 72

Hetepheres II, Queen, 93–94

Hetepsekhemwi, 41

Hezekiah, 292

Hierakonpolis, 22, 33, 39, 42

Hieratic, 282

hieroglyphs, 20, 29, 34–35, 67, 69, 80, 128, 195, 218, 304, 305

hippopotami and crocodile, 84

History of Egypt (Breasted), xiii, 27, 210

Hittites, 218–19, 233–34, 235, 245, 247, 248, 249, 251–53, 258, 263

see also Hatti

Hordedef, 97

Horizon of Aton, 236, 238

Horns of the Earth, 139–40
horses, 136, 171, 174, 183, 191, 199, 290
Horus, 22, 35–36, 41–43, 44, 64, 187, 201–2
Huni, xxii, 54, 56, 57
Hyksos, xxii, 127–41, 151, 259, 283

Ikui, 102
Imhotep, 47–48, 49–50, 52–53, 97, 203
immortality, 3, 80–81, 83, 98–99, 101, 125
Ineni, 140–41, 147, 153
inheritance, 195–98
Instruction literature. *see* wisdom literature
Instructions for King Merikare, 100
Intef, xxii, 102, 180
Intef II, Wahankh, 102
Intef VI, 131
Intef VII, 131
Intef VIII, 131
Inundation, 12–13, 30, 62, 63
Ipuwer, 96
iron, 295
irrigation, 12–13
Isis, 41, 42, 144, 187, 305
Israel, Israelites, 258–59, 263, 292
It-tawi, 107–8, 109, 110, 118
ivory, Ivory Road, 34, 36, 40, 85, 90, 150

Jerusalem, 222
jewelry, jewels, 38, 99, 116–18, 151, 175, 206, 232, 261, 274
Jews. *see* Hebrews
Johnson, W. Raymond, 203
Joppa, 180
Joseph, 128, 129
Josephus, 28, 127
judgment of dead, 99, 101, 125
justice, 99, 125, 144, 181, 182, 211
    see also maat

ka, 54, 70–71, 148, 263
Kadesh, 171, 173–75, 176–77, 182–84, 245, *246*, 247, 248, 250–51, 252, 263
Kamose, xxii, 132–34, 135

Karnak, 132, 138, 140, 149, 151, 159, 165, 169, 176, 179, 194, 201, 238, 241–42, 243, 252, 254, 258–59, 268, 284, 305–6
Kashta, 287–88
Kerma, 113, 114, 115, 140
Khafre, xxii, 63, 64, 74, 76, 78, 108, 123, 212
Khasekhem, 44–45
Khasekhemui, xxii, 44–45
Khentkaus, 93
Khety, 100
Khnum, 148
Khufu, xxii, *46*, 59, 62–63, 64, 65, 66, 67, 71, 72, 75–76, 78, 108
Kipling, Rudyard, 110
Kiya, 208, 230–31
Kush. *see* Cush

Labyrinth, the, 119–20
Lahun, 108, 117
Lake Nasser, 15, 112
language
    Babylonian, 217
    Egyptian, 27, 51, 213, 305
    Hamitic, 20
    Hebrew, 302–3
    Hittite, 218–19
    Meroitic, 295
    Semitic, 20, 128
Late Period, xviii, xxiii, 273, 300
Lauer, Jean-Phillipe, 48–49
law, 41
Layer Pyramid, 54
Lebanon, 50, 175, 245
leech book, 50–51
Libby, Willard F., 24–25
Libyans, xxiii, 93, 104, 108–9, 139, 257, 258, 263, 283
Lisht, 108
literature, 78, 100, 300–302
Loret, Victor, 280
Lower Egypt, 10, *11*, 12–13, 22–23, 36, 37
Luca, 257
Luxor, 14, 102, 189, 201, 254
Luxor Museum, 137
Lycians, 258

Maadi culture, 15
maat, 96, 144, 167, 210–11, 264
Maatkare, 145
magic, 8, 51–52, 60–61, 70–71,
  72–73, 75–78, 80–81, 99, 264
Malkata, 201
Manetho, xxi, 28–29, 41, 54, 92, 93,
  100, 127, 130, 270, 284, 291, 300,
  304
Maraye, King, 257
Marfan's syndrome, 236
Mariette, Auguste, 102–3
Maspero, Gaston, 5, 103, 278, 279,
  282
mastaba, pyramid, 47–48, 71–72,
  92–93
Mazghuna, 123
medicine, 50–53, 74
Medinet Habu, 262–63, 267
Medjay of Nubia, 186
Medum, xxii, 55–56, 57, 58
Megiddo, 169, 171, 172, 173–75, 176,
  178, 222
Meketaton, 216–17
Meketre, 105
Memphis, 36–37, 39, 85, 96, 102,
  107–8, 187, 231, 290, 293, 294
Men, 36
Menes, xxii, 1, 23, 32, 33–34, 36–37,
  39, 40, 42, 101
Menkaure, xxii, 63–64, 92
Menkheperre Thutmose III, 144, 188
Mentuemhat, 300
Mentuhotep I, xxii, 102
Mentuhotep II, 103, 104, 152
Mentuhotep IV, 106
mercenaries, 247, 303
Meresankh, 72
Merikare, 100, 101, 103
Merimde culture, 15
Meritaton, 224, 231
Meritre Hatshepsut, 188
Merneith, xxii, 35–36, 40
Merneptah, xxii, 257, 258–59, 260,
  263, 274, 283
Mernere, xxii, 87
Meroe, xxviii, 140, 294
Mesehti, Count of Assiut, 105
Meshwesh, 283

Mesopotamia, 19, 20, 38
Metropolitan Museum, 74, 103, 105–6,
  117, 118, 158, 162
Middle Kingdom, xvii, xxii, 29, 74, 97,
  99, 107, 112, 113, 114, 115, 116,
  118, 122, 123–24, 125, 135, 286
Mitanni, 178–79, 197, 198, 218, 219,
  245
  see also Naharin
models, tomb, 105–6
Montet, Pierre, 273–74
Montu, 102
Moses, 215
mummies, mummification, 50, 61,
  81–83, 154, 235–36, 237, 243, 267,
  276–77, 278, 279–83, 306
Mursilis III, 233
Museum of Fine Arts, Boston, 70, 74
Mutemwiya, 197
Mutnefret, 139
Muwatallis, 245, 248
Mycerinus. see Menkaure

Naharin, 178–79, 182, 183, 184, 199,
  218
  see also Mitanni
Nahas, 280, 281
Namlot, 288–89, 290
Napata, 191, 287, 291, 292–93, 294
Naqada I, 15, 22, 36
Naqada II, 15, 17
Naqada III, 15, 22
Narmer, xxii, 33–34, 36
Narmer palette, 22, 33–34, 36
Naville, Edouard, 163, 164
Nebka, 76
Nebmaatre, 201
  see also Amenhotep III
Nebtawi, 106–7
Nebti, 36
Necho, xxiii, 299
Nectanebo, xxiii, 304
Neferneferuaton, 208, 223, 224
Nefertari, 255, 256
Neferti, 96
Nefertiti, 154, 208, 212, 223–24,
  227–28, 230, 235, 238, 242
Nefret, 74
Nefrure, 144, 158, 188

Nehsi the Nubian, 147, 150
Neitkrety, 92
Neolithic era, 3
Nesubanebded. *see* Smendes
New Kingdom, xvii, xxii, 29, 51, 80, 82,
    103, 137, *170*, 286
Nile River, *11*, 12–13, 14, 30, 89–90,
    92, 112–13, 118
Nineteenth Dynasty, 29, 74, 240–41,
    242, 273
Nineveh, 294
Ninth Dynasty, 29, 100
Nitokris, 92, 93
Niy, 179
nomes, 84
Nubia, Nubians, 14–15, 55, 66, 85,
    86, 91, 104, 108, 111–12, 115, 133,
    135, 149, 171, 185, 191, 192, 194,
    195, 198, 215, 242, 255, 286–87
    see also Cush
Nynetjer, 41

obelisks, 149, 158, 161, 166, 185, 187,
    194
Oedipus, 296–97
Old Kingdom, xvii, xxii, 29, 31, 47,
    59, 72–73, 74, 83, 95–96, 98, 99,
    101–2, 107, 120, 123, 125, 301–2
Oriental Institute, Chicago, 28, 262,
    281
Orontes River, 183, 247
Osiris, 37, 41, 42, 106, 125, 128, 187,
    202, 211, 244, 286
Osorkon III, xxiii, 289

Paleolithic era, 3
Palermo Stone, 32
Palestine, 8, 115, 135, 198, 219, 221,
    245, 259–60, 263, 270, 284
palette, Narmer, 22, 33–34, 36
Panehsy, 267
papyrus, papyri, 13, 31–32, 51–52, 80,
    88, 102, 265–66, 274, 278
Paser, 275, 276
Paweraa, 275–76
Peleset, 263
Pelusium, Battle of, 304
Peoples of the Sea, 257–60, 263
Pepi I, xxii, 84, 87

Pepi II, xxii, 87, 88, 91–92
Pepinakht, 88
Peribsen, xxii, 43, 45
Perring, John, 58
Persia, Persians, xxiii, 29, 273, 304
Petrie, Sir William Flinders, 4–10, 37,
    38, 61, 102–3, 117–18, 121, 123
pharaohs, 15, 29, 32, 145, 201–2, 219,
    237, 266, 279, 286, 303, 304
    see also specific pharaohs
Philae, 255, 304, 305–6
Philistines, 263
Phoenicia, 177, 178, 293
physicians, 53
Piankh, 267–68
Piankhi. *see* Piye
Pinudjem, xxiii, 279, 282, 283
Pithom, 260
Piye, 288, 289–91
pots, pottery, 3, 4, 5, 7–10, 15, 17, 19,
    21, 25, 39, 53, 55, 112, 128
predynastic cultures, 1–10, 15–22,
    24–27, 33, 37, 39, 89
Protodynastic culture, 15, 22
Proverbs, 302–3
Psamtik I, xxiii, *269*, 299–300
Psusennes I, xxiii, 273–74, 283
Ptah, 53, 187, 247, 248, 249, 258
Ptahhotep, Instructions of, 100, 301
Ptolemaic Period, xxiii, 304
Ptolemy, xxiii, 28, 304–5
Punt, 85, 87, 88, 149–50, 180
Pyramid Age, 59, 95
pyramid complex, 58–59
pyramid mystics, 60–62
pyramids, 56–59, 72, 79, 305–6
    see also tombs; *specific pyramids and sites*
Pyramid Texts, 80–81, 83, 99, 125

Qa'a, 40
queen, position of, 195–98
queens' pyramids, 64
Quft, 5

radiocarbon. *see* carbon 14
Rahotep, 74, 131
Ramesseum, 252, 254
Ramesside Period, 273, 301
Ramses (city), 260

Ramses I, xxii, 243
Ramses II, xxii, 91, 188, 189, 201,
    240, 244–45, 247–57, 262, 263,
    281–82, 305
Ramses III, xxii, 245, 262, 263–64,
    265, 283, 287
Ramses IV–XI, xxii, 232, 264, 265,
    266, 267, 270, 273, 274
Raneb, 41
Re, 75–78, 83, 99, 159, 187, 194, 202,
    213, 247, 248, 249, 251
Reisner, George, 68–69, 70, 113, 115,
    192, 225, 293
Rekhmire, 180–82, 184
religion, 41–45, 54, 123, 213–16,
    265–66, 267–68
renaissance, 273, 300
revisionism, historical, xvii, 40, 168–69
Rhomboidal Pyramid, 56
Ribaddi, 221
Roman Period, xviii, xxiii, 304, 305
Rosetta stone, 195

sacrifice, human, 39
Sais, 284, 288, 289, 299
Saite Dynasty, xxiii, 300
Sakkara, 39–40, 41, 44, 48–49, 79–80,
    84, 108, 242
sarcophagus, 40, 53, 54, 62, 68, 69,
    70, 71
Sargon II, 292
Satamon, 204, 208
scarabs, 20, 127, 199
sculpture, 50, 73–74, 83–84, 122–23,
    202, 203, 207, 212–13, 238, 241,
    244, 254, 271, 300
seals, stamp, 20, 41, 43
Sea Peoples. see Peoples of the Sea
Sebni, 88
Second Dynasty, xxii, 29, 41–45,
    47–48, 244
Second Intermediate Period, xvii, xxii,
    122, 287
Sed festival, 202
Sekenenre, xxii, 130, 131, 132, 135,
    138, 281
Sekhemib Peribsen, 40, 43–44
Sekhemkhet, 54
Semainean culture, 15

Semenkhkare, 224
Semna, 112–13, 115
Senakhtenre, 131, 138
Senenmut, 147–48, 151–52, 154–57,
    158, 167
Sennacherib, 292, 293
Senusert I, xxii, 95, 107, 108, 109–10,
    111
Senusert II, 111, 117
Senusert III, 111–12, 113, 115, 116,
    123, 212, 286
sequence dating, 7, 9–10
Serapeum, 39
serekh, 35, 43, 44
Sesostris. see Senusert III
Set, 41, 42–43, 44, 45, 128, 247
Sethe, Kurt, 163, 164
Seti I, xxii, 242, 243–44, 245, 282
Seti II, 260, 261, 280
Setnakhte, 262
Set the Enemy, 244
Seventeenth Dynasty, 29, 130, 131,
    132, 148
Seventh Dynasty, 29, 100
Shabaka, xxiii, 291, 292
Shabatka, 292
Sharuhen, 135
Sheklesh, 257
Shepherd kings. see Hyksos
Sheshonk I, xxiii, 283, 284
Shishak, 284
Shu, 213
Shubilulliuma, 219–20, 233, 234, 235,
    245
Sicilians, 258
Sidon, 220
silence, 301–2
silver, 174, 188, 252, 261–62, 270–71,
    274
Simyra, 220, 221
Sinai, 55, 67, 88, 110, 265
Sinuhe, The Story of, 110–11, 115
Siptah, 260–61
Sirius, 30–31
Sit-Hathor-Iunet, 117
Sixteenth Dynasty, 29, 130
Sixth Dynasty, xxii, 29, 39, 84, 90, 92,
    93
slaves, slavery, 175, 186, 187

Smendes, xxiii, 270, 272, 283
Smenkhkare, 208, 224, 225, 228–29,
    230, 231, 235–36, 242, 280
Smith, Sir Grafton Elliot, 168, 282
Snefru, xxii, 25, 54–58, 59, 65, 67, 76,
    77, 78
Sobekneferu, Queen, xxii, 122–23, 143
soldiers, 89, 104–5
Sothis, Sothic cycle, 30, 31
Sphinx, 64, 194, 297
statues. see sculpture
Step Pyramid, xxii, 39, 46–50
stimulus diffusion, 19
Strabo, 119
Sudan, 68, 85, 90, 180
Sumer, 19, 20
sun, 75
Sutekh, 247, 249
Syria, 110, 115, 149, 160, 161, 171,
    176, 177, 178, 179, 182, 183, 184,
    191, 192, 194, 198, 215, 219, 220,
    221, 222, 242, 245

Taa (the Brave), 131
Tadukhepa, 199, 230
Taharka, xxiii, 292, 293, 294, 300
Tanis, 128, 272, 273–74, 284
Tanutamon, 294, 295
Tasian culture, 15
Tausert, xxii, 261, 262
Teaching of Amenemhat, The, 109
Tefnakhte, 284, 288, 289, 291
Tell Asmar, 7
Tell el Amarna, 209, 212, 217, 223,
    238
Tell el Dab'a, 128, 135
tells, 6–7
temples, 22, 254–56, 265, 266,
    274–76, 286–87
    see also specific site names
Tentamon, 272
Tenth Dynasty, 29, 100, 101
Teti, xxii, 84, 87
Teti-en, 135
Tetisheri, 137–38
Thaneni, 169, 174, 180
Tharu, 171
Thebes, 102, 104, 130, 133, 137, 139,
    175, 176, 180–81, 191, 201, 209,

223, 231, 233, 236, 237, 238, 254,
    265, 266, 268, 273, 274–76, 284,
    285, 287, 288, 291, 293, 294, 300
Thinis, 22, 91
Third Dynasty, xxii, 29, 39, 46–50,
    53–54, 70, 73
Third Intermediate Period, xviii, xxiii,
    273, 300
Thirteenth Dynasty, 29, 123, 129–30
Thirtieth Dynasty, xxiii, 304
Thirty-first Dynasty, xxiii, 304
Thoth, 50, 187, 289
Thutiy, 180
Thutmose I, xxii, 139–40, 141, 147,
    148, 151, 153–54, 160, 163, 164,
    177, 179, 219, 283
Thutmose II, 141, 143–44, 146–47,
    163
Thutmose III, 144, 146, 150, 153, 157,
    158, 159, 160, 161, 162, 163, 164,
    165, 166, 167, 168, 169, 171, 173,
    174–91, 198, 219, 220, 241, 243,
    245, 250, 259, 263, 266, 279
    annals of, 250
Thutmose IV, 61, 194, 197–98, 201,
    202, 280
Thutmose (sculptor), 212
Thutmose (son of Amenhotep III),
    204
Thutmosid succession, 141, 163–64
Thuya, 199, 200, 234
Ti, 84, 264
Tiaa, 193–94
Tigris River, 6
titles, of king, 145–46
titulary, 35, 75, 145, 223
Tiye, Queen, 154, 199, 200, 204, 208,
    223, 225, 234, 235
Tomb of Queen Tiyi, The (Davis), 225
tomb robbers, 38, 53, 68, 71–72, 83,
    116, 120–21, 141, 152–54, 189,
    192, 193, 204, 225, 232, 237, 238,
    266–67, 274–78, 293
tombs, 22, 68–70, 71, 72–73, 83–85,
    93, 96, 99, 189, 205–6, 238,
    306–7
    see also mastaba, pyramid; specific tomb sites
Tombs. Treasures. Mummies. (Forbes), 283
treaty, 252

truth. *see maat*
Tunip, 183, 184, 220
Turin Papyrus, 31–32, 92, 127
Tursha, 257
Tutankhamon, xxii, 69, 70, 186, 189,
    204, 206–7, 208, 216, 223, 229–30,
    231–34, 236–37, 238–39, 241,
    242, 267, 274, 280, 306
Tutankhaton. *see* Tutankhamon
Tutimaois, 126
Twain, Mark, 24, 60
Twelfth Dynasty, 29, 31, 32, 107–8,
    111–12, 114, 115, 116–18, 120,
    122, 232, 264
Twentieth Dynasty, 262, 263, 265, 266,
    273, 283, 287
Twenty-first Dynasty, xxiii, 273,
    276–77, 282, 283
Twenty-second Dynasty, xxiii, 283, 284,
    285
Twenty-third Dynasty, xxiii, 284, 285,
    289
Twenty-fourth Dynasty, xxiii, 284, 291
Twenty-fifth Dynasty, xxiii, 291
Twenty-sixth (Saite) Dynasty, xxiii,
    300–301, 303
Twenty-seventh Dynasty, xxiii, 273, 304
Twenty-eighth Dynasty, xxiii, 304
Twenty-ninth Dynasty, xxiii, 304
Tyre, 220
Tyrsenoi, 258

UNESCO, 91
Unfinished pyramid, 54
Uni, 87
unification, 21–23, 32–33, 41
Unis, xxii, 79–80
Upper Egypt, 10, *11*, 12–13, 22–23,
    36, 37, 42
Ur, 38

Valley of the Kings, 103, 141, 146,
    153–54, 189, 192, 197, 204, 222,
    224–25, 236, 237, 242, 256, 261,
    262, 266–67, 280
Valley Temple, 59, 62–63, 64
vizier, 129, 181
Völkerwanderungen, 128, 263
Vyse, Richard, 58

Wadi el Hammamat, 107
Wadi Halfa, 112
Wahkare Akhtoy III, 100–101
Walls of the Ruler, 108, 110
War of Liberation, 132–37
Wassukanni, 178
weapons, 1, 10, 104, 105, 136
Weeks, Kent, 256
Wenamon, 269–73
Wente, Edward, 283
Who Was Who in Egyptology, 277
Williams, Bruce, 14–15
Winlock, H. E., 103, 104, 105, 188
wisdom literature, 78, 100, 300–302
women, Theban importance of, 137,
    138
Woolley, Sir Leonard, 38
writing, 18, 19, 20, 34–35, 123, 128,
    217
    see also cuneiform; hieroglyphs

Xois, 130

Yam, 87–88, 89–91
Yehem, 171
Yuya, 199, 200, 223, 234

Zaghlul, Saad, 280–81
Zawaiyet el Aryan, 54
ziggurats, 19
Zoser. *see* Djoser